THE PO...
OF BIG F...

THE POLITICS
OF BIG FANTASY

The Ideologies of *Star Wars,*
The Matrix and *The Avengers*

John C. McDowell

McFarland & Company, Inc., Publishers
Jefferson, North Carolina

LIBRARY OF CONGRESS CATALOGUING-IN-PUBLICATION DATA

McDowell, John C.
  The politics of big fantasy : the ideologies of Star wars, The matrix and The avengers / John McDowell.
      p.   cm.
  Includes bibliographical references and index.

  ISBN 978-0-7864-7488-2 (softcover : acid free paper) ∞
  ISBN 978-1-4766-1820-3 (ebook)

  1. Star wars films—History and criticism.   2. Matrix (Motion picture)   3. Marvel's The Avengers (Motion picture : 2012)   4. Fantasy in motion pictures.   5. Myth in motion pictures.   6. Motion pictures—Philosophy.   7. Motion pictures—Political aspects.   I. Title.
  PN1995.9.S695M47 2014
  791.43'75—dc23   2014016952

BRITISH LIBRARY CATALOGUING DATA ARE AVAILABLE

Cover illustration by Mark Durr (based on the 1942 "We Can Do It!" poster by J. Howard Miller for the War Production Co-ordinating Committee)

Printed in the United States of America

McFarland & Company, Inc., Publishers
  Box 611, Jefferson, North Carolina 28640
  www.mcfarlandpub.com

To the memory of my late grandfather, Thomas Manson (1920–2013),
to whom I owe a considerable debt of gratitude

To Sandra and my children: Archie, Jonathan,
Joseph, Margaret (Meg) and Robert

And to the most excellent of doctoral students,
Ashley Moyse and Scott Kirkland

CONTENTS

ACKNOWLEDGMENTS

A constant source of stimulation has been two of my very best doctoral students, Ashley Moyse and Scott Kirkland. Not only have they been excellent partners in the process of conducting sophisticated reflections on popular culture, but they have deepened my insight into the cultural and religious significance of the likes of *The Walking Dead*, Christopher Nolan's Batman trilogy, the Coen brothers' *A Serious Man*, and Ridley Scott's *Alien* and *Prometheus*. This extraordinary pair has been an intellectual light and has kept hope alive. On saying that, Scott, I would like to encourage you to develop a greater appreciation of Jar Jar Binks' characterization! Ash Cocksworth has not only flourished intellectually almost in spite of my obsession with popular culture, but has contributed to my appreciation of *The Dark Knight*. My Newcastle colleague Dr. Kath McPhillips has provided the opportunity to enjoyably lecture for the past four years on "The Ideology of *Star Wars* as Modern Myth" in her Sociology of Religion class. Dr. Chris Falzon has graciously given me a copy of a recently delivered seminar paper on "The Limits of Film as Philosophy."

The various studies in this book are indebted to the practical support of my family. My five children have followed my delight in all things *Star Wars* and superheroic, and are now themselves beginning to appreciate the need to investigate and interrogate deeper cultural resonances of the "entertainment" they consume. Archie McDowell significantly helped guide my reading of the history and development of Marvel's Avengers, and is always a good source of conversation regarding the various Marvel and DC universes as well as the *Star Wars* universe. My long-suffering wife's task is now one of even more intensely heroic endurance! It is my father whom I thank for encouraging my fascination with popular culture, science fiction and superheroes in particular. Yet it was especially my beloved late maternal grandfather, Thomas Manson, who demonstrated an intense suspicion of the "culture industry," and aided in the formation of the desire to understand and critically engage with deeper insight. I dedicate this book in the first place to him, and I deeply regret not having been able to present him with a copy.

This book in two main places reworks the arguments developed in material I published earlier. Consequently, I am grateful to the requisite publishers for permitting the use of previously published material from:

- "National Treasures: Joss Whedon's Assembling of Exceptional Avengers," © Anthony R. Mills, John W. Morehead and J. Ryan Parker (eds.), *Joss Whedon and Religion: Essays on an Angry Atheist's Explorations of the Sacred* (Jefferson, NC: McFarland, 2013), 183–195, by permission of McFarland & Company, Inc., Box 611, Jefferson, NC 28640, www.mcfarlandpub.com

- "From Sky-Walking to the Dark Knight of the Soul: George Lucas' *Star Wars* Turns to Tragic Drama," in Douglas Brode and Leah Deyneka (eds.), *Myth, Media, and Culture in Star Wars: An Anthology* (Lanham, MD: Scarecrow, 2012), 65–82, by permission of Rowman & Littlefield.

- © John C. McDowell, *The Gospel According to Star Wars: Faith, Hope and the Force* (Louisville, KY: John Knox, 2007), ch. 4, by permission of Westminster John Knox.

PREFACE

When I was a young boy, Friday evening's entertainment involved watching the late 1970s television series *The Incredible Hulk* or the reruns of the 1960s cult show *Star Trek* with my father. Most importantly, his taking me to *Star Wars* as a seven-year-old was undoubtedly a lasting highlight of my childhood. Like many youngsters of my generation, comic book and science-fiction/fantasy comics, movies and books were an important staple of my growing up. So too were Jesus movies at Easter time. And, at least with *Star Wars*, quite early on I realized that there was something going on that was more interesting than simple distraction of the entertainment industry. In the Preface to my 2007 book (renamed *The Gospel According to Star Wars* by the publisher) I jested that my study was partially written in response to my wife's question as to why I spoke so frequently about *Star Wars* to my children rather than "deeper" topics. The present book is a further indication of why I continue to have an *intellectual* enjoyment of many screened works, and still find some movies and television series like *Breaking Bad*, *The Walking Dead*, *The Wire*, *Farscape* or Moore and Eick's version of *Battlestar Galactica* surprisingly rich amidst the tiring banality and triviality of the increasingly formulaic productions of the popular movie industry in Hollywood.

My aim in this book is to bring intensively focused critical attention to a particular set of movies: Larry and Andy Wachowski's *The Matrix*, George Lucas' *Star Wars* saga, and Joss Whedon's *The Avengers*. But I have an abiding and pervasive interest in several other visual events such as, for example, Ridley Scott's *Alien*, *Prometheus* and *Blade Runner*, the most recent and rebooted version of *Battlestar Galactica*, Christopher Nolan's Dark Knight trilogy, Alex Proyas's *Dark City*, Terry Gilliam's *Brazil* and *12 Monkeys*, Zach Snyder's *Watchmen*, and Lucas' *THX 1138*. There are several reasons for selecting these movies, largely all coming from the science fiction and fantasy generic stables, in particular their phenomenal cultural appeal. The box office success (which I tend to measure in terms not of simple revenue but of *adjusted* revenue) and subsequent cult following of the recent movies *The Matrix, Star Wars,* and *The Avengers* has been extraordinary. The imagery, language and narratives of *Star Wars* are frequently referred to intertextually in other popular cultural products. *The Avengers* has capped off a significant turn of the popular blockbuster to superhero stories in a way that may save the otherwise struggling comic book industry. Its promised sequel has launched a further round of cinematic attention to Thor, Captain America, and Iron Man, as well as a television series *Marvel: Agents of S.H.I.E.L.D. The Matrix* provided to be the surprise of 1999, the year expected to be dominated by *Star Wars Episode I: The Phantom Menace,* and apart from spawning an expansion into a trilogy, it has encouraged Matrix-inspired hyperreal religiosity, as well as the now commonplace special effect of the bullet-time sequence. And yet, precisely as a consequence of their popularity, and the fact that they are relatively lightweight populist and child-focused texts, they tend to be ignored in film scholarship, being left instead to the type of film philosophy/theology crowd that still wants to ask about Plato's Cave and Descartes' epistemic dreams in relation to *The Matrix* and *The Truman Show;* or the temporal metaphysics of time travel from the likes of *12 Monkeys, The Butterfly Effect, Donnie Darko, The Time Traveler's Wife, Looper,* and, more recently *About Time;* or the nature of human identity in relation to the question of artificial intelligence and the post-human depicted in the likes of *Blade Runner, Terminator 2, Independence Day,* and *A.I.: Artificial Intelligence;* or the historical accuracy of the claims about Christianity in *The Da Vinci Code.* Yet as Patricia Kerslake argues specifically of science fiction,

> Despite its ambience of fantasy, SF is not the literature [or movies] of ageing children. It is frequently brutal and condemning as it examines our today and our tomorrow through the microscope of the future and, equally as often, through the lens of the past. It permits us to see more clearly what we have been and what we may become.[1]

In bringing a wide-ranging set of critical tools to the reading of these texts I hope to illuminate their political ideologies, while also being attentive to any identifiable folds that the material may provide.

A second reason for choosing these movies is that I am unconvinced by much of the little critical scholarship that has been interested in them. What they all have ideologically in common is that they, or at least the genres they belong to (this is the case with Whedon's *The Avengers*, since he could not be accused of neo-liberal politics), tend to be regarded as belonging to politically conservative frames of socio-cultural reference, although it is with the *Star Wars* saga that I particularly argue this reading to be superficial and weak. In fact, the reason for my studies in *Star Wars* begun in 2005 has largely been disquiet over the accounts of the saga provided by scholars. Some have been distinctly shallow, although more sophisticated and intellectually challenging treatments have begun to emerge over the past few years.

ABBREVIATIONS

ANH   *A New Hope*
AOTC   *Attack of the Clones*
BSG   *Battlestar Galactica*
ESB   *Empire Strikes Back*
ROTJ   *Return of the Jedi*
ROTS   *Revenge of the Sith*
SW   *Star Wars*
TPM   *The Phantom Menace*

Introduction:
Why So Serious?

At one moment in the 1999 box office smash hit *The Matrix*, Cypher reveals his deep desire to be someone important, "like an actor." Many cultural theorists might want to question this understanding of what it means to be "important." But there is little doubt about the cultural significance of what tends to be referred to as "popular culture," and in particular movie and television culture. In the contemporary West, although certainly not only there, the entertainment industry has become one of the most culturally significant and commercially profitable areas of production that markets its products to those with increasing time for leisure and disposable income. George Lucas, creator of the *Star Wars* (*SW*) franchise, acknowledged in an interview published the month following the theatrical release of *Return of the Jedi* that "film and [other] visual entertainment are a pervasively important part of our culture, an extremely significant influence on the way our society operates.... But, for better or worse, the influence of the church, which used to be all-powerful, has been usurped by film."[1] Lucas continued by indicating a keen awareness of not only the teaching possibilities available through contemporary forms of media, of having what he later called "a very large megaphone," but also of the moral responsibilities of filmmakers.[2] This is a notion he has mentioned on a number of occasions, and he has done so particularly by appealing to the possibility of mythmaking. So as early as an interview published in April 1977, prior to the release of *Star Wars* (from 1979 known more fully as *Star Wars Episode IV: A New Hope*), Lucas lamented that "there was not a lot of mythology in our society—the kind of stories we tell ourselves and our children, which is the way our heritage is passed down. Westerns used to provide that, but there weren't Westerns anymore."[3] In that context, he continued,

5

"I wanted it [viz., *SW*] to be traditional moral study, to have palpable precepts ... that children could understand.... Traditionally we get them from the church, the family, and in the modern world we get them form the media—from movies."[4] The connecting of *SW*, morality tales for children, and mythology is something Lucas has done on a number of occasions. At some point prior to October 1982, he admitted to Dale Pollock, an early biographer of the director, that "I wanted to make a kids' film that would strengthen contemporary mythology and introduce a basic morality."[5] Just prior to the general theatrical release of *The Phantom Menace* he declared that "somebody has to tell young people what we think is a good person. I mean, we should be doing it all the time. That's what the *Iliad* and the *Odyssey* are about—'This is what a good person is; this is who we aspire to be.' You need that in a society. It's the basic job of mythology."[6] So Pollock claims that "Lucas offers more than just escapist entertainment; he gives us a vision of what should be."[7] However, the notion of "mythology" is not a straightforward one, as will be see throughout this study, and Lucas has tended to employ it as a reference to Joseph Campbell's work in depicting a decontextualized understanding of the "monomyth" of the heroic journey that underlies and shapes mythic tales. *SW*, he claims, is designed to be "mythological," and through this observed "mythic" template Lucas consciously attempts to provide a form of moral instruction. (Michael Kaminski's challenge to the connection of Lucas and Campbell in the design process of 1977's *SW* will be discussed in Chapter 2.)

The cinema, then, can be influential in the construction of identity through the expression of philosophical, economic, political, and moral assumptions that shape the cultural artifact. Bryan P. Stone, for instance, argues that "it is naïve to believe that film, either as an art form or a medium for communication, is somehow unbiased. The cinema may function both as a *mirror* and as a *window*, but primarily as a *lens*. We see only what the camera lets us see, and we hear only what the writer has scripted. Movies do not merely portray a world; they propagate a worldview.... The cinema is a double-edged sword. It helps us see what we might not otherwise have seen, but it also shapes what and how we see."[8] One needs to ask Lucas, and other cultural producers like him, then, what he hopes to educate his audience in and what he is permitting his audience to see, and subsequently to hold that lens on the world up to critical light. Consequently, Stone continues, "the worldview and values propagated by the cinema—however subtly or implicitly this may occur—must be critiqued through a posture of constructive engage-ment.... And this critique must be both rigorous and extended far beyond the narrow scope of values and behaviors typically critiqued by standard rating systems concerned only with whether a film features profanity, nudity, or violence."[9]

In an important development of the notion of moral accountability, Ursula K. Le Guin reminds us that artists not only have a duty to teach but equally a duty to be very careful about what is being taught through their work. She claims that "there is … [a] responsibility to ensure that one's work does not, even if inadvertently, employ and continue deroga-tory stereotypes, appropriate for selfish purposes elements of other's cultures, and present women and minorities as Other."[10] Le Guin's pro-nouncement suggests that there is a deeper significance in considerations of mythology, and therefore of the "educational" or formative signifi-cance of film and television, that cannot be exhausted by speaking of intentionality—whether of the *auteur*, as Lucas is close to being (as author, director of two-thirds of the movies in the saga, and producer), or the larger cast of those involved in the production of a movie or other cultural artifact. Cultural, religious, and morally significant values can shape the artifacts in all kinds of ways, and "by being repeatedly por-trayed on screen such attitudes, behaviors, and values are reinforced as 'natural' and 'right.'"[11] As Rowan Williams once observed, "A society's mass fantasies are anything but trivial" and should not be treated through forms of banal evasion of their cultural significance.[12]

Kevin Wetmore, Jr., claims that "behind it [viz., *Star Wars*] … lurks assertions and assumptions and a complex interaction between the imag-inative world of the films and the real world which it can and does reflect."[13] So in response to the common deflation of the academic project of intensive analysis of popular cultural products, "It's just a movie!," Wet-more announces that "there is no such thing as 'just a movie'; all films are the product of the culture and individuals who produce it, even if the implications in the film are unintentional. No culture is innocent."[14] By "innocent" he has in mind the task of subverting the naïveté of assump-tions of hermeneutical "purity," what might be called more simply "objec-tivity." Yet the choice of the term "innocent," connected with notions of moral judgment as it is, is itself not innocent. Scholars of culture from an ideological critical bent, work to unmask cultural power relations and to suggest ways in which they hinder the flourishing of life in various ways. The difficulty is that the task of criticism is itself a contextual one, and therefore the liberationist moral enterprise can likewise slip into utilizing modes of rhetoric that suggest its own innocence. Therein criticism would mask its own array of determinative assumptions about power and the good life. A further danger that needs to be borne in mind is that such ideological criticism, unless sophisticatedly attentive to and humbly honest about, the complexities of discourse, can tend to circumvent the dominant ways in which cultural products *are* received in practice by offering a hegemonic interpretation that appears like scholarly assertion—"the movie looks like this, but *I* tell you that it is rather like this...." Those considerations relate particularly to understanding the cultural artifact as "text," and reflecting on what kinds of approaches are required in order to properly provide a deep "reading" of them.

Philosophies of the Banal, or How Shallow the Rabbit-Hole Goes

The cultivation of critical attention to "popular culture" and its artifacts has taken a particular turn over recent decades among academic cultural commentators. One of the reasons for this is that, as scholar of religions Adam Possamai argues,

> today, the old border between "high" and "low" culture is not easy to recognize, as there is no longer a clear consensus within the field of cultural production and consumption. Art uses popular culture and vice versa.... We are no longer bound to traditional values of (dis)taste which give a general agreement on what is good and bad. In this postmodern society, there is no longer any self-evident consensus on the cultural hierarchies, such as the opposition between the high bourgeois culture and the low working-class taste of the nineteenth-century.[15]

Much work has been done contesting the older distinctions between "high" and "low" culture, but some of it can appear a little intellectually lazy. It is certainly arguable that there remains a sense in which meaningful distinctions do indeed still have to be made. The intellectual value of reading *Twilight* instead of Plato's *Republic*, for instance, would require some considerable justification, especially if the context was an upper level university Philosophy class. Yet even within so-called popular or mass culture there are distinctions to be made—for instance, there are layers of complexity in David Cronenberg's directorial work or in the thick texts of Christopher Nolan, for example, that one would struggle to find in either the products of the Farrelly brothers or Judd Apatow. That, of course, does not invalidate the latter works if they are properly contextually located. But it does suggest that there remain considerations of cultural depth that require reflection without deflationary recourse to a banal and crude "anything goes" cultural scheme. While Theodor Adorno is frequently criticized for being elitist in his regard for "high" culture, especially since he tends to be less attentive to the ideological issues of power and control in "high culture" in his critique of the massification involved in "the culture industry," he at least wanted to indicate the conceptual layering of cultural artifacts that cannot be simply flattened out without a loss of the ability to ask about quality, insight, sophistication, and so on.

Adorno's work on "the culture industry" has been an important tributary in the flow of critical perception that popular culture is more important than any reduction to "escapist entertainment" would permit. Popular cultural artifacts are certainly entertaining for a great many (hence the notion of *popular* culture). But even this deserves scholarly comment and reflection. What is happening to a culture that becomes leisured, a society that requires some or even much of its time to engage in being entertained? Intensive versions of entertaining products are themselves deeply formative of consciousness and imagination, so that "reality" not only influences entertainment but entertainment influences reality in a doubling of the mimetic conditioning. This occurs, in fact, in non-trivial and politically interesting ways. For example, even the public or political life has been shaped by the entertainment industry, and politicians' statements slip easily into the mode of a manageable sound bite, an echo of a memorable advertising slogan. This is a point developed more fully some time ago in Neil Postman's work. Not only does he recognize the popularity of television, but he views it as a lens through which the world is mediated. "There is no education so exalted that it is not modified by television. And most important of all, there is no subject of public interest ... that does not find its way to television. Which means that all public understanding of these subjects is shaped by the biases of television."[16] So, he observes, "our politics, religion, news, athletics, education and commerce have been transformed into congenial adjuncts of show business, largely without protest or even much popular notice. The result is that we are a people on the verge of amusing ourselves to death."[17] Running through his study is a connection of the entertainment society with Aldous Huxley's vision in *Brave New World*, and in its turn, Postman's critical analysis echoes Adorno's emancipationist critique of cultural massification in "the culture industry." What has emerged in late modern society is a form of distraction, and one that is detrimental to society's health, according to Postman's account. As Jean Baudrillard claims, "It is useless to fantasize about state projection of police control through TV.... TV, by virtue of its mere presence, is a social control in itself."[18] Such a claim is highly suggestive of the relations of the spectacle, cultural ideology, political agency, and the possibilities of imagining a healthy counter culture. Scott Bukatman explains: "The spectacle controls by atomizing the population and reducing their capacity to function as an aggregate force, but also by displacing a surfeit of spectacular goods and lifestyles among which the viewer may electronically wander and experience a simulation of satisfaction."[19]

In the *Dialectic of Enlightenment*, Adorno and Max Horkheimer argue that the adversary of the individual is "the absolute power of capitalism" and that forms of popular culture, like Hollywood movies (as opposed to fine arts), are just forms of manipulation and dominance. They describe popular film, for example, as "the triumph of invested capital...; it is the meaningful content of every film, whatever plot the production team may have selected."[20] Their argument is twofold: that the culture industry creates the values that serve its own purposes, namely, to do its business of entertainment more profitably; and that these values are inauthentic and alienating to the mass of people who are compelled to adopt them. The culture industry, then, induces a kind of passiveness and bland receptivity in individuals that is the very opposite of the point of real art.

Adorno has been criticized for assuming an ideologically determinist relationship of the culture industry and its consumers when he depicts the productive mechanisms of "mass" culture. He tends to operate too neatly with a sense of a "grand men of history" motif that imagines that culture is dictated and consequently that the mass audience is passive in the process. He then presumes that cultural products are always blandly formulaic.[21] Matters are nevertheless considerably more complicated than the critics' rejoinders to Adorno at this point would suggest, and consequently his theoretical perspective on the industrialized productions of popular culture continues to maintain an important influence. As John Lyden observes, "the idea that popular films function primarily as ideology continues to be the dominant paradigm for feminist film theory, leftist political film theory, psychoanalytic film theory, screen theory, genre studies, and cultural studies."[22] Adorno's critique, therefore, in one way or another fruitfully persists in disruptively interrogating the mechanisms of cultural creativity and the regulating commodifying "aestheticization of everyday life," a creativity that brings with it a form of apolitical distraction that is generated by a self-referential entertainment culture.[23] Adorno's critique remains effective without the critic having to understand matters of audience reception in flatly passive terms. No overly constructivistic narrative of human subjectivity can adequately mask the multiple determinations involved in the formation of conscious agents, the various forms of dependency or learning that occur in human development. According to Lyden, then, "ideological criticism of popular film is essential because one of the major ways in which cultural hegemonies involving gender, race, or class are promoted and perpetuated is through the images of popular media, including film." Likewise, Gordon Lynch argues that "there are reasonable grounds for suggesting that such [ideological] representations do indeed matter. Research on audience responses have suggested that people are likely to adopt the way of understanding the world that is offered to them through the media unless they have some other experience or way of interpreting the world that contradicts this media perspective."[24]

It is precisely the growing recognition of this that has led to the explosion of academic interest in popular cultural artifacts. Lyden observes that "the growing [academic] interest in film ... indicates a growing appreciation for the role that technological media play in our lives, from television to computers. We are beginning to realize that we cannot understand or interpret our society except in its relation to these unavoidable additions to it."[25] Nevertheless, it still remains the case that for many professional academics, products of popular culture (such as pop art, music, magazines, television and movies) are treated only cursorily and therefore as intellectually lightweight subjects for study. In Adorno's critique, for instance, "the universality of the art of the culture industry ... is the universality of the homogenous same, an art which no longer even promises happiness but only provides easy amusement as relief from labour."[26] Consequently, it is "one good reason why people have remained chained to their work, and to a system which trains them for work, long after that system has ceased to require their labour."[27] In this account, the entertainment industry occupies the role that Christianity once did in Marx's analysis as the opium of the masses. "The phrase, the world wants to be deceived, has become truer than had ever been intended."[28] The promise of happiness shifts into the feeling of "the most fleeting gratification," and thus people "desire a deception which is nonetheless transparent to them." For Adorno, Bernstein comments, this movement of cultural acceptance involves a "degraded utopia of the present."[29] It constitutes the stupefaction of thought, the ending of democratic society, the "fettering [of] consciousness" that "impedes the development of autonomous, independent individuals who judge and decide consciously for themselves."[30]

Lynch warns that there are two problems facing many students of popular culture: the perception among other scholars, and the mitigated rigor of much of the scholarship conducted. "One of the dangers of the study of everyday life," he laments, "is that it risks descending into the trivial and the banal. In its worst forms, the study of popular culture can appear to be an academic holiday, in which scholars have a break from their more normal weightier interests, and write texts on forms of popular culture that particularly interest or amuse them."[31] Steven Sanders finds both an increasing enthusiasm among philosophers for the study of popular culture, and film more specifically, and in equal measure an approach to film that tends towards intellectually unsophisticated readings.[32] He admits that while there are conspicuously significant differences in quality among those who academically discuss films, it is lamentable that "good science fiction film criticism remains in perilously short supply." Various reasons for this are offered. Firstly, and most damningly, he assesses that "some bad science fiction film criticism is simply attributable to sheer incompetence."[33] Is this a reference to the fact that too few of the most erudite of intellectuals tend to offer sustained reflection on popular culture, and even they, when they do provide comment, do so without intensive knowledge and understanding of an ever-complexifying area of research? Popular cultural comment, in many cases, seems to attract much argument by assertion, the bluff of opinion, and an impatience with long-term reflection.

The second reason Sanders provides is that "some is due to the pervasive influence of various disfiguring intellectual tendencies in academic circles that are estranged from what were once the humanizing methods of the humanities." There are various places in which this problem can be detected. It is particularly evident in the kinds of philosophical approaches that exploit popular culture for illustrative effect, for example. For instance, philosophical commentators on film have a propensity to ask questions concerning the relation of Plato's Cave and René

Descartes' epistemic doubt from his dream argument to *The Truman Show*, *The Matrix*, *Dark City*, and *The Thirteenth Floor*; or the temporal metaphysics of time travel with regard to the likes of *12 Monkeys*, *The Butterfly Effect*, *Time Cop*, *Donnie Darko*, *The Time Traveler's Wife*, *Source Code*, *About Time* and *Looper*; or the nature of human identity in relation to the question of artificial intelligence depicted in the likes of *Blade Runner*, *Terminator 2: Independence Day*, *The Thirteenth Floor*, *A.I.: Artificial Intelligence*, and the recent television series *Almost Human*. Of course, it is not an illegitimate use of a text to attempt to find connections in order to more effectively communicate a set of ideas in what one might call a *metaphorical mode of film study*. However, on its own terms, this is an intellectually shallow approach since it does not "read" films textually in and for themselves, and also it does not utilize the necessary intellectual conditions for deep reasoning through contextualized reflection; therefore, it can be prone to providing some impoverished, problematic and even deeply distorted readings of the movies it treats.[34]

A particular favorite of philosophers is *The Matrix*, having attracted considerable attention from and excitement among philosophical publishers. Tellingly, however, much of the discussion leans towards the culturally uninsightful and rather philosophically banal. Connections between the narrative and both Descartes and Plato are frequent, as mentioned above.[35] Likewise, a documentary entitled *Return to the Source: Philosophy and The Matrix* (2004) explores certain perceived philosophical connections, functioning much like The History Channel's *Star Wars: The Legacy Revealed* (2007), which uncritically explores George Lucas' pair of trilogies from the perspective of a Joseph Campbell–inspired understanding of myth. These references do at least emerge from the movie itself, but the studies press them insufficiently hard. More astutely, at least, Christopher Falzon mentions a further set of philosophical connections, that of issues of technology and scientific hubris.[36] However, this too enacts a certain reading decision that largely emerges from within one part of the extensive story arc. As the backstory mentioned only allusively in *The Matrix* but displayed more intensively in the Wachowski brothers–approved *Animatrix* makes clear, the issue is not so much one of hubris as of abuse and instrumentalization (or, certainly, this is not their main concern)[37]—the sentient constructions (artificial intelligences) are denied the appropriate legal and political-economic conditions that recognizing the agential subjectivity of their independent consciousness would demand. In that regard, the story would be one of slavery and liberation, the narrative conceptuality that underlies *I, Robot* and the rebooted *Battlestar Galactica*, and less that of the *Terminator* movies. (James Cameron's *The Terminator* offers indications of forms of technophobia, and *Terminator 2: Judgment Day* displays hubris with regard to Miles Dyson's initial response to the Terminator's horrific revelations of the impending hostilities.) The backstory, filled in by the movie itself, then has to do with the machines repaying the favor, not in an act of retribution but for survival. Reading the movie from this particular angle, then, would permit one to explore the reduction of life to mere a mechanized form for the exploitative use of others, a theme pertinent to, for example, *The Running Man* for which criminals participate in a gladiatorial game show on television; Lucas' *Attack of the Clones* (*AOTC*); Peter Jackson's *Lord of the Rings* trilogy, with its depiction of Saruman's making of the Uruk-Hai for the sole purpose of making war on Rohan; *Gamer*, which echoes many of the concepts of *The Running Man*, but with death row inmates being controlled on a game "Slayers"; *Repro Men* (2010), in which a medical corporation treats its patients as purchasers of vital organs and, in the event of non-payment, sends the Repro Men to repossess their property. Furthermore, the references to Jean Baudrillard's material on late capitalist hyper-reality (Neo's fake copy of *Simulacra and Simulation* is visible early in the movie) cannot go unnoticed. This *potentially* offers deeper and more contemporary cultural possibilities for reading, although there is considerable disagreement among commentators as to how far the movie realizes this philosophico-political potential, and what its actual hermeneutic potential is. These possibilities and scholarly contentions are simply not mentioned by most philosophical commentators. They too neatly tend to decontextualize the movie in several respects: by not taking into consideration the way in which the post–*The Matrix* films, like the sequels and the animations, enable, nay necessitate, rereading; by not reflecting on the movie in the context of its culture; and by not considering it in the light of the traditions of the cinema, for instance those of dystopian science fiction and the literature of cyberpunk.[38]

This metaphorical mode of philosophical reasoning concerning film is well exemplified in the predominantly rather intellectually meager "Philosophy and Culture" series of books published by Open Court, and more recently by Wiley Blackwell. Among the numerous examples of how this approach distorts understanding of film, it is worth picking up on the notion of instrumentalized life mentioned above and reflecting briefly on Richard Hanley's paper on the use of the biotechnology of cloning in *Star Wars*. He argues in general that "if cloning is not inherently bad, and harms no one (or does relatively little harm), it's not wrong."[39] Even the genetic manipulation of the clones in order to diminish their autonomy does not deny the worthwhileness of the resultant life. He compares this to Obi-Wan's manipulative use of Jedi mind control on the death-stick pusher in the bar in *AOTC*, which serves a greater goal. The practice of clone engineering, he argues, could count as the product of a justifiable need for self-defense. However, Hanley has drastically missed the crucial point in the cloning process, the matter that is vital for understanding the larger symbolic value that this process has in the *SW* saga. The Republic's senators and even the Jedi unwittingly provide some moral legitimacy for supporting the Clone Army Creation Act (Jar Jar Binks even proposes the granting of emergency powers to the Chancellor, powers which are first utilized to create the Grand Army of the Republic), and are therefore complicit in the events that result in their downfall with the rise of "the first Galactic Empire." Padmé Amidala is almost alone in appearing to be well-equipped to remain interrogative and suspicious of the swift drive to war. (In her suspicions she is joined in *Revenge of the Sith* by, among a handful of others, Mon Mothma and Bail Organa.) Moreover, the issue of cloning is of the instrumentalizing of life—sentient life is created in order to do another's bidding, and *only* another's bidding. Clones are denied any semblance of independent life, which is illustrated by the fact that they are given and known only by numbers, at least until later in the Clone Wars (we can see an example of this with the reference to an Imperial storm trooper as TK421 in *A New Hope*). The clones are little more than biological versions of the Separatist Confederacy's battle droid armies constructed from a logic of utility, obsolescence and waste. They are, in short, disposable biomechanical entities. Certainly towards the end of the Galactic Civil War many members of the Senate and the Jedi Council believe the clones to be almost human and hence the commanders are accorded names. Yet these commanders and the commanders *alone* have some (distinctly limited) semblance of human personality by virtue of the fact that the process of their cloning is designed with enhanced programming in order to enable them to display strategic initiative and battle leadership capabilities. Consequently, what we are reminded of is the fact that the practice of valuing others' lives *only insofar as it contributes to one's own personal gain* is clearly the ethical way of the Sith (Obi-Wan's use of

mind control is purely momentary—it does not make the instrumentalizing action a permanent one.) Hence, it is symbolically significant that
the contribution of the Jedi to this process of instrumentalizing is precisely the main means of their own destruction.[40] There is a perverse
justice in this.

Likewise, there are numerous textually insubstantial and distorting
religious readings of the *SW* saga, each of which fails to perform a hermeneutical archaeology (digging deeply in order to read or understand
the artifact). The result is a body of work that sees its own spiritual reflection in the water deep in George Lucas' well. Orson Scott Card observes,
"Hardly anybody can answer the easy Bible questions on Jeopardy anymore, but almost everybody can tell you about Obi-Wan Kenobi, Darth
Vader, Yoda, and The Force."[41] The classic trilogy in particular has created a pool of memories, a shared stock of images, ideas, and knowledge
for three or more generations of film fans. In relation to religious education, James L. Ford claims that "one might well argue that popular
epic films like *The Matrix* and *Star Wars* carry more influence among
young adults than the traditional religious myths of our culture."[42] It is
because of this, and also their love of the material itself, that Christians
like Dick Staub make use of the movies to tell the Christian story to two
generations of *Star Wars* fans. He likens his Christian use of *Star Wars*
to St. Paul's speech on Mars Hill in Athens in Acts 17. Here the apostle
famously used "the cultural icons of Greek culture to build a bridge to
Christian truth.... Because *Star Wars* is the prevailing epic filmic myth
of our era, and Christianity is the prevailing faith tradition in the West,
I think relating them to each other can help us understand both more
fully."[43] In an interview in *Christianity Today* he speaks of *Star Wars* as
"True Myth,"[44] and his book *Christian Wisdom of the Jedi Masters* shows
how Luke's development is analogous to a serious Christian's progression
as a follower of Jesus.

> My book is ... a look at Luke's development from a directionless young
> man who discovered his life purpose after encountering Obi-wan and
> Yoda and learning from them about the "unseen Force." Today, many
> young people are seeking meaning, and my generation has failed to pass
> on the authentic and radical adventure offered by Jesus.... The progres-
> sion of the aspiring Jedi involves recognizing the existence of the Force,
> then seeking, understanding, and using the force against the dark side.
> The progression in Christian discipleship involves recognizing that there
> is a Lord, then seeking, understanding, and serving the Lord, which
> involves a battle against the dark side.[45]

Staub is one of a growing number of more spiritual writers on *Star Wars* who unmistakably fudge the gaps between this set of movie texts and the Christian tradition's texts, or indeed of any and every particular religious tradition. A similar process animates the work of Matthew Bortolin, John Porter, Caleb Grimes, and Russell Dalton.[46] Moreover, this blurring of the texts distorts the cinematic text itself, compressing its significance to its ability to demonstrate, illustrate or aid in the depiction of the particular religious story being told.

Moreover, religious readers of film have reduced the culturally interesting *The Da Vinci Code* and *The Passion of the Christ* to questions of the historical accuracy of the claims about Christianity rather than tackle them as culturally specific readings of the Christian tradition; others search for religious themes and imagery, such as Paul Fontana who spends his time searching for "God" in *The Matrix*, rather than critically analyzing the cultural values and ideological assumptions of the movie texts that contribute to the formation and sustenance of sociopolitical identity.[47] Like Staub and others on *Star Wars*, Gregory Boyd and Al Larson simply ransack and distort the cultural particularity of *The Matrix* in order to make it do an evangelistic work of illustrating Christian conversion.[48] As Sanders concludes, "virtually all bad writing about science fiction film reflects poor thinking about it, not only cheapening science fiction film criticism but also trivializing science fiction film itself."[49] Given the all-too-brief considerations of ideology above, one could argue that it is naïve to uncritically regard popular culture as providing forms of pure and simple "entertainment." Likewise, it is a distinctly shallow move to "read" movies for illustrative purposes, as often occurs in writings on religion or philosophy and film. Both of these moves are indications not so much of the infantilization of culture provided by the cinema but of the ideological illiteracy, particularly with regard to religion and the political, of contemporary late modern society and its "scholarly" commentators. And so for Frederic Jameson the important question needing to be asked is whether "culture [can] be political, which is to say critical and even subversive."[50]

An Outline of the Chapters

According to Gilbert Perez, we "respond to the movies of our youth with something like the feelings of first love."[51] Only one of the sets of

movies (and merely three of the six movies from the six within that set)
studied in this book involve, properly speaking, movies from my youth—
the "classic" trilogy of the *SW* saga—and I hope not to be dewy eyed in
relation to it. My aim in this book is to intensively bring into focus my
critical attention on certain political features of a particular cluster of
movies: Joss Whedon's *The Avengers*, George Lucas' *SW*, and the Wachowski brothers' *The Matrix*. In bringing a wide-ranging set of critical tools
to the reading of these texts, I hope to illuminate their political ideologies, while also being attentive to any identifiable folds that the material
may provide. As Jes Battis argues, "Politics are an integral part of all
popular media, but they infuse [science fiction] even more so, because
SF remains a genre that is closely concerned with ethics and cultural
development.... As Althusser insists, we can't get away from ideology,
because there is no 'away.' The exit sign is ideological, the rear entrance
is ideological—even the getaway car is tainted."[52] Of course, that also
ironically entails that the critics' sounding of the ideological siren is
itself ideological. The ideological rabbit hole is endlessly deep.

In his own inimitable way Stanley Hauerwas announces that "we"
(meaning Americans, although his observations have a relevance more
territorially expansive than that) do not know how to think as a society
about questions of importance, in particular about who we are. It has
variously been claimed by cultural observers that all "our" relations are
determined ultimately by a free market economy that is much more than
merely a set of procedures regulating goods exchange—it is instead, a
regulator of the Good itself and thus identity forming and disposition
determining. Cultural meaning is limited to that grand economic story.
Consequently, Zygmunt Bauman, for instance, argues that even the
potential for resistance is subsumed and domesticated into its territory.[53]
Moreover, many have claimed that politically American culture has been
shaped by a plenitude of longstanding and overlapping myths: American exceptionalism, messianic missiology, Manichaean dualistic sensibility, and redemptive violence. Given that "popular culture" exists as
an expression of cultural values, many of these ideologies are exhibited
in some form or another in the most popular of mass produced cinematic texts.

Where these critical claims are particularly noticeable, to varying
degrees, is through texts as diverse as Lucas' *SW*, the Wachowskis' *The
Matrix*, and Joss Whedon's *The Avengers*. These are in many ways all
deeply religious texts in that they suggest forms of the regulation of per-

sonal and social identity, and they embody a politics that shapes the political imagination in ways that can disrupt the potential for imagining a global social body—what Rowan Williams calls a "body of grace." Despite the domination of Manichaean readings of George Lucas' *SW* saga, these particular texts are considerably more ambiguous and resistant to ideologies supportive of American political and cultural hegemony. While these three sets of texts all exhibit in various ways the postsecular presence of religion, they exist in markedly different relationships to it and thereby exemplify the intensive differences between forms of religious commitment in the contemporary United States. After all, *SW* and *The Matrix* have contributed to the growing number of hyper-religions (in *SW*'s case, Jediism), and they themselves both express a pluralistically eclectic sentiment, a type of liquid religiosity, especially in terms of *SW*'s portrayal of "the Force" and *The Matrix*'s multiple references. Suggestively, Joss Whedon's *The Avengers* is considerably more religiously thin in its use of religious images and motifs, but it fundamentally rewrites the Captain America character that had been rendered more interestingly complex in the recent Marvel series *Civil War*. Equally, these texts embody many of the particular political tensions that characterize the United States after 9/11.

My exploration of these films begins with a lengthy chapter that raises significant questions regarding Whedon's superhero movie. His entertaining *The Avengers* harks back in its mood to an older period of comic book lore, with its rather flat characterizations of "the good" and "the wicked," "the heroes" and "the villains." However, as Paulo Freire observed some years ago, "there is no such thing as a neutral education process." Consequently, cultural theorists recognize that so-called "popular culture" cannot be accorded the status of "entertainment" *simpliciter*, but its relation to deeper ("religious") senses of identity are to be acknowledged, understood, and tested. Even if popular culture is particularly thin in its explicit religious imagery, it expresses a religion-liteness for a spiritually consumerist religious landscape. It reflects the massive "subjective turn of modern [Western] culture" that puts the onus on the theological reading of the movie's consumer as a religious "seeker." And yet the connection between *The Avengers* and the religious is more complex and more interesting. In fact, Robert Jewett and John Shelton Lawrence's questions concerning the politics of the "Captain America" "myth of the American superhero" take on a particular resonance with this piece of Whedon's work and its potential for embracing a form of American civil religion.[54] The contention of the chapter is that Whedon's piece binds religion to the civil religion of the national project, the commitment to the wellbeing of the state. This (unwitting?) move is intensified by the way in which the Captain America character is construed, and a comparison with Marvel's *Civil War* series and other complex post–9/11 cultural artifacts (like Ronald Moore and David Eick's *Battlestar Galactica*, Zack Snyder's *Watchmen*, and Christopher Nolan's Dark Knight trilogy) indicates the politically interrogative possibilities that have been circumvented by what emerges as Whedon's rather politically conservative text.

Emancipatory considerations shape the book's study of *SW* in the even lengthier Chapter 2. Years ago, Susan Sontag grandly proclaimed that "there is absolutely no social criticism, of even the most implicit kind, in science fiction films. No criticism, for example, of the conditions of our society which create the impersonality and dehumanisation which science fiction fantasies displace onto the influence of an alien 'It.'"[55] Making such grand gestures is always an unwise affair. Sontag had in mind the 1950s, but even this earlier period of cinematic science fiction does not entirely fulfill her rather unwisely uncomplicated observations. For instance, Jack Arnold's *It Came from Outer Space* (1954) tells the story of benign aliens who attempt to conduct repairs on Earth only to be confronted by hysterical violent human beings. These themes had partially been developed by Robert Wise's *The Day the Earth Stood Still* (1951). This movie offered a quite different set of political possibilities from those of the increasingly familiar alien-threat motif, possibilities for promoting international co-operation during a period of intense Cold War hostility, in particular the Korean War. Klaatu is sometimes spoken of as a "Christ-like alien" figure (he assumes the name "Carpenter," for instance, and he is resurrected) who benevolently comes to rebuke humans for their conflicts and to warn them about an impending destruction should their self-destructive behavior not be curbed.[56] However, the alien's arrival with a message of peace only brooks xenophobic fear and aggression against the alien "others." According to Keith Booker,

> *The Day the Earth Stood Still*, with its resplendent vision of benevolent aliens who have come to Earth on a mission of peace (only to be greeted with suspicion and violence), thus went against the grain of both anti–Soviet and anti-alien hysteria.... Thus, if the paranoid treatment of the possibility of alien invasion in many SF films of the 1950s can be taken as an allegorical representation (and sometimes even endorsement) of the fear of communist invasion or subversion, the critique of xenopho-

bia in *The Day the Earth Stood Still* can be taken as a sort of counter-allegory—as a critical commentary on the anticommunist hysteria that was then sweeping the United States. This aspect of the film includes an extensive interrogation of the role of the media in producing and stimulating mass hysteria by sensationalizing accounts of the dangers posed to Earth by the alien visitors.[57]

Booker notes that the director "himself has stated that he was entirely unaware of these parallels until they were brought to his attention after the film had been completed. On the other hand, these parallels are so obvious that Wise's claim seems a bit difficult to believe; the film even ran afoul of 20th Century–Fox's censors over the scene in which Klaatu rises from the dead, a scene that the censors felt made the parallel between Klaatu and Christ all too clear, causing them to insist on the insertion of the line concerning the limited nature of Klaatu's resurrection."[58]

According to George Lucas, "being a student in the Sixties, I wanted to make socially relevant films, you know, tell it like it is. But then I got this great idea for a rock & roll movie, with cars and all the stuff I knew about as a kid."[59] In 1973, as he closed in on completing *American Graffiti*, he "turned to the stars," working on slowly designing and scripting a project that he had had on his imagination's radar since 1968.[60] *THX 1138* had proven a financial disaster a mere two years earlier, costing Francis Ford Coppola's fledgling production company American Zoetrope its very existence as Warner Brothers demanded that Coppola repay the $300,000 loan it had provided to source some of his scripting projects. Lucas had also had problems selling the idea of *Apocalypse Now* to the studio a year before, a script he had himself been working on for some four years by that point in time, with Vietnam movies being too controversial at the time. What was to become known as *Star Wars* was conceived against a backdrop of cultural turmoil in the United States, as the messy Vietnam War limped to its end, with many in the nation suffering the trauma of severe introspection; as President Richard Nixon was implicated in the Watergate scandal; and as economic misery loomed on the horizon. Lucas has famously announced that he wrote *SW* in order to give wonder and an enjoyment of story back to the post–Vietnam age. This might sound like a return to the older American myths of heroism, the kind Lucas himself grew up with, and thus as a simple escapism that mitigates the important possibility of learning from the mistakes that took the United States into Vietnam in the first place.[61] By outfitting the Empire out with a Nazi look, for instance, the impression can be of a less morally complex war in the minds of an American audience, and thus return something of a romance to American conflict after the politically divisive and psychologically traumatic Vietnam War. Influential film critic Pauline Kael describes Lucas' *SW* and Steven Spielberg's *Jaws* (1975) as an infantilizing of the cinema that reconstitutes the spectator as a child, and then overwhelms her with sound and spectacle that has the effect of obliterating any sophisticated sense of irony, aesthetic self-consciousness and critical reflection. While Kael's reading hobbles on some readings of the saga, it has become particularly difficult to sustain in the light of the burgeoning direction the *SW* movies have come to take with their account of Darth Vader, especially in the narrative arc that has determined the trilogy of prequels as a tragic drama.

Chapter 3 presses a socio-political critique of the dystopian imagination, but does so by assuming that there are varieties of dystopianisms. Not all dystopianly charged texts can function as effective critical aids to the "emancipatory utopian imagination."[62] Some slip, in fact, into forms of anti-utopian nihilism, while others provide what Peter Fitting describes as "false utopian solutions to the dystopia of the present."[63] Specifically, the chapter focuses on Larry and Andy Wachowskis' *The Matrix*, arguing that it subverts its own critical dystopian potential, to use Frederic Jameson's terms, "of making us more aware of our mental and ideological imprisonment," and thereby utopianly slips back into the mode of celebrating the simulated realities it attempts to criticize.[64] Only its sequels disrupt the Idealist subjectivity that sustains the first movie in the series, pushing the trilogy towards a flashy nihilism only to offer a fragilistic and contingent form of transcendence of systemic determinism.

Formal Disclaimers: Reader Guides

There are four disclaimers I would like to make in advance, and I offer them in order to help with reader expectations of what will be studied and argued in the pages of this book. Firstly, as mentioned above, each of these chapters is particularly lengthy. While that may have something to do with a natural verbosity on the part of its author, there is a more substantive and material reason for this. The book tackles several texts that have generated a wealth of commentary, but commentary that has frequently been uninsightful, problematic, not well informed or reasoned, and also mimicking of a set of readings that have too neatly become commonplace. My accounts, therefore, have considerable work to do in order to provide their resistant readings.

Secondly, these textual studies might appear to be couched in a formal style that makes extensive effort to suppress the investments that different readers bring to the texts, and therefore hegemonically impose a flattening ideological reading on them. Without wanting to engage in the complex territory of hermeneutics, and to reflect on "reader-response theory" in particular, I maintain, however, that my readings are actually considerably more modest than that. This is indicated by the fact that where they diverge from those of other commentators, I offer mine through critical engagement with other perspectives, and through *argument*. In other words, I try to avoid the intellectual indolent approach that takes the form of *assertion*. In fact, one of my concerns in several of the chapters is with commentators who tend to be too hasty in providing their own readings, especially when identifiably sidestepping disruptive complexities and tensions in the texts and their contexts. Even where my rhetoric appears to be at its most assertive, my readings are offered as invitations for others to engage, even if that engagement involves disagreement, and offer their own critical perspective on the material and the variety of accounts of it that are burgeoning among the commentators. To adapt a point made by Stanley Hauerwas about the writing style of Karl Barth, the description offered "is already an argument just to the extent that his descriptions and redescriptions cannot help but challenge our normal way of seeing the world."[65] My readings may well be quite wrong, but I offer them as arguments regarding the socio-political significance of the texts as being considerably more ambiguous than is often, perhaps even regularly, suggested.

Thirdly, much of the book is written in a quite dense style and is therefore reader-demanding. Despite the ever-complexifying field of cultural and media studies, there still remains too much film-scholarship that leans towards the intellectually lightweight, especially those that come from professional Anglophone philosophers, theologians and those commentators with religious interests. In contrast, I tackle these movies as "texts" in a similar scholarly fashion to the way I have discussed theological and philosophical texts in my other publications. Consequently, this book enables me to be much less constrained by things such as word limits, frequent use of allusion and technical terminology, expectation of at least some background knowledge, and complexity of argument, than was permitted by the publishers of what ended up as a more general readership book, *The Gospel According to Star Wars: Faith, Hope and the Force* (Louisville, KY: Westminster John Knox Press, 2007). Of course, this point does not self-justifyingly mask my awareness of my own limited writing style.

Fourthly, I admit that while my understanding of these selected texts continues to develop I remain very much an amateur scholar of film. In his celebrated study *Orientalism*, Edward Said makes the striking statement about his engagement in political and ideological analysis: "there will always remain the perennial escape mechanism of saying that a literary scholar, a philosopher, for example, are trained in literature and philosophy respectively, not in politics or ideological analysis. In other words, the specialist argument can work quite effectively to block the larger and, in my opinion, the more intellectually serious perspective."[66] Given the responsibility to tell appropriately and well the stories of our lives and those of others for whom one claims to speak as a witness, the contemporary proliferation of specialisms cannot morally release the so-called amateur from responsibility to probe, interrogate and imagine matters differently. Said's assertion can be broken down into the following two broad claims: in the first place, ethically significant matters are much too *important* to be left to specialists, and thus cannot properly be dealt with at the rather thin and distorting hermetic level of the "history of ideas."[67] It should be a matter of real political concern that a vast array of academics are fiddling (debating and arguing among themselves) while Rome burns around us. In the second place, even those identified as specialists are not free from the formative operation of special "interests." Likewise, I am convinced that it remains *morally* important for scholars to be intellectually interested in concerns, desires and so on that take them out of their scholastic "comfort zones."

Fifthly and finally, my professional academic commitments are as a theological scholar, with abiding interests in philosophy, history and studies in culture and religion. However, while at various points this book does attempt to engage with what might be called "civil religion," it deliberately offers very little of what might be recognized as "theology." There are only the barest and vaguest of hints of a theological reading of matters of social formation and the distorting effects of wickedness in my reading of George Lucas' *SW* saga. In this regard, this book is markedly different in theoretical concern as well as in tone from *The Gospel According to Star Wars*.

1

THE SUPER BODY-POLITIC
Nationally Assembling
Joss Whedon's Exceptional
The Avengers

Entertaining Difference? Late-Modern Religion

According to Paulo Freire, "people are manipulated by … [a] series of myths."[1] This statement comes in the context of Freire's book on education, and the implication of his argument is that reflections on education need to be considerably more demanding than any simple concern with pedagogical techniques, practices, and skills of learning would be. Popular culture has often reflected currents and shifts in the zeitgeist and its supporting mythologies, and in this science fiction and fantasy genres are often in the vanguard. As Kevin Wetmore argues, "science fiction has served as a distancing form, allowing analysis of and commentary on contemporary issues under the guise of the distant future or a fantasy world."[2] For instance, much science fiction had trained its sights on Cold War paranoia during the 1950s and 1960s, and George Lucas' *THX 1138* displayed its writer/director's concerns with American hostilities in S.E. Asia a few years later. *Dr Strangelove* expressed apprehension over the nuclear arms race, and Stanley Kubrick's *2001: Space Odyssey*, among other things, raised questions about the wisdom of technological ingenuity. Ridley Scott's *Alien* and James Cameron's sequel *Aliens* echo the cultural angst of the late 1970s and post–Vietnam and post–Watergate sense of the end of the myth of progress, focusing on questions of the self-interest of corporations, the trustworthiness of the military–industrial complex, the over-dependence on technologies, and even "the precariousness of our human identity."[3] In this pair of movies, there are demonstrably also expressions of dread over the fragility of life in the face of nature's instinct to survive, anxieties over gender fluidity, and the ongoing horror over a monstrous otherness.

According to Richard Gray and Betty Kaklamanidou, "the Hollywood film and television industries" have not only cashed in on "some of the most recognizable American pop culture symbols," but have "turned ... them ... into modern day myths (according to the Barthesian definition which views myth as discourse).... Indeed, popular culture is a domain that ... produces multilayered narratives that contain and spread ideological and political messages to a wide audience."[4] Consequently, in a move not unlike that of Freire, cultural theorists recognize that so-called "popular culture" cannot be contained by being reduced to simple "entertainment"; they argue that its discursive relation to deeper senses of identity should be understood and tested.

A particularly critically acclaimed dramatic performance with deep political-cultural resonance has recently appeared in a quite surprising place. This place has involved a metanarrative return to a kitsch and relatively mediocre, even if nostalgically well-remembered, television offering originally conceived by Glen A. Larson. But where the 1970s version offered child-friendly entertainment, Ronald D. Moore and David Eick's reconceived *Battlestar Galactica* (*BSG*; 2004–9) has been widely regarded as a gritty exploration of the crisis of American consciousness after 9/11. So, while distancing the show from any direct allegory, Moore announces that it provides the possibility to "comment on things that are happening in today's society, from the war against terror to the question of what happens to people in the face of unimaginable catastrophe."[5] The broad story arc of Larson's series has remained intact—the brutal enforcing of the Cylon "vision of existential hygiene on humanity" in a genocidal nuclear holocaust against the inhabitants of the twelve Colonies of Kobol, the humans' flight and search for a home on earth with the mythical 13th tribe, and so on.[6] Yet gone are the charmingly naïve Boxey character, the lovable daggit, the relatively psychologically uncomplicated portrayal of good and evil, and the light and uncomplicated mood of pre-pubescent fantasy adventure. These have been replaced by an atmosphere burdened with foreboding and wracked by consequential conflict; by gritty handheld camera work; by political intrigue and the moral questions raised by the bare life of survivalism; by the introduction of terrorist sleeper-cells, political assassinations and *coup d'états*, and suicide bombings; by more prominent and interesting female characters who challenge the older version's gender stereotypes; and by common evidently allegorical reflections on recent socio-political events (such as concerns about an untidy election, monotheistic-inspired violence against a decadent society, torture as a self-protective interrogation technique, and so on). According to Eick,

> To me, the old sci-fi novels—the [Robert] Heinleins, the [Isaac] Asimovs, the [Ray] Bradburys, the [Philip K.] Dicks and so forth—were all about allegorical sociopolitical commentary. So it really wasn't so much about coming up with a new idea. It was going back to an old one, which is, Let's use science fiction as the prism or as the smokescreen—as it was sort of invented to be—to discuss and investigate the issues of the day.[7]

What is particularly noticeable is the attention given to religion in the four seasons of the space drama. As was noted in *The New Yorker* the show brings "into play religion and religious fanaticism, global politics, terrorism, and questions about what it means to be human."[8] To go back a few years to George Lucas' *Star* Wars (*SW*) of 1977, a short time prior to Larson's show, one interesting scene had suggested that "the Force" did not lie with the secular, or at least with a secure and self-confident secularism. So Darth Vader threateningly announces to Admiral Motti, "I find your lack of faith disturbing." More recently, James Cameron's *Avatar* has sympathetically exhibited the theme of moral responsibility to the lives and cultures of others by contrasting its sympathetic treatment of the pantheistic spirituality of the Na'vi with the considerably less sympathetically portrayed greed of the corporation that enacts an instrumentalized version of rationality and is sustained by the power of a privatized military enforcement complex and an operative *realpolitik*. Equally, the theological terms used in both Ridley Scott's *Prometheus* and Zack Snyder's *Man of Steel* are worth mentioning in this context. While the likes of Richard Rorty continue to forcefully intellectually defend the American secular political arrangement, the compromise arrangement that emerges with the peace Treaty of Westphalia (1648), and critics of religion like Sam Harris and Richard Dawkins sound the alarm, a wider range of voices have begun to be powerfully asserted in public with respect to not only the presence and importance of "religion" but even over the very nature of the "public" itself. Sociologist Bryan S. Turner observes the modern emergence of "religion" in a "privatized" mode:

> One consequence of the global spread of western Christianity has been to construct a model of religion as a special institution in which religion is essentially a private matter of individual subjectivity. This model of

religion was basically an expression of the political attempt to prevent religious wars in the Treaty of Westphalia of 1648. In response, intellectuals in Asian cultures [for instance], especially in Japan and China, started inventing new terminology to give local expression to this new phenomena. The religious cultures of the East were slowly transformed into formal religious systems with leaders, theologies, texts and hierarchical institutions as "Eastern Religions"...[9]

BSG, *Avatar*, *SW* much earlier, and *The Matrix*, however, suggest that religion is considerably more fluid than the restrictive boundaries of "public" and "private" space might permit. In the late 1970s Larson's creation carried strong overtones of Mormonism: a mythic 13th tribe had ventured off to the "new world," even if there were numerous references to ancient Greek paganism set over against it (is this to emphasize the series' mythic qualities, and therefore the ancientness of the issues at hand?). Yet the religious dimension was largely underplayed in relation to the political arrangements of the civic life of the refugee communities fleeing (atheistic) Cylon genocide. In contrast, and in a distinctly darker mood that is more culturally resonant with the shifting sands of American consciousness, the newer version of *BSG* explores something considerably more religiously and culturally interesting. Wetmore argues that "In addition to apocalypse and salvation, *BSG* is repeatedly concerned with prophecy, creation, sin, exile, resurrection, and betrayal. In short, it is a narrative that is rife with religious meaning, and contains many echoes of the concerns, concepts and beliefs of American Christianity."[10] However, this comment limits the range of *BSG*'s concerns. The series engages a variety of available and clashing religiosities, and it does so by drawing them into "public," expressing their political nature and the pressure they exert on political or civic life—the religion-lite civil religion which is the public face of the religious pluralism of the 12 tribes of Cobol; the religious intensity of self-confident monotheistic fundamentalisms; secularism; and even cynical nihilism.[11] Moreover, it portrays these complex conditions and religious traditions by offering "viewers a rich tapestry in which degrees of faith and differing doctrinal positions are treated sympathetically and sincerely."[12] For instance, by exploring the series' early cynic Dr. Gaius Baltar later in religious terms, the show "explodes the opposition of science and religion."[13]

Under contemporary religio-cultural and socio-political conditions the older liberal "logic of certainty" is shifting into a self-reflexivity close to a "logic of uncertainty" so that "nothing escapes close critical examination" and reimagining.[14] The so-called "public" is becoming a distinctly more contested (and in the process more pluralized and fragmented) space that more adequately reflects the heterogeneity of the nation's population, its multiculturalism. Questions of what the nation-state now is surface particularly from the late modern capitalist process of globalization. Even so, while many theorists have been claiming the end of the modern nation-state with the globalized economic conditions and increasingly labor mobility, with the liquid societies of late capitalism (Bauman), Turner, for one, argues that "nation state sovereignty in fact is being forcefully re-asserted in the 'war on terrorism'" amid the trauma of a post–9/11 sense of fragility and the fervor of a wave of patriotic sentiment and its muscular military power.

> Because state formation by definition makes people into either citizens or aliens, the modern nation state creates rather than solves the problem of multiculturalism. States need to create formal identities for their citizens, and these legal boundaries typically coincide with territorial boundaries, thereby producing a binary division between insiders and outsiders, that is, between aliens and citizens.[15]

In some ways it might appear that Samuel Huntington's "clash of civilizations" thesis is better equipped to describe some of the tensions and pressures of contemporary globo-politics than Fukuyama's optimistic portrayal of "the end of history and the last man." Yet even here there are political tensions that Huntington's thesis is particularly ill equipped to expose.

The Religion of the National Experiment

As cited in this book's introduction, Freire observed some years ago that "there is no such thing as a neutral education process." That goes for the "education" provided by cultural artifacts. And this is a political claim given the way culture forms the soil for identifiability and binds otherwise disparate communities together culturally and imaginatively. "Education," Freire argues, "either functions as an instrument that is used to facilitate the integration of the [learner] into the logic of the present system and bring about conformity to it or it becomes the practice of freedom."[16] Consequently, cultural theorists recognize that so-called "popular culture" cannot be accorded the status of "entertainment" *simpliciter*, but its relation to deeper senses of identity are to be acknowledged, understood, and evaluated. For one thing, it has become clear that in some cases "spiritual" value has been claimed to be generated, in one way or another, by forms of popular culture. Here instances of the hyper-real religiosity of Jediism, for example, appear to be more religiously significant than being simply moments of religious expression, illustration or inspiration (such as one finds with Christian groups' love of C.S. Lewis' *The Lion, the Witch and the Wardrobe*), or enrichments of already existing religiosities, in the liquid spirituality of late modernity.[17] The superhero culture, for its part, has provided a stock of images, phrases, themes and stories now often better known around the world than many religious texts. Siegel and Shuster may have been imagining a Samson for our times with shades of Moses (this emancipatory status is clear in Jor-el's missiological description in Richard Donner's *Superman the Movie*) in *Action Comics* 1 of 1938, but in many ways familiarity with Superman may have now even surpassed religious progenitors. So Roz Kaveney, for instance, relates how when she was an adolescent she learned an important moral lesson from the *Daredevil* comics and accordingly emphasizes that "I learned it not from religion, nor political economy, nor from great literature, but from superhero comics."[18] Reflecting on her education, she adds that comics "helped teach me to play with paradox, and with the complex and double-natured; they are one of the reasons I enjoy the postmodern condition without needing to dignify it with elaborate structures of theory."[19] These claims are interesting for a number of reasons: for instance, what kind of "teaching" can or do comic book superheroes provide? Secondly, what is going on with anti-theoretical play that refuses to reason publically its understanding that these sites are educationally significant?

According to Richard Kearney, "in our own postmodern era of fragmentation and fracture, ... narrative provides us with one of our most viable forms of *identity*—individual and communal."[20] John Shelton Lawrence and Robert Jewett's critical engagement with modern popular culture takes the form of identifying certain identity-generative narratives or myths that have for some time contributed to the shaping of the American imagination. In their *The Myth of the American Superhero*, and in Campbellian fashion, they explain that an "American monomyth" has directed American sensibility since the earliest times of the European settlement of North America, and that this is detectable in much popular culture.[21] In fact, "these problematic tendencies of American culture are significantly nourished by a post-civic popular culture that has become a new center for shaping political beliefs and impulses to action."[22] In their critical political narrative they particularly detect "a broad mythic stream that flows through superheroic comics" that amounts "to a kind of mythic induction into the cultural values of America."[23] Accordingly, the popular texts not only display or express a political vision, but reinforce that idea by making it a natural, or ideological, part of the fabric directing the readers' imaginations of nation and the individual's place within it. Stanford Carpenter claims that artifacts are not to be read simply as "texts," but more ethnographically.

> Artifacts—in this case comic books—are more than the images, texts, representations, or discourses that they seem to contain. Artifacts should not be "read" as text. To do so denies the fact that artifacts—as "things"— are part and parcel of a vast array of cultural, economic, political, and social relationships.[24]

This generative stream exhibits "problematic tendencies of American culture" such as the stress on the individualized agent or vigilante with intense moral certainty (without self-reflexivity), the post-civic anti-democratic political action, the delineation of solution-by-violence, and the simplistic us-vs.-them depiction of "good" and "evil."[25] To use Idealist philosophical language, an individuated subjectivity has been expressed in the archetypal lone hero who with intense moral certainty (without self-reflexivity) self-sacrificially acts redemptively. In its turn, moreover, this heroic mythology not only displays or expresses a political vision, but serves to significantly nourish and reinforce these tendencies by making it a "natural" part of the fabric that directs the readers' imaginations of nation and the individual's place within it. What is equally important, culturally speaking, is the fact that, as Richard Gray and Betty Kaklamanidou argue, "these new superhero texts, however, not only comment on contemporary socio-political events, but also disseminate American ideology throughout the world. [Daniel] Franklin claims that each American motion picture contains part of the nation's political ideology, which is based primarily on classical liberalism put forth by John Locke during the 17th century."[26] Among their vast array of arguments, Jewett and Lawrence's critique tends to focus on three main areas: the national political expression of "the vigilante tradition," the moral purity of the agent(s), and the violence involved.

With regard to the first of these, Jewett and Lawrence are concerned for the health of a democratic system when the underlying narratives design "unelected, law-transcending figures [who] exercise superpowers to overcome foes."[27] They cite Donald McDonald's complaint about the militarization of American foreign policy "when, at critical moments, it is the military who seem to offer the crisp, definite, tangible options— while those who argue for negotiation, diplomacy, and respect for the decent opinion of mankind seem to be offering the unattractive, end-lessly prolonged, and inconclusive options."[28] This state of unaccountable "exceptionalism," flowing from the action of those who are morally pure against the corrupt and wicked, is referred to by Jewett and Lawrence as the "pop-fascist dimension" in American cultural-political life. In this way, then, claims to national mission sit uncomfortably close to totali-tarian politics, in that they sinisterly and muscularly secure their refusal to listen to others' opposing voices, and repudiate the entertaining of any possibility that "the Good" transcends their conceiving and can crit-ically measure their envisaged practices, but instead self-assertively impose their own accents on dissenters and identify "the Good" with their performance. In other words, such a myth involves refusal to co-operatively converse or even to admit the need to be guided or held accountable by others. This refusal, the critics contend, contributes to the difficulty the United States frequently has with submitting itself to what is perceived to be the unwarranted restraint imposed by the United Nations, whereas it instead asserts for itself the right of unilateral action. Jewett and Lawrence continue by claiming that "many of the superheroic stories," for instance, "carry an invitation for the audience members to emulate the zealous action,"[29] and the form of this zealous action is unde-mocratic in ethos. "Personal crusades against evil, so perfectly exempli-fied in the American monomyth, hardly qualify as standing within the tradition of democratic sentiment."[30] As will be argued later, there is a quite different way in which this can be read, however, and dealing more carefully with the particularities of the text can make for not only for a more satisfactory reading of the superhero culture they critique but also an account of the cultural-political context they belong to. For now, though, it is important to continue to indicate the connections Jewett and Lawrence make between the concept of the superhero and conser-vative political ideology.

In order for this ideology to function, the superheroic figure not only has to have "an extraordinary capability for effective acts," but it also has to embody "transcendent moral perfection."[31] Frequently, Jewett and Lawrence spend time excavating the historical texts in order to claim that this kind of mythic sensibility is traceable to considerably earlier days in the formation of the set of free states that became known as the United States.[32] Covenantally focused Puritans brought a sense of their own isolation from the Christianities of the "old world," righteous and redemptive presence with them to the "new world," the place where the consummation of God's ways would messianically occur through their work. This notion morphed early on into a messianic millenarianism with a national sense of missiological destiny for the building of the holy commonwealth, the eschatologically "new world." According to Ernest Lee Tuveson, Jonathan Edward's idea was that with the conversion of the New World "divine providence is preparing the way for the future glorious times of the church, where Satan's kingdom shall be overthrown throughout the whole habitable globe."[33] A famous instance of this developing millenarianist mythology was John Winthrop's sermon delivered in 1630. While this has been described as "a kind of Ur-text of American literature," he was, of course, neither American nor was speaking to an American audience. (In fact, to further indicate the anachronism, there was no "America" at that time.)[34] A particularly memorable claim in Winthrop's homiletic rhetoric likened the nation to a city on a hill, and this imagery has been picked up more recently by both Ronald Reagan and George W. Bush: "Wee shall finde that the God of Israell is among us, when ten of us shall be able to resist a thousand of our enemies, when hee shall make us a prayse and glory, that men shall say of succeeding plantacions: the lord make it like that of New England: for wee must Consider that wee shall be as a Citty upon a Hill, the eies of all people are uppon us."[35]

In a like manner, a Henry Melville wrote later, "we Americans are the peculiar, chosen people—the Israel of our time; we bear the ark of the liberties of the world.... Long enough have we been skeptics with regard to ourselves, and doubted whether, indeed, the political Messiah had come. But he has come in us, if we would but give utterance to his promptings."[36] Jewett and Lawrence indicate the importance of this mythology in the frontier narrative. This version of the myth operates with a sense of an "Other" in the form of an uncivilized and barbarically destructive native who threatens the morally pure settlers, and the frontier myth's missiological sensibility comes to underlie appeals to "Manifest Destiny and the allegedly selfless imperialism of earlier American civil religion, when seizing other countries surfaced as the nation's mission during the Spanish-American War."[37] Consequently, H.W. Brands observes, "if a single theme pervades the history of American thinking about the world, it is that the United States has a peculiar obligation to better the lot of humanity.... Americans have commonly spoken and acted as though the salvation of the world depended on them."[38]

The myth of "American exceptionalism" has led to the widespread American (religio-political) belief that American national self-interest is problematically identical with global altruism, so that "what was good for America was good for the world."[39] This "good," then, gives to American consciousness a sense of moral leadership for, and a driving feeling of destiny "under God" to, the (barbarian) nations for the sake of their civilization. So Jewett and Lawrence notice that "While the language of 'chosen people' and 'political Messiah' is no longer used by sophisticated Americans, the values and emotions associated with such ideas continue to exercise their power. A sense of mission 'was present from the beginning of American history, and is present, clearly, today.'"[40] It was for that reason that while President Ronald Reagan was elected with a mere 28 percent of the vote in 1980 (voter apathy produced only a 53 percent voter turnout), not long after was "Flush with a sense of power and destiny" and himself came to pronounce the American mission under God.[41]

Julia Ward Howe's 1861 *Battle Hymn of the Republic* is equally an instructive moment in this burgeoning national ideology since it particularly connects national destiny and violent action. In it the biblical images that refer to the work of God in Christ are applied to the coming and presence of the Union armies, the armies of the *United* States. On this Jewett and Lawrence comment:

> In the marching of the Union soldiers was "the glory of the coming of the Lord"; and with God marching on the side of the Northern armies, it saw victory as inevitable.... Who is this martial God who leads the Northern troops into battle? Who is the "Lord" who crushes the grapes of his wrathful wine by the feet of his troops? It is none other than the loving Christ seen through the lens of the Book of Revelation. The contradictory images of the peaceful suffering servant and the marching Lord of battle are joined in the final stanza. The redemptive task of the northern soldiers is neatly shifted from annihilating the enemy to altruistically setting people free. The unselfish mission of the suffering, dying servant is incorporated into that of the warrior. He soldier dies—not killing others, but suffering for others.[42]

With regard to violent action, Jewett and Lawrence argue that the overriding of the democratic process results in assertive action and the inability to be hampered by ideals of conversation, argument, reconciliation and compromise. They observe that "the American monomyth betrays deep antagonism toward the creative exercise of reason on the part of the public as well as the individual."[43] What it entails therefore, they continue, is that "careful deliberation, knowledge of law, and mastery of book learning are usually presented in monomythic materials as indicators of impotence and corruption. In the exercise of redemptive power, purity of intention suffices." The ideology of what Jewett and Lawrence speak of as the American monomyth slips into a conflictual ideology, and so according to Richard Slotkin, "tales of strife between Americans and interlopers, between dark races and whites, became the basis of our mythology."[44] Several cultural-political commentators have used Walter Wink's notion of the "myth of redemptive violence" to identify a crucial element in the development of the idea of America, although for Wink this is itself *the* myth of America.

Jewett and Lawrence, however, focus on the character of the hero, and the political implications of his (the protagonists are generally gendered male) action, and they do so with a view to the underlying ideological system that forms political self-understanding. But among other things, they do not press the possibilities for systemic economic critique as substantially as they could. Batman is a good example of what is at issue here, with his Andrew Carnegie–like philanthropism. Frank Miller in *Batman: Year One* describes Wayne Manor as having been "built as a fortress generations past, to perfect a fading line of royalty from an age of equals."[45] The Spencerist equation of power, success and superiority are notable in the stories, and such a socio-economic concern is mentioned by Selina Kyle in Christopher Nolan's inspired rebooting of the Batman franchise. To Bruce she announces, "there's a storm coming, Mr. Wayne. You and your friends better batten down the hatches, cause when it hits you're all going to wonder how you ever thought you could live so large and leave so little for the rest of us." Yet even here the critique is insufficiently pressed by the director, and the economic liberation motif (the rhetoric and imagery associated with Bain in *The Dark Knight Rises* are, to a significant degree, allegories of the French Revolution)[46] is distinctly masked since it is associated with fear (the people under nuclear threat), madness (the Scarecrow, Dr. Jonathan Crane), and the contested notion of justice (The League of Shadows' spirit of just vengeance and Manichaean sensibility). In this case, the myth or even the myths that the cultural artifacts express and visually suggest lie in *both* what they *say* and also in what they do not say—or better yet, what they do not contest.

Differently Entertaining: Religion in Joss Whedon's The Avengers

The American national experiment, unlike that of the "old world," has become determined by the immigration of *different* peoples. Initially the sense of the civic was broadly similarly predicated on common ethnicity, that of white northern European Protestants. While tensions remained and exploded at various pressure points, the idea of the United States shifted into a common civic frame. The idea of the nation, then, is one of a civic society gathered around certain core values represented by the flag rather than as ethnically composed tribalistic commonality, and therefore one in which the nation itself is the focus of unity, even if particular governments and political parties themselves are not perceived to embody that unity sufficiently. Therein a different kind of us-them/good-evil binarism has politically developed than an ethnically charged one.

Joss Whedon's multi-ethnic *Firefly* exemplifies these post-ethnic conditions by displaying without comment ethnic and spiritual diversity, and therein providing a set of conditions in which "the diversity of religion and spirituality is celebrated in a technological advanced society."[47] His *Buffy the Vampire Slayer* references not only the Romantic counter-modernity of the Gothic but also a sexual fluidity through Willow (lesbian) and Angel (non-human because "undead"). This series echoes the shifting values and pluriform social performance of late "liquid" modernity, and it further expresses the irrepressibility of the spiritual and the magical in cosmopolitan and religiously plural societies. *The Avengers* seems to strike a related ethnic cord with its gathering of such an array of vastly different persons into "the Avengers initiative." In 1975 Marvel's Chris Claremont revamped the mutant X-Men into something more ethnically diverse and nationally global, and this radicalized the superhero team-ups. The origins of the idea came from the success of DC Comics' reworking of its earlier experiment with the Justice Society of America into the Justice League of America in 1960 and Marvel's subsequent Fantastic Four (November 1961). What is significant about the JLA, however, is that it contained several "aliens" (the Amazonian Wonder Woman, the Atlantean sovereign Aquaman, Kryptonian Superman, and later J'onn J'onzz or Martian Manhunter) who had, for all intents and purposes become naturalized *American* heroes. Marvel followed with *The Fantastic Four* a year later in November 1961, and then with the Avengers in September 1963. The grouping appealed to an audience which desired to see its heroes team-up, and even to test their strength and skill when their tempers overtook their collegiality.

It is intriguing, and perhaps suggestive, that Whedon has altered the original line-up (September 1963) in order to include the thawed out Captain America, and a reimagined Black Widow, replacing Wasp and Ant-Man in the process. Even Mark Millar's and Bryan Hitch's *The Ultimates* of 2002, which appears closer to Whedon's vision, retains these two displaced characters. (Ant-Man here, however, takes the form of Giant-Man.) It is in this context that Whedon, himself a self-proclaimed atheist, offers a few underdeveloped references to religion.

There is a thin recognition of religious plurality through including both Thor and Steve Rogers (Captain America) alongside the absence of mentions of religious matters among the other (more secular?) characters. While Whedon's many imaginative cinematic and televisual projects inhabit an imagined post-secular pluralization, the hints in *The Avengers* are not explored any further. In other words, if religion is not invisible or discredited by broad critical swipes, it is hardly visible either. It is both noticeable and noteworthy that Whedon does not make much of the reductionistic potential involved in the religious imagery attributable to the design of Thor, or at least not directly. This is a character developed by Marvel Comics at a time when much science-fiction and fantasy literature was suggesting that the gods were simply primordial extraterrestrial beings mistakenly taken as deities. As Kenneth Branagh's *Thor* indicates, the Asgaardian "gods" are super-beings from another realm who have "slipped into myth and legend" [Odin, in *Thor*]. The type of godness that Thor characterizes is certainly quite different, then, from that of the ancient Nordic tales. Yet there is something also quite un–Feuerbachian at the same time about Marvel's depiction: the power of these "gods" is protective rather than inversely detracting and negating. Loki is not an exception to this since his conflictual colonialist drive, revealed in attempted genocide against Jotunheim in Branagh's movie, is born specifically of the angst of a very human-like identity-crisis and as a psychologically reactive move to take control of his destiny in response to his discovery of his true lineage. Something of this has been explored more recently in Ridley Scott's *Prometheus* (2012), taking its cue from Erich von Däniken's pre-visitation idea proposed in *Chariots of the Gods*. Here the creative "Engineers" are construed as moving to destroy life on earth as a result of human wickedness.

Theological language continues to be used of Thor throughout Branagh's *Thor*, and this is picked up by Whedon. In a humorous reference, Whedon's Captain America claims that "there is only one God, maam, and I'm pretty sure he doesn't dress like that." This theological reference may be particularly significant by virtue of the fact that it is offered by a character who hails from a now temporally displaced and culturally remote society. Is this, then, a reference to a form of Christian nostalgia or even to Captain America as a religious anachronism? Agent Phil Colson's earlier comment on the continuing contemporary relevance of Cap's patriotic attire might find a parallel here: "people might need a little old fashioned." Moreover, not only does the narrative not display any explicit contestation of Cap's claim, it is interesting that the theological statement is made by someone whose super abilities are the product of the *scientifically* developed super-serum research. In this regard, Cap actually embodies a refusal to understand scientific progress as inversely related to religious commitment.

The most one can say, then, is that Whedon does not studiously avoid religious motifs and their political implications, even if he does not use them to challenge the dominant Hollywood secularism or the atheism prevalent in 1960s and 70s science fiction, or to indicate the contemporary tensions over the clash of "publics."[48] In this regard, his work reflects what Possamai and Lee declare to be increasingly the case among science fiction, and one should add fantasy and superhero, writers: that a narrative "dealing with faith issues no longer needs to justify its existence (or lack thereof) of religion against a backdrop of atheism. Rather, religion is often presented as a regular and visible narrative prop."[49] They continue, "although science dominates the super hero universe, magic and religion persist, and live side by side with atheism."[50] Even so, Whedon's is a religion-lite for a spiritually consumerist religious landscape.

Whedon's Politics of National Pleasure

Something more religiously significant but simultaneously politically problematic emerges for critical consideration at this point, however. The slender nod to religion that *The Avengers* provides occurs in the context of a piece that does not challenge American nationalism, the equation of God and nation that Frank Miller's President Ronald Reagan announces in *The Dark Knight Returns*, and that is partly conceptually connected with the most nationally symbolic and patriotically associated of the characters. This deflects the kinds of tensions that religious commitment can generate for the consciousness of identity as national citizens. As David Rapaport argues, "religion has been an essential and quite possibly the most important ingredient in the state's legitimacy."[51] The danger here, in other words, would be that Whedon's piece binds religion to the national project, the commitment to the well-being of the state and the state's frequently violent relations to other states. Religions are transnational, and the so-called "world religions" of the post-axial period tend to be trans-ethnic, and this is particularly so among the aggressively evangelistic religions of Islam and Christianity. Consequently, there are tensions and difficulties for the relation of citizenship in the modern nation-state and one's trans-national religious identification. As a result, the national comes to adopt more formally religious features—national "civil religion," in Robert Bellah's phrase, for a civic and multi-ethnic state, for the minimalist unity of populations ethnically, culturally and religiously increasingly fragmented.[52] Observing this, William Cavanagh claims that the nation organizes "bodies around stories of human nature and human destiny that have deeply theological analogues. In other words, supposedly "secular" political theory is really theology in disguise."[53] In this regard Samuel Huntington's much cited "clash of civilizations" thesis comes to look distinctly limited—there is no stable West versus a stable Islam, but only ever mobile and porous communities loosely held together by commitment to certainly common nationally defined values. Hence the cultural and political importance of the Bush-era's move against Islamicist terrorism, and imagistically the deep connecting of this with multiple forms of Christian imagery (language of "crusade," for example), and the vision of a remodeled Middle East operating on the "civilized" principles of the United States. Moreover, it equally contextualizes the so-called "fundamentalist" projects that attempt to create conditions for the securing of identifiable markers against the liquidity of the flattening of commitment and consciousness in an age of globalized information technologies, pluralized media values, cultural heterogeneity, and the blandly minimalist identifiability of persons as consumers. In other words, the questions are particularly important in the context of contemporary global political events.

One might argue that Whedon's purpose was not to do this—his attentions lie elsewhere. But I want to suggest that matters are substantially interesting for the religiously informed and ideologically suspicious reader than simply looking for explicit religious references, commenting on their infrequency, or even paying naïve attention to the director's intentions. To put it at its starkest, the danger would be that *The Avengers* can suggest (either wittingly or not) a binding of religion to the national project, the commitment to the well-being of the state and the state's frequent violent relations to other states. In this way, it could imply and reinforce the ethos of national "civil religion" that bonds a civic and multi-ethnic state as a minimal national unification.[54] In order to sustain such a critical reading, much work needs to be done in analyzing the political significance of Whedon's movie.

The film's scenes in India and Russia are utilized in order to provide a sense of the global, but the new breed of hero (the Russian spy Black Widow, and the Norse "god" Thor) is then drawn back to the United States in order to do heroic business. The sense here is less that of Claremont's X-Men and more that of DC Comics' post–1950 redevelopment of Kal-el. The socially minded crusader for justice from the late 1930s becomes the Kryptonian immigrant who is integrated *into* the nation, emerging as both one of the people and as a national idea referred to as "truth, justice and the American way." As Geoffrey Hodgson claims, "the professed goal of immigration to America is integration. Wherever immigrants come from, as they and their children become Americans, they cease to be representative of the whole world."[55] Kevin Smith recognizes the connection between this heroic character and the American dream. Superman is the "Ultimate Immigrant ... who came here and made something of himself. He works hard, pays his bills and finds time to stop Brainiac from enslaving Earth."[56] Commenting on this set of claims, Jewett and Lawrence assert that "here Smith encapsulates the preferred persona of the civil religion: the power to save earth combined with an ego that seeks nothing for itself."[57] Promotion pictures for Richard Donner's *Superman the Movie* of 1978 visually illustrate this with Superman standing against the backdrop of the star-spangled banner, and the theatrical version of *Superman II* of 1980 (i.e., not Donner's pre–re-edited and partially refilmed edition) had a scene with the hero returning the White House's dome with the flag proudly flying on top of it. Bryan Singer's 2006 version of the Kryptonian's story, *Superman Returns*, however, at least suggest a modest shift in this sensibility. At one point Perry White instructs his reporting team on the questions the paper has to address regarding the return of Superman. "Does he still stand for truth, justice, all that stuff?" The omission of "and the American way" is particularly noticeable.

The *Action Comics* character originally had been offered as a defender of the "New Deal," of social justice, as a supporter of the outcast, and as an opponent of the political and economically corrupt. In other words, with his appearance in 1938 he had a quite socioeconomically radical comic book origin. Despite the privilege that the alien Kal-el was born into, this refugee was adopted and raised as Clark Kent by a simple, honest and modest midwestern farming family, and rather than simplistically uphold the law (which supports the powerful and wealthy) he came to support the economically disenfranchised against their unjust victimization, "clearly the champion of the underdog, displaying a sense of class consciousness virtually absent from later comic book stories."[58] According to Aldo Regalado, then, "Superman directly engaged the terms of modernity in America, embodying popular longings to challenge the inequities of its systems of corporate capitalism."[59] However, the ethos soon shifted. According to Umberto Eco, this character's growth in popularity led to the franchise being commodified as a consumer leisure product, and this had an effect on his socio-political role.[60] It was particularly during the Second World War and the subsequent period in which the government expressed intense suspicion of the comic book genre in the 1950s that the character was reinvented for the Cold War. From this point, "the American way" become as much a part of his identity as his letter "S" emblazoned on his garishly conceived costume. The character was reimagined as something of a super policeman or reactionary law-enforcer. As Tony Mills argues, during the Second World War, "Superman—formerly a champion of the oppressed whose first few years were drenched in social commentary and judgment—became a state-sponsored tool of the establishment. Even the grim and gritty Batman, who is usually associated with the dirty underbelly of the nation, fully endorsed American patriotism by urging readers to buy war bonds."[61] Accordingly, even Zack Snyder, director of the nationalism-disruptive *Watchmen*, has his *Man of Steel* respond to General Swanwick's question, "How do we know that one day you won't act against America's interests?" with "I grew up in Kansas, general. I'm about as American as it gets." There is no contesting of the ideology of national self-interest here, and while Kal-el mentions that he will help on his own terms there is the danger that the superpowered American resident will not only not contest the *realpolitik* of American self-interest but will, as in the second part of Frank Miller's celebrated *Dark Knight Returns* graphic novel, actually fearsomely act in its interests.

That connection between Superman, the world and the American way, nonetheless, is itself politically telling, as Jeph Loeb and Tom Morris imply when suggesting that the Kryptonian orphan is "an ongoing example of ... [what] the genuinely *human* way should look like."[62] However, given the deep connections made between this character and the nation-state, this universalizing consequently reflects the long-standing mythology of national exceptionalism which is proclaimed in George W. Bush's early 2003 State of the Union Address: "The liberty we prize is not America's gift to the world, it is God's gift to humanity."[63] As with the so-called "Golden Age" of comic books, right up through the 1960s, this mythos portrays the U.S. as a righteous and ideologically unique nation, possessing a messianic mission on behalf of the global good. It "forcefully set[s] forth the United States as the embodiment of all that is right."[64] As Jewett and Lawrence observe, "Superman is conservative about challenging the community's failing institutions. Like the Lone Ranger, he always delivers the evildoers to the police rather than killing them or dishing out his own punishment."[65] The latter sentence here is meant to support the first one, although it requires remodeling to circumvent its carelessness. The important issue is not whether a superhero metes out his/her own justice as if that solves Jewett and Lawrence's worry, since their critique of superhero texts is precisely that they tend to operate with a vigilante sensibility. Moreover, Judge Dredd remains part of a corrupt and violent governing system even while delivering fatal justice. The issue is, instead, that Superman is a political conservative who deals only with surface crime and not with the corrupting system. *Superman vs. the Elite* offers intriguing suggestions in this regard in a scene in which the Kryptonian is questioned in the United Nations about his decision not to destroy Atomic Skull. In his defense, Superman iterates that his powers are not to be used to be judge, jury, and certainly not executioner, and he emphatically declares that his superpowers do not stand above the law. The interrogator, however, asks why he does not use his powers "to fix the world." The response is telling: "I do not believe the world is broken.... It has always been my belief that, at its core, people are good."

At this point, Richard Wagner's *Flight of the Valkyries* might start to resound in the ideology critic's ears, as the disturbing scene in *Watchmen* depicting the nationalized heroes' victory in Vietnam comes to mind. (The political irony of the historical revisionism is suggested by virtue of the fact that Snyder's scene musically echoes the most famous moment in Coppola's *Apocalypse Now* which had been distinctly critical of an America involved in the conflict in S.E. Asia).

Frank Miller develops this connection of the man of steel with the state apparatus to dramatic effect in *The Dark Knight* graphic novel series. *The Dark Knight Returns* offers an aging Batman who is confronted by Ronald Reagan's state in the guise of Superman, and portrays the Man of Steel destroying Soviet jets and tanks, as well as a nuclear missile (the Coldbringer), during a moment of US–USSR tension—the Corto Maltese crisis. Miller's later *The Dark Knight Strikes Again* offers a more self-reflective Superman criticizing his choices. To Wonder Woman and Captain Marvel he laments, "Look at us—hiding on the dark side of the moon like a pack of cowards—skulking about the same rooms where we used to strut as the glory-born Justice League of America—all the while letting monsters rule the world. What have we become?"[66] At this point the face of Lex Luthor appears on the video screen and an answer is provided: "You've become exactly what I always dreamed you'd be, Kent. Pliant, obedient servants, each of you, to the will of your betters." To return to Miller's drama of *The Dark Knight Returns*, the two old friends confront each other in a brutal conflict over their relation to the state, with near fatal consequences. Of course, the more recent *Superman-Batman Public Enemies* depicts the pair fighting alongside each other against the presidency of Lex Luthor. The DC universe has reconceived the relation of Miller's characterizations to the constantly evolving narrative DC arc by attributing it to one of the "alternate worlds."[67] Not merely a narrative thought-experiment, the highly complicated series *The Crisis on Infinite Earths* depicts a multiverse with multiple parallel Earths that were in the process of being destroyed by Anti-Monitor, with five surviving Earth-histories being merged into one by Monitor, his heroic mirror-image, only to be fractured into 52 different universes by Alexander Luthor. The setting for Miller's story is now depicted as Earth–31.

A quite startling challenge to the nationalist simplicity of the man of steel's appeal appears in Mark Millar and Dave Johnson's graphic novel of 2003, *Superman: Red Son.* The work constitutes a thought experiment,

imagining what it might have looked like had Kal-el crash landed in the
Soviet Union rather than the United States. Tony Spanakos relates the
highly significant reconstrual of the character in the thought experiment:

> The result is frightening. Their Superman continues to be moral (unlike
> the characters in *Watchmen*), wanting to do good with his powers, defend-
> ing order and justice. But the problem is that the order and justice are
> those of Stalin's Soviet Union. When Stalin is poisoned by his son, Super-
> man becomes the new head of the Soviet Union and uses his superpowers
> and his alliances with Wonder Woman, a reprogrammed Brainiac, and
> others to engender a utopia in the USSR, a utopia that, terrified of, he
> eventually leaves behind.... As *Marvels* and *Watchmen* make clear, the
> presence of superheroes who constitute an Other to us, almost unrecog-
> nizable as humans, should make humans more insecure. *Superman: Red
> Son* shows how moral superheroes in nondemocratic contexts, in the
> absence of checks and balances, could similarly tend toward utopia—
> making activities that have inevitably dystopian results.[68]

It is not merely with DC Comics that there is such testing of the
American nationalist experiment. While in *Iron Man* Tony Stark declares
his lack of comfort with the "system" of weapons manufacturing and
trade that brings death, he in no way moves against the system of political governance that puts stock in the power of its arsenal, or the system
of international relations that requires expensively equipped military
complexes. It is not insignificant, then, that it is the politically conservative Stark who leads the pro-registration group in Marvel's *Civil War*
event series. As a critical take on this notion, Miller's Batman comes to
realize the limitations in his life's work as the Dark Knight late in his life.
Bruce tells Barry Allen (a.k.a. the Flash), "We blew it, Barry! We spent
our whole careers looking in the wrong direction! I hunted down mug-
gers and burglars while the real monsters took power unopposed!"[69] In
the first book of Miller's *The Dark Knight Returns*, Bruce Wayne is seen
to be reflecting on the differences between the killer of his parents and
the mutant gang currently terrorizing Gotham City, and of the former
he reflects, "he flinched when he pulled the trigger. He was sick and
guilty over what he did. All he wanted was money. I was naive enough
to think him the lowest sort of man."

The images in Whedon's superhero movie certainly do not receive
the kind of explicitly nationalized treatment that directly co-opts the
heroes into the national project in the way that Marvel's epic comic book
series *Civil War* comes to, or as is explored in the revisionist politics of

the *Watchmen* with the drafting of Dr. Manhattan and the Comedian by Richard Nixon during the Vietnam War. In many ways that fact is deserving of comment in relation to Whedon's *intentions*. Even Whedon's Captain America is more understated than a more jingoistic director could have constructed. Yet, the potential for a globalized politics is circumvented, and the heroes' involvement with what appears to be a largely American shaped S.H.I.E.L.D (Supreme Headquarters International Espionage Law-enforcement Division) venture reinforces the conditions conducive to the so-called myth of American exceptionalism, the project rhetorically launched by Winthrop's sermon. S.H.I.E.L.D. is, after all, supposed to be a powerful international organization responsible for *global*-security introduced into the comics in August 1965 and that answers only to the United Nations. This is not suggested by Whedon's piece, however. Not only do those working on the S.H.I.E.L.D. helicarrier who speak in the movie display an American accent, but the main figure of "the Council" directing Nick Fury's group is likewise American. Even the former KGB agent and defector to the U.S., Natasha Romanov, now comes complete with an American accent. The only other member of the Council to address the Director, and does so very much in a subordinate role to the American Councilman, is English. But the underlying suggestion here is not so much one of global co-operation as of a British government aligned with the U.S. (as with foreign policy in the Middle East since at least the invasion of Afghanistan). While the narrative does contest the governance of those in power, with S.H.I.E.L.D.'s ordering of the Avengers to avert a governmentally approved nuclear strike on Manhattan, the movie does not contest America's leadership as such but only the motives and poor judgment of particular persons in power. After all, the comic books of the 1970s with which Whedon himself was familiar develop their frequently morally unambiguous forms of vigilantism against a backdrop of disillusionment with the Vietnam War and Watergate, and slip into the early 1980s with Ronald Reagan's appeal to the myth of the Wild West and American moral and political supremacy. One could make a case from *The Avengers* for a conservative politics of "small-government" and the altruistic actions of well-placed individuals, but not for a globo-politics that challenges the myth of America as beacon to the world. (There is too little reference to the world to sustain much sensible democratic reflection here.) With a theological flourish, on the first anniversary of 9/11 George W. Bush proclaimed,

America strives to be tolerant and just.... We fight, not to impose our
will, but to defend ourselves and extend the blessings of freedom.... And
the duty we have been given [by God]—defending America and our freedom—is also a privilege we share.... And our cause is even larger than
our country. Ours is the cause of human dignity; freedom guided by conscience and guarded by peace. This ideal of America is the hope of all
mankind.[70]

Moreover, Whedon's film falls into the trap of portraying a plot
mechanism required by the Manichaean undertones within the mythos
of exceptionalism, that the threat is from the "other," the wholly and
irreconcilable alien. While not tending to trade in explicitly dehumanizing insults, much superhero literature is pervaded and even framed
by this broad sensibility of the utterly irredeemable "other," particularly
in the comics that predate the 1970s. As Stan Lee once admitted, "the
battle between a hero and a villain (which is what virtually all our stories
get down to) is basically a conflict between a good guy and a bad guy,
or between good and evil."[71] Of course, one could argue that the ethnic
connection between Loki and Thor mitigates that vulgar ideology somewhat, since they are both alien Asgaardians. And yet, Loki is revealed
to not be a child of Odin at all, having been stolen by Odin from the
Frost Giants of Jotunheim with a view to someday enabling an alliance
between these two realms. In this sense, his menace is an echo of older
fears of illegitimacy (Shakespeare's Edmund in *King Lear* is a good example), and of a form of familial disruption (with the sins of the fathers
rebounding on them) and otherness. Whedon does make much of this
origin story which is more fully and Shakespearianly explored by Branagh, and he also softens any potential Manichaean blow through Thor's
attempts to make familial connection with his half-brother.

But the use of the colonializing alien race the Chitauri nevertheless
remains significant. In a moment of post–9/11 angst and catharsis, and
in an echo of the *Transformers* movie franchise, Whedon's New York suffers an act of terrorism sustained by an imperialist threat, only to be
saved (not without sustaining heavy property damage, of course) by the
morally uncomplicated and selflessly motivated superhero squad. The
heroes are presented towards the end of his movie not with the kind of
public fear that forces the Batman into the shadows as *vigilante*, or the
government to move to control the superpowered as in season 10 of
Smallville and in Bryan Singer's two X-Men movies, or the attempt to
publicly curtail the heroes' activities in Alan Moore's *Watchmen* (with

its Keene Act of 1977), Pixar's *The Incredibles*, and the recent television series *The Tomorrow People*. Instead, they are icons of a publically celebrated *militia* organization. Unlike in Frank Miller's Batman series and Marvel Comics' *Civil War* event series, for instance, there is no ambiguity regarding the heroes' relation to civil society or public debate concerning civil rights, vigilante action, extreme violence, and so on. The mood of *The Avengers* is instead akin to Lucas' *SW*, or *A New Hope* (*ANH*), of 1977, even if the latter did begin to substantively deconstruct that sensibility in and through the appearance of each new movie in the saga. The heroes never face the kinds of tragic dilemmas that complicate moral existence, or are caught by the enforcement of the governance of others who themselves are more self-interested. According to Danny Fingeroth,

> We have a need for a champion who will know the right thing to do, the right amount of force that needs to be applied, and who has the resources to muster that force and set right everything that has veered off track. Although, in reality, when mere humans try to do these things the results are often messy and muddled, the superhero ideal exists because we want and need it to on many psychological levels. We need to dream, and superheroes are the embodiment of what C.G. Jung termed the collective unconscious.[72]

In an evident contrast to this, Marvel Comics has tended to conspicuously design Tony Stark in morally ambiguous terms. For example, he is deeply self-destructively compulsive, hedonistic and narcissistic. According to Spanakos, "Although Stark's private life is exciting, it is not exactly moral. Stark's conception of the beautiful and the good are too superficial and material and he is too much a slave to his passions."[73] As a result of these character flaws he struggles in particular with alcoholism and this struggle occasionally leads to tragic incidents. This imperfect armored warrior-hero often has to repair the very conditions he has consciously or unintentionally created. So Christopher Robichaud observes that the Iron Man has to be very much understood as a flawed idol. "Tony Stark often finds himself having to right the wrongs that he, inadvertently or not, helped bring about."[74] In many ways it is his intransigent and uncompromising enforcing of the government's registration of all costumed heroes that makes for the tragic conditions of Marvel's superhero *Civil War*. Moreover, he even attempts to manipulate a war with Namor's Atlantis in order to unite the heroes, and misguidedly uses the Green Goblin to do so with catastrophic results. Whedon's movie sug-

gests little of this Stark, even if he does have him announce to Agent
Colson that he "does not play well with others." Equally, the writer-
director's instinct-driven Hulk eventually becomes domesticated and
harnessed to the defensive task at hand. The frightening unleashing of
raw aggression so violently turned initially and momentarily on Thor
and Black Widow gives way to a character who stands in the outward
facing circle of the hero initiative, a circling of the wagons moment as
the little group heroically faces a seemingly overwhelming enemy bent
simply on annihilating human life. There is in the narrative no sense of
the destructively rampaging beast who in the comic books and the two
recent big screen outings (*The Hulk* and *The Incredible Hulk*) is intensely
suspicious of General Thaddeus Ross and the American military complex[75]; or whose rampage leads to the very formation of the Avengers in
the first place in *Marvel's Avengers* origins story; or who has to be ban-
ished from earth by Stark and Reed Richards after devastating Las Vegas.
As Spanakos argues, the monstrous Hulk is an ontological exception
who is utterly uncontrollable by the state, and a constant threat to its
legitimating military presence. Such a beast instead becomes considerably more politically domesticated when handled by Whedon. Here he
is able to harness his bestial rage, and is co-opted to work for a political-
military complex.[76]

   Again the contrast between this unproblematized sense of the ideal
"hero" and the increasingly more psychologically tortured and morally
ambiguous Batman, exemplified in Frank Miller's work and assumed by
Christopher Nolan, is significant. So Miller, in *Batman: Year One*, depicts
Bruce reflecting on his parent's death as the night when "all sense left
my life."[77] Despite the moral transformation of Bruce Wayne in *Batman
Begins* (he emerges from his need to avenge his parents to rejecting the
Manichaean apocalypse promoted by The League of Shadows), he
refuses to save the soldiers of The League of Shadows from the exploding
building, or Ducard from the train, and this latter action (a moral non-
doing) is itself the tragic result of his earlier action in saving his former
teacher, and it will rebound again with further tragic repercussions for
the city of Gotham and more personally for Wayne himself in *The Dark
Knight Rises*. In the second of the trilogy, *The Dark Knight*, Batman
appears a little more morally ambiguous again, or he does at least at one
point since it is not clear that Nolan has sufficiently created a sense of
the complexity of moral evil—he brutally engages in torture of the Joker,
with the latter tormenting him with the thought that the "hero" is but

a mirror image of the "villain." Desperate times, one might argue, calls for desperate measures. The question is what kind of person engages in such morally ambiguous action, the kind of action conspicuously absent from Whedon's superhero movie. It is little wonder, then, that the contrast is drawn between the self-sacrificiality of "earth's mightiest heroes" and the self-serving imperialist Chitauri. This echoes President George W. Bush, who puzzles after 9/11 over why people hate America so much when the U.S. is so evidently good. This also echoes the strand of American exceptionalism iterated by Harvard Professor Irving Babbitt, for instance, when he naïvely exaggerates about, or perhaps propagandizes concerning, national benevolence in 1924, missing the power interests it so profitably serves and the interests it does not:

> We are willing to admit that all other nations are self-seeking, but as for ourselves, we hold that we act only on the most disinterested motives.... If the American thus regards himself as an idealist, at the same time that the foreigner looks on him as a dollar-chaser, the explanation may be due partly to the fact that the American judges himself by the way he feels, whereas the foreigner judges him by what he does.[78]

Of course, Nolan's Batman is interpreted not merely in the aftermath of 9/11, but after Miller's celebrated redesign of the Dark Knight (and with Nolan, Miller's vision is more dramatically realized than in the Tim Burton depictions). Pushing the psychological complication of the character, *The Dark Knight Rises* offers a Bruce Wayne on whom the emotional turmoil of his past has taken its toll. This is a man who is so scarred by his experiences that not only does he hang up his vigilante cape and his detective efforts, but he retreats for years into solitude. With Miller's graphic novel entitled *The Dark Knight Returns*, the psychologist Dr. Bartholomew Wolper is depicted as persistently questioning the state of Batman's mental health. The costumed "hero," he argues, displays a "psychotic sublimative/psycho-erotic behavior pattern." "You might say," Wolper continues, "Batman commits the crimes using his so-called villains as narcissistic proxies." In many ways Bruce Wayne is the alter-ego of a man consumed by his loss on that fateful night on a Gotham street at the hands of a mugger. So Scott Beatty in his *Batman: The Ultimate Guide to the Dark Knight* claims that "Bruce Wayne does not exist. In many ways, Bruce Wayne also perished the night his parents were murdered in Crime Alley by Joe Chill all those years ago. In Bruce's own mind, Batman has become the dominant reality from that moment forward as his quest for justice overshadowed all other personal needs or desires. So single-minded in his crusade, obsessive-compulsive to the point that long-term relationships become impossible for him, Bruce thinks of himself only as the Dark Knight."[79]

In fact, in _Batman: Holy Terror_, from the "Elseworlds" series of graphic novel thought experiments, America is conceived of as a theocracy and Thomas and Martha Wayne were victims of a government hit for their treason against the political terror of the inquisitorial state.[80] Bruce, here the Rev. Bruce Wayne, embarks as a man of conscience on his career as the Dark Knight openly for _vengeance_, and the catharsis for his personal rage lies in his acts of violence in the guise of the Batman and his resistant acts against the state system. And so Miller, in his _The Dark Knight Strikes Again Part 1_ shows Superman reflecting critically on Batman's mission by questioning his judgment, and thereby his mental health: "Bruce, you sociopath. You monomanic. You megalomaniac. Our world is a glass menagerie, easily shattered—a poorly balanced house of cards, set to topple. And you're just the man to bring the whole works down…. You monster."[81]

Grant Morrison and Dave McKean's _Arkham Asylum_ questions Batman's sanity further.[82] Early on in the graphic novel the Joker demands the vigilante come "in here, with us, in the nuthouse, where you belong." To Jim Gordon, Batman admits that "I'm afraid that the Joker may be right about me. Sometimes I question the rationality of my actions. And I'm afraid that when I walk through those asylum gates … when I walk into Arkham and the doors close behind me… it'll be just like coming home." This psychological questionability is acknowledged by Rachel Dawes in _Batman Begins_ when she speaks of Bruce Wayne's face as "your mask. Your real face is the one the criminals now fear. The man I loved, the man who vanished, he never came back at all. Maybe he's still out someone. Maybe someday, when Gotham no longer needs Batman, I'll see him again." On the other hand, Nolan subverts this sense by having Bruce long for a (transcendent) life beyond the Batman with Rachel, and then with Selina Kyle in _The Dark Knight Rises_. Partly this responds to the years of the Dark Knight's absence in Miller's narration, although that is echoed to a degree in the absence between Nolan's second and third instalments.

Moreover, Bruce, suffering from among other things his failure with Jason Todd, who as Batman is now not averse to using explosives, is conceived throughout as continually tortured, not only by the image of his parents' death but by his feeling of complicity in numerous deaths caused by letting the Joker live.[83] For instance, in a poignant moment of self-revelation, the billionaire parts from his evening with Jim Gordon admitting the ineffectualness of his earlier vengeful crime-fighting life and the emotional emptiness of what has largely become a bare life: "I leave my car in the lot. I can't stand to be inside anything right now. I walk the streets of this city I'm learning to hate, the city that's given up, like the whole world seems to have. I'm a zombie. A flying Dutchman. A dead man, ten years dead... I'll feel better in the morning. At least, I'll feel it less."

Where this sense of the corrupting effects of deep human angst, the fragilities caused by ignorance of all ends, and the complexity of motivation is dramatized particularly well is in *Watchmen*. This text, which Iain Thomson describes as a "work of postmodern deconstruction" of the cult of the hero, puts in question the very nature of the hero, and those revered in the comic book culture as being morally worthy of our adulation.[84] As Mark White insightfully observes,

> in *Watchmen*, Alan Moore and Dave Gibbons gave us a glimpse of what a world with costumed heroes might *actually* look like—and it wasn't pretty. This was not the shiny "world of tomorrow" that was so familiar from the Superman comics. The world of *Watchmen* surpassed even the grim and gritty Gotham City and Hell's Kitchen of Frank Miller's Batman and Daredevil stories. These were not your noble, perfect, shiny heroes either—Nite Owl could be your Uncle Al, and Rorschach could be the crazy guy down the street who talks to pigeons (and thinks they talk back). Even Dr. Manhattan doesn't know what to do with his nearly limitless power. And the Comedian, a man with no superpowers who is allowed to run amok with the sanction of a very corrupt state, may possibly be the most frightening—and realistic—aspect of *Watchmen*.[85]

In fact, neither Rorschach nor the Comedian are merely crazy, or at least not obviously so with regard to either the former's fanatical devotion to justice (since that is shared feature in the superhero world, such as with Marvel's Punisher and The Extremist) or his understanding of justice as retribution (given the Manichaeism that pervades both the real-life socio-political conditions, and the portrayal of wickedness and the Good in much popular culture), or the latter's sociopathic disdain for life in a brutal world. Rorschach's is certainly an extremity that comes through the familial brokenness, the abuse of maternal neglect and resentment of her son, and social alienation suffered by the young Walter Kovacs. But his obsessive compulsion as a moral agent in his vengeful move against a corrupt and corrupting society appears to lie elsewhere. As Aperlo observes, "Quitting [after the Keene Act of 1977] was never an option for Rorschach, because becoming a masked avenger was never a choice, but a calling."[86] What is so disturbing is not so much the visual demonstration of his uncompromising brutality, but, as with Marvel's Punisher, the performance of what consistent and untainted retributive justice looks like when set in the context of vigilantism. His insanity is the display of what kind of person it takes to purely embody without self-aggrandizing self-interest the Manichaeism that characterises the "us-vs.-them" so prominent in political discourse and the sense of the righteous nation on a just mission. In other words, what makes him disturbing is that he holds a mirror up to his socio-political context as it makes for monstrously retributivist persons. He is the ugly consequence (an extreme one certainly, but nonetheless a logical outcome) of this society (and for which this society is complicit in the creation of). "Rorschach," Jacob Held maintains, "as befitting his name, lets us see ourselves. Through him, we see our desire for justice pushed to its limits."[87] The ink-blot mask is a sign of this projectionist function of his character—on his face the audience is to see itself as the analysand and he the projection of its most deeply held or unconscious desires for vengeance by those desiring a world perceptibly clear-cut in its revelation of good-evil. In fact, Thomson maintains, "By opening (and "closing") the comic with Rorschach, Moore implies that comic book heroes are projections of the fantasies of their readers—as well as their authors."[88] Eddie Blake, or the Comedian, acts in denigrating mockery since nothing has meaning, and therefore anything "morally" goes (including rape and murder) and everything is worth destroying. His is a nihilistic perspective for those who have the power to willingly laugh in the face of the void. According to Keeping, "unable to create, he instead takes pleasure in destruction, and being a superhero gives him license to do so."[89] The movie's director Zack Snyder makes this suggestive social comment about the character: "He is as American as he can be, but he is also the dark side of what America has the potential to be."[90]

To return to the distinctly contrasting piece of work that is Whedon's *Avengers*, at its best, it offers characters who, put most starkly, appear to be stripped of recognizable human psychology at key points. The movie's earlier portrayal of conflict among the group has considerable potential for offsetting that concern, but this is insufficiently pressed, and when placed under threat their differences dissipate and they all pull together as one—as is visually stated in the moment of their defensive circling. The team, and presumably then their mutual trust and friendship, forms by default in a moment of facing a mutual threat. This is a process reflecting Marc Copper's observation very soon after 9/11: "Domestically, the attacks produced a spontaneous outpouring of mutual solidarity and community compassion.... Twenty years of Reaganite individualism appeared to melt overnight."[91] Consequently, Jewett and Lawrence's claim about one of the key features of what they call "the American monomyth" characterizes Whedon's work with *The Avengers*: "In the exercise of redemptive power, purity of intention suffices. Heroes are either static, innately possessing all the wisdom they need, or they learn all they require from a single incident."[92]

At worst, something quite different in sensibility emerges. The initiative is largely saved by virtue of Fury's visual discourse—the display of bloodied Captain America trading cards that were (or rather for effect placed by Fury after the fact) on Coulson's dead body. (Of course, the television series *Marvel's Agents of S.H.I.E.L.D.* has rewritten the murderous incident in order to keep the agent's character alive.) The connection between the moment of the group's uniting (albeit here it is only Stark and Rogers who are present) and the display of Americanness—the cards celebrating the patriotically *American* costumed and entitled hero—is suggestive. Coulson's (apparent) death not only makes poignant the notion that he died for something, but indicates the intensive wickedness of the deadly perpetrators of the hostility whose action preemptively strikes against the city. This latter idea is particularly crucial in the development and maintenance of war-time nationalism. So Bernard Brandon Scott argues that in a Manichaean scheme "conflict is resolved by having a purified savior destroy the enemy. Our villains must be morally evil so that we may be morally pure and our violence justified."[93] Therefore, even if the covering by one's flag should give us a certain protection from the chill of the winter of national crisis, it should not obscure our view of what has been going on underneath the covers that others wear. In the wake of 9/11 and the pervasive Manichaeism of President Bush's rhetoric, Rowan Williams warns about this ethos:

> Bombast about evil individuals doesn't help in understanding anything. Even vile and murderous actions tend to come from somewhere, and if they are extreme in character we are not wrong to look for extreme situations. It does not mean that those who do them had no choice, are not answerable, far from it. But there is sentimentality too in ascribing what

we don't understand to "evil"; it lets us off the hook, it allows us to avoid the question of what, if anything, we can *recognize* in the destructive act of another.... If we act without questioning, we change nothing. It is not true to say, "We are all guilty"; but perhaps it is true to say, "We are all able to understand *something* as we look into ourselves."[94]

It is little wonder, then, that the contrast is so evidently drawn between the self-sacrificiality of "earth's mightiest heroes" and the evidently and morally simplistically self-serving Loki and the imperialist Chitauri. This echoes the strand of American exceptionalism cited earlier from Babbitt, for instance. Not only that, but an old tradition among popular cultural artifacts identified the villain by his aesthetic otherness as well, and this was a caricaturing step particularly visible in certain portrayals of ethnic minorities. J.R.R. Tolkien's orcs, goblins, uruk-hai, and even the Gollum character are all good examples of this tendency, in contrast to the identifiably human-like design of the hobbits, elves, and dwarves. So too is Ridley Scott's monster in *Alien* as designed by H.R. Giger. From the Superman narratives, special mention could be made of Lex Luthor's imperfect clone Bizarro, who differentiated from the "last son of Krypton" as a monstrous and villainous "other" by virtue of both his physicality and his name; or Darkseid from Apokolips, the greatest threat to the DC universe; or the even more aptly named Kryptonian clone, the living weapon Doomsday. With *The Avengers* the Chitauri are a race provided by the Titanian Eternal Thanos (whose name itself is an ominous play on the Greek *thanatos*, or death) bent on a brutal colonial project of enacting cosmic hygiene against disorder and free will. Brian Ott claims that "the path to [morally questionable] torture begins long before even the capture of 'enemy combatants.' It begins with the naming of the Other, for if one does not see an enemy as human, then one does not feel compelled to treat 'it' humanely."[95] According to Ott, "In the original *Battlestar Galactica*, for instance, the Cylons were overtly mechanical and robotic. They symbolized the dual fears of unbridled technology and the loss of humanity to technology at a point in history marked by rapid (even rampant) technological innovation and adoption.... Whereas the Cylons in the original series represented our social fears about technology, the Cylons in the new *BSG* represent our social fears about cultural difference—a point that is emphasized by the repeated contrast between the messianic monotheism of the Cylons and the secular polytheism of the human colonists."[96] One difficulty with this reading, however, is that the rebooted series ended on a controversial note, with a rather Romantic voluntary destruction of the colonialists' communication technologies, and the images of the robotic against the playing of Bob Dylan's "All Along the Watchtower." More fundamentally, however, the contrast between Larson's Cylon "other" and the more recent *humanization* of the Cylons is marked and unequivocally politically significant. As Ronald Moore suggests, "The audience has always seen them [viz., the Cylons] as people by virtue of the fact that we made them look human in the mini-series."[97] Drawing this depiction directly in to the theme of torture, an episode writer on *BSG* admits that "if people see the Cylons as just machines, they can do anything to them. But we also wanted to explore the Cylons' claims that they do have souls."[98] Purposely or not, then, Whedon colludes with an ideology of a threatening *racial* "other," an other that is itself given no complicating psychological backstory, and not only is this psychologically lazy but it potentially politically valedicts a Manichaean sensibility that colors the current politico-cultural fear of the racially stereotyped Middle Eastern Muslim "other."

The contrast between this and the most recent adaptation of *BSG* is stark, and the political implications of the difference are pronounced. Moore and Eick take the Larson model of the Cylon as the genocidal agent the Colonies' destruction and do some radical things with it. For a start, the clinical aesthetic of the technology of the Cylon race (that is so directly contrasted with the bodily flesh of the humans) has been subverted. And this is done through the introduction of 12 humanoid Cylons. Secondly, Larson's destroyers of worlds are given no backstory, whereas in Moore and Eick's rebooted version the Cylons themselves pre-emptively strike against the very agents of their oppression. In that regard, the nuclear holocaust is arguably a self-defensive move, even if it is an apocalyptically catastrophic one. The Colonies become complicit in their own destruction, a fact noted by Colonial William Adama in a speech given at the decommissioning ceremony for the Battlestar Galactica prior to the Cylon attack: "We decided to play God, create life, and when that life turned against us, we comforted ourselves with the knowledge that it really wasn't our fault, not really. You cannot play God and then wash your hands of the things that you've created. Sooner or later, the day comes when you can't hide from the things that you've done anymore." Finally, as the series progress, the Cylons are "humanized" at the level of will as much as at the level of displaying fragile physicality by themselves fracturing into conflicting factions, with one faction demanding peace with the humans, rather than annihilation, for their old enemy. According to Hal Shipman,

> In the new series, the root of the conflict with the humans and the Cylons is the robots' revolution against their status as slaves in human society. The Cylons have shifted from being clearly evil to occupying a more morally ambiguous position.... In altering the relationship between human and Cylon, the new series also changes the relationship between the viewer and the two groups, putting us in a space somewhere between the two, where we were previously firmly in the humans' camp.[99]

What Shipman notices, then, is not only the moral complication involved in the series, but equally the invitation to engage in reflexivity. It is this form of reflexivity that demands an explicitly political reading. Dinello argues that

> *Battlestar Galactica* made a starling, mind-boggling shift—morphing the hated Cylons into American Occupiers and the beloved Humans into Terrorists ... the show's geopolitical focus shifted from terror alert America to war-torn Iraq and, in the process, went where no other work of fictional pop culture dared. It provided a devastating, incisive, and subversive critique of the American occupation of Iraq. It did so by dramatizing an unprovoked invasion, portraying the damaging effect on those occupied, sympathizing with a morally ambiguous but legitimate insurgency, and aligning itself with the violent radical philosophy of black French revolutionary Frantz Fanon.[100]

However, something particularly interesting emerges for further critical reflection at this point. Whedon tellingly does not utilize the themes, characterizations or symbols from Marvel's controversial epic event, Mark Millar's *Civil War* (2006–2007), and yet this series offers a potentially rich set of materials for politically complicating the psychology of the "national consciousness." It is this series that Roz Kaveney argues "is the closest Marvel has ever come to writing political satire and protest."[101]

> At a time when most of American popular culture was avoiding political issues like the plague and when even quite casual protests against the Iraq war ... were greeted with howls of vilification, it is interesting that superhero comics produced a work of significant protest art, significant because it supplied a lot more than protest.[102]

One character in particular demands reflection, that character most iconically associated with the nation, "Captain America."

To Cap It All Off..., Whedon Captains a Team Without a Super-Challenge

According to Ott, the rebooted "*BSG* invites viewers to adopt a critical, self-reflective frame toward our post–9/11 world. By dramatizing the moral dangers and pitfalls of unrestrained fear, *BSG* furnishes viewers with a vocabulary and thus with a set of symbolic resources for managing their social anxieties."[103] In particular, this commentator is impressed by the reflexive patriotism that is dramatized by the politically daring series. He connects this both to notions of the way in which the enemy "Other" is continually humanized, and the homogenization of others as "the Other" is broken open by the increased individuation of the carnal models of the Cylons, and he subsequently draws out the political implications.

> A group that has only a common enemy will not have the will to fight. It must also share a common set of values and beliefs that define it as substantially one. This is why appeals to patriotism and nationalism increase in times of conflict. Internal dissent poses a particularly troublesome problem for a leader intent on war. Even as dissent affirms democratic principles, it potentially threatens the sense of collectivity essential for conflict. One prominent strategy for addressing internal dissent is to cast the dissenters out of the collective.[104]

In science-fiction such as *BSG* and in comic books, something interesting is being done, socio-politically speaking. As Terry Kading observes,

> The superhero comic, in response to 9/11, provides a distinct medium from which to reflect on and explore the fears, insecurities, and varied individual reactions generated by the attacks. On the one hand there is the ability to recapture the terrifying and horrific images of 9/11 through vibrant colors and striking detail, a style that has been perfected through decades of expressing the dramatic action between superheroes and supervillains to date. On the other hand there is room to present commentary on thoughts, emotions, and insights as events unfold, thus rendering a novel appreciation of 9/11 and the post–9/11 environment.[105]

Among other things, Marvel's *Civil War* event series provides comment on the decline of civil liberties. In the process it depicts the character most heroically associated with the American nation since his first comic book appearance, Captain America, in such a way as to make him a focus of political engagement against the current political regime and the forms of nationalism that are invoked to maintain its power. The significance of this cannot be overstated. Jewett and Lawrence identify Cap as a particularly good exemplar and expression of the American superiority complex and the "contradictory form of civil religion" whose mission occurs through "violent crusading."[106] They briefly offer a case study of his origin in which patriot Steve Rogers' superpowers were a product of the military industrial complex. In the origin narrative that first appeared in March 1941, the enthusiastic patriot was a physically weak and sickly man who was rejected by the American army. However, the military reject was transformed in the laboratory into a physically impressive and powerful (as well as mentally more agile) American savior through the experimental application of Professor Reinstein's super-soldier serum. On perceiving the success of the experiment, the scientist proclaims, "We shall call you Captain America, son! Because, like you, America shall gain the strength and the will to safeguard our shores."[107] In the conflict with the Axis powers that was looming, Cap's stories offered a way for comic book reading children to patriotically cheer on the coming American war effort. Jewett and Lawrence comment: "Taking on the role of civic instructor, *Captain America* issued an invitation to its young readers to become involved in the fight for freedom as 'Captain America's Sentinels of Liberty.'"[108] The *Marvel Chronicle* relates that this 1940s superhero was designed to be "an individual who could take on the great threats that menaced the world."[109] Accordingly, Joe Simon and Jack Kirby's Nazi-bashing flag-draped champion of freedom proved to be a highly bankable character—in his wartime outing he sold almost a million copies per issue.

What relevance does the character have today, however? The Steve Rogers of Whedon's spectacular drama makes a self-critical suggestion to Coulson when he asks, "Aren't the [viz. his] stars and stripes not a little old fashioned?" The agent's response exhibits the unifying relevancy of the new patriotism. This entails, then, a quite particular and uncomplicated reading of the character in *The Avengers*, and the political impact of this is pronounced. Jewett and Lawrence, for instance, use Cap for their title in order to express the very shape of the mythological complex that accounts for the crusading politics they critique. The *Captain America* comic books' "crudeness," they comment, along with the "broad mythic stream that flows through superheroic comics," amounts "to a kind of mythic induction into the cultural values of America."[110]

As a typical embodiment of the American civil religion, offering regeneration of a helpless democratic society by selfless superheroism, Captain America stands squarely within the narrative tradition that can be traced back through earlier forms of American entertainment to the biblical paradigms employed in the Indian captivity narratives ... in these and countless other examples, superheroes and -heroines exercise the powers otherwise reserved only for God in dealing with evil. They are the individuated embodiments of a civil religion that seeks to redeem the world for democracy, but by means that transcend democratic limits on the exercise of power.[111]

Yet the linking of Cap and the American politicians and soldiers in the war against terror is actually distinctly misleading, and it is a similarly quite particular and uncomplicated reading of the character that Whedon likewise offers in *The Avengers*. Jewett and Lawrence's thesis may work for the super-soldier's earliest depictions, but it works particularly badly in relation to his later character development in which he is more aligned with those who understand America as a developing and politically ambiguous *project*. In a context devoid of his original setting-in-life, the comic series involving this character came to its end in February 1950. When reintroduced the nature of this protagonist morphed, and so by the 1960s Cap, as he is often referred to for short, was uninvolved with international defence, but rather was engaged in a variety of socio-cultural issues closer to home. Even during the Vietnam conflict, he was only involved on two occasions, and less in a belligerent role than as the rescuer of American soldiers. In many ways his was a questionable existence. Whatever his reasons for continuing to wear the stars and stripes, Rogers' flag certainly did not drape over his eyes so as to obscure his perception of the messy realities of the political life of his nation or to secure his identity as uncritical patriot. As early as 1970, Stan Lee admitted that Captain America is "beginning to have second thoughts.... He realizes he can't really side with the establishment 100 percent."[112] He is closer to the good patriot who carries "on a lover's quarrel with their country," to use William Sloane Coffin's terms.[113] As with the political spirit of many at the time, after the Watergate scandal of 1974 the comics depict Cap in conflict with his government. In *Captain America* issue 169 (January 1974), the Committee to Regain America's Principles frames Cap for murdering the Tumbler. Rogers, in consequence, becomes so disillusioned with his nation, learning that the Secret Empire has been led by none other than the President himself, that he even lays aside his stars and stripes costume in December 1974 and dons the garb of the superhero Nomad for a period (four comic book issues, until April 1975) instead. At this point he becomes the man without a country. By 1980 the national Populist Party seeks Cap to run for the presidency, but his refusal to accept the challenge is the fruit of the realism of his dedication to American values that would be mitigated by the realities of public office. Rogers was even challenged for the role of Captain America in October 1986 by the Super-Patriot, and resigned from his position in August 1987 (briefly returning for issue 335 in November), being rebooted by Jeph Loeb and Rob Liefeld in November 1996 and further rebooted by Ed Brubaker in January 2005. With his character development, the prominent moral certainty and muscular self-assertiveness of the nation is continually questioned and is frequently portrayed as imperialistically self-interested.

From this complication of the most patriotic of the mainstream superhero characters, it makes sense that he be the one to be re-imagined after 9/11. According to Terry Kading, "The superhero comic, in response to 9/11, provides a distinct medium from which to reflect on and explore the fears, insecurities, and varied individual reactions generated by the attacks."[114] The Civil War, resulting from a massive catastrophe at Samford and the consequent suppression of certain civil liberties, significantly makes Captain America the focus of political engagement against the current political regime and the forms of nationalism that are invoked to maintain its power. This epic Marvel miniseries event registers doubts about the U.S. government and brings them to the fore when the Super-Human Registration Act requires heroes to register their identities with the federal authorities. In response, Cap helps form an underground rebellion to oppose what he conceives to be an unconstitutional Act, an invasion of privacy for those heroes requiring secret identities for the protection of their loved ones, an erosion of the civil liberties, and an undemocratic step on the way to an abusive totalitarian political system with the heroes functioning as government agents. In consequence, he comes face-to-face with his former friends (led by Stark) in brutal (and eventually—seemingly—fatal) conflict. The ambiguity of the character is well captured in a comment of Marvel writer Ed Brubaker in 2007 concerning the fans' expectations of him: "What I found is that all the really hard-core left-wing fans want Cap to be standing on and giving speeches on the street corner against the George W. Bush administration, and all the really right-wing fans all want him to be over in the streets of Baghdad, punching out Saddam Hussein."[115]

Nevertheless, even here with the deeper political complexity of the *Civil War* series and of its use of the character of Captain America, it remains only partially interrogative. It can query forms of unquestioning patriotism, the blind faith that is put in governments that legitimates them in such a way that they become considerably less contingent, fragile, and morally responsible than they might otherwise be on proper critical reflection. However, it does not contest or complicate the very sense of commitment to national particularity, to what Benedict Anderson calls the "imagined community" that disciplines self-identifying spatiality and temporality, and the narrated myth of the nation-state as something more than contingent body for broad forms of managing the conditions for social, cultural and political life.[116] Zygmunt Bauman gives his study *Globalization* a haunting subtitle: *The Human Consequences*.[117] It might be argued, that a book that remains needing to be written is *Patriotism: The Human Consequences*. It is to these consequences—primary but arbitrary geographical self-identification, national competitiveness so often destructive of other nation-states, triumphalist self-assertion, blindness to one's nation's flaws, and so on—that the politically astute moral agent needs to attend.

Conclusion

According to Gray and Kaklamanidou, "if we consider mainstream films to be a form of escapism, which offer a mixture of education and entertainment, superhero films of the new millennium lean greatly toward the latter characteristic."[118] This, according to several commentators, tends to be the case during periods of trauma as the need for consolation and escape become the psychological order of the day. After 9/11 "we all wanted desperately to believe that good can defeat evil," argues John Muir, "and, perhaps more to the point, that there is a clear line differentiating these opposing philosophies.... Superheroes became comforting and safe, like creamy vanilla ice cream, reflecting pure American values and innocence."[119]

This might account for the recent tremendous box-office success of the superhero genre of movies. Superhero imagery, characterization, and supporting narratives tend to provide just such a sensibility. After all, in Joe Johnston's 2011 movie *Captain America: The First Avenger*, Steve Rogers' time in the 1940s ends as he redirects a plane bound destructively for New York by the terrorist cult Hydra led by the Red Skull. As Johannes Schlegel and Frank Habermann argue, "one of the basal narrative patterns of superhero films (and comic books alike) is the eternal Manichaean struggle of good versus evil."[120] So Stan Lee once admitted that "the battle between a hero and a villain (which is what virtually all our stories get down to) is basically a conflict between a good guy and a bad guy, or between good and evil."[121] There is an innate conservatism in the superhero mythology, as Richard Reynolds argues: "the normal and everyday enshrines positive values that must be defended through heroic action—and defended over and over again almost without respite against an endless battery of menaces determined to remake the world." "The superhero," Reynolds continues, "has a mission to preserve society, not to re-invent it."[122] The justice enacted in superhero activity is reactive, a responsive to some lack. This reading is echoed in Fingeroth who argues that "without being overtly ideological, superheroes champion the consensus views of most residents of Western democracies. They are not in favour of violent revolution to change political power."[123]

Inactivity makes for complicity, and this is equally morally problematic. This is true, says Fingeroth, even where they do not speak up or out against unjust systems. "We can say that not opposing the status quo is in effect supporting it."[124] Fingeroth does recognize that this general statement does not fit all cases, *Watchmen* being just such a resistant example. Yet "the results in such works are for the most part disastrous. When superheroes try to change society proactively, things end up worse than they were at the beginning." Of course, the psychologically focused commentator continues, "what Reynolds sees as weakness of the superhero—the reactive nature of the archetype—is, it seems to me, the thing that makes people actually able to relate to such characters." While that Manichaeism is something that permeates much of popular culture, it is resisted by what amounts to more complex portrayals. For instance, Hellboy is a more ambiguous figure, rendering the good-evil boundaries permeable.

As I related several years ago in my *The Gospel According to Star Wars*, George Lucas once admitted that he offered simpleminded solutions to complex problems, "but if someone would just take one of those simpleminded solutions, the world might be a better place to live."[125] The problem is that the complexity of problems, by the very nature of their complexity, defies simpleminded solutions. Anything less endangers the usefulness of the proposed solution. Dramas such as Moore and

Eick's *BSG* and to a lesser extent Nolan's Dark Knight trilogy, in contrast, refuse to capitulate to untransformed desires for solace and vengeance. For instance, *Batman Begins* conducts an extended critical conversation between two different accounts of justice, with Bruce Wayne opposing The League of Shadows' Manichaean sensibility with something more differentiating and reformist. Henri Ducard, representing Rā's al Ghūl, announces, "I warned you about compassion, Bruce.... Then [we will] watch Gotham City tear itself apart through fear.... Only a cynical man would call what these people have lives. Crime, despair! This was not how man was supposed to live.... It should be you [Bruce] standing by my side saving the world." Ducard, here, understands the city's salvation to occur only through its "natural" purging destruction in the "movement back to harmony," his account of justice being forged as one of retribution. In contrast, Bruce counters with a threat: "I will be standing where I belong—between you and the people of Gotham." His role will be to protect the people from destruction, as far as he can. For Ducard, Wayne is a misguided idealist who refuses to do all that is necessary to enact "true justice." With respect to *BSG*, for its part, the viewer perceives how this small screen text

> interrogates how, when confronted with an Other who seems so alien, yet so familiar, we find ourselves questioning our most fundamental notions about humanity and civilization, about who and what we are, and what we hope we might be. In blurring the boundaries between human and inhuman, between barbarism and civilization, and by exposing that anyone might find himself in the no-man's land of the exception, stripped to bare life, *BSG* asks us to resist the Manichaean logic of "with us or against us" when its only possible outcome is not only the dehumanization of the other, but the dehumanization of ourselves.[126]

John Scott Gray observes that Larson's 1978 version of *BSG* "presented a cut and dried world in which the viewers found themselves collectively supporting the Colonials as they were pursued by the clearly mechanistic Cylons. "This enemy," Gray continues, "represented a class of beings that could easily be disregarded, in large part because the glaring differences between us and them allowed us to view the Cylons as a totally alien outsider."[127] Even in the new *BSG* specism runs through the numerous narratives, with the surviving Colonists dismissing the very identities of the Cylons by referring to them as "toasters," "machines," and even in an echo of the racist charge used by police-captain Bryant in Ridley Scott's *Blade Runner*, as "skin jobs," for example. The difference between Moore and Eick's *BSG* and that of Larson, however, is that this specism is itself part of the new series' *narrative* which is then reflexively complexified and contested from within that narrative, whereas it is part of the political framework for Larson's narrative.

Nonetheless, it is not possible to compare such very different types of dramas. That, however, is not the point being made here. Rather, where critics perceive *BSG*, *Watchmen*, the Batman trilogy, *SW* Episodes II–III, and other cultural artifacts as offering possibilities for penetrating cultural-political analysis and self-reflection, Whedon's superhero work has the potential for destabilizing the interrogative mood. At its best, *The Avengers* is a visually impressive superhero "shoot-em-up" that has proven to be a box-office smash hit with both children and adults alike. Yet while it is a visually impressive spectacle and is hugely entertaining with its quick pacing, it remains nonetheless a narratively and psychologically lightweight superhero action movie. It possesses little of the narrative and character depth and sophisticated philosophical complexity of, for instance, Ang Lee's earlier *Hulk*, Christopher Nolan's Batman trilogy, or Bryan Singer's *X-Men*. However, at its worst, *The Avengers* is simply too loose and focused to challenge and transform increasingly dominant and "official" forms of patriotism, something Spanakos sees occurring in, for instance, *The Incredible Hulk*, *Iron Man* and *Avatar*, with their portrayal of "the global superpower's tendency to both exploit and colonize the other."[128] As General Thaddeus Ross explains about Bruce, after discussing the earlier super-soldier experiments, "as far as I'm concerned, that man's whole body is property of the United States army." Ross' chase for the Hulk is a chase to harness his power for military purposes. Of course, several versions of experimental sera are injected into the special forces soldier Emil Blonski with abominable repercussions. For Spanakos, official versions of patriotism are often dominated by disqualifying the determinative influence on the self by the other, as in any way aiding in "finding one's authentic self and struggle." Many of the post–9/11 superhero movies, according to Spanakos, are "fantasies of self-preservation, but what is noteworthy is that the consistent enemy is not the distant other, but the military industrial complex ... which gave initial life and meaning to the protagonists. The heroic struggle is to offer an alternative patriotism by defending what is just against official versions and representatives." Spanakos continues by observing that "interestingly, these post–September 11 Hollywood blockbusters deliberately contest an official and simplistic version of patriotism and disqualification of the other, presenting awareness of the other as central to finding one's authentic self and struggle. They do this by showing the global superpower's tendency to both exploit and colonize the other, while identifying an authentic patriotism with recognition of the other."

The Avengers, in contrast, is in danger of slipping into simplistic and cathartic forms of characterization of self and other, and of glib portrayals of the conflict between the two, ideologically shrink-wrapped in the civil religion of a flag. It harks back in mood to the older period of comic book lore, with its crude representations of the good/wicked, heroes/villains, and its flat characterizations of the psychology of the main protagonists. As Kaveney recognizes, Whedon has had a comic-book "obsession."[129] The consequent danger is that it will not be taken seriously by commentators as a cultural artifact. It would seem, in its conscious mood of moral nostalgia, that it has utterly ignored the moral ambiguity of character and the necessary hermeneutic of suspicion learned from histories of corrupt and corrupting forms of governance, and the political potential for hero-myths with the "righteous us vs. evil them" type ethos. It rides roughshod over proper political self-reflection and reasoned scepticism, by offering a morally simplistic and unambiguous universe. Its violence is not portrayed in terms either of complex causalities or of bloody, unpredictable, and harrowing loss and tragic catastrophism—it is the clear-cut war of good against evil, and therefore, in a sense, the "good war" in which everything works out and the good wins out in an anaemic happy ending aided by the emotion-regulating score of Alan Silvestri. Not only does this violence not resonate "realistically" but as fantasy it therefore has the emotional feel of dealing death at a distance, which cannot adequately explore the horrors of loss, but it is ideologically important that this violence is redemptive. Instead, the dealing of death in this war is evacuated of its complexity, its harrowing emotional resonance, and its forcing of self-questioning. In the end, it is difficult to shake off the nagging sense that the climax suggests that the war is justified because of the victory of good over evil. The consumable surface spectacle offers a way of containing and limiting the depth of involvement with issues of war, and invites a kind of awed passivity in the audience, a visceral aesthetics of this cinematic event that negates its suggested teaching of morality. In this it does not depart from some of the more childish versions of the superhero narratives, those characterized by Kading:

The appeal of the superhero narrative is not just the power of "good" triumphing over "evil" but that the superhero spares us from the plodding, messy, and often unfulfilling dynamics involved in organizing peoples and nation-states in a collective response against further vile acts and continued insecurity. The superhero offers everything: rapid and effective action, a just and proportionate response, and above all, in achieving results no more innocent lives are lost. In the superhero narrative "evil" is not addressed through "evil" (more innocents injured or killed), and we are not brought down to their level and forced to combat villains by vile tactics. There is a clear and persistent separation between "good" and "evil," in that the "good" is able to act and respond with superior means. There are no compromises with questionable characters or nations, calculations concerning the loss of more innocent lives, or limits to freedom/liberty to achieve a safe and secure end. Supervillainous figures are defeated, the sanctity of the innocent preserved, and we quickly return to a secure context knowing that superheroes assure our continued prosperity and progress.[130]

Russell W. Dalton's reading of the counter-cultural "message" of the movie as one of heroism and self-sacrifice in protection of others is not so much incorrect as ideologically superficial—after all, these are values demanded by the modern nation-state.[131] The potential moral radicality of this form of heroism is distinctly muted by the way heroism is presented and co-opted within a larger and deeply determinative politically significant mythology. Long gone are the more complex and tragic clashes of different ideologies in the likes of, for instance, the post–9/11 Marvel *Civil War*, *Battlestar Galactica*'s reboot, Bryan Singer's *X2*, and Snyder's version of *Watchmen*, Christopher Nolan's Batman, and the Wachowski brothers' *V for Vendetta*, among numerous cinematic texts that reflect critically on the uses and abuses of power. Naturally, in saying all this one must be careful not to use extratextually other materials from which to critique Whedon's superhero movie in any straightforward fashion. The point, rather, is to indicate the ways in which identifying complex motivations and identity determinations can be, and indeed have been, handled in considerably more morally satisfying and complex ways in these texts. In other words, these texts set in sharp relief Whedon's labor. The questions, then, are why his work here takes the specific form that it does, of what it is that directs his directorial selections and revisions, and what the religio-political implications of these are. The answers may not be what most fans of the talented Whedon expect or hope to hear.

2

"HE WAS DECEIVED BY A LIE"
Tragedy and the Dark Plague
of the Politics of Fear
in George Lucas' *Star Wars*

It is May 25, 1977, and little is known about the movie that opens this evening, *Star Wars* (*SW*). "Gigantic lines [have] formed ... in each town, city, or suburb" largely as a result of word-of-mouth.[1] In fact, due to the length of the queue, only those who are near the front, and have accordingly queued longest, will be lucky enough to be admitted. The lights go out, the screen retracts fully and after attraction-promoting advertisements and a viewer health warning (the film-board classification certificate), audience anticipation builds. What appears first on screen is the impressive Twentieth Century–Fox studio logo—thickly blocked gold writing lit by spotlights on the ground, sitting high on a pedestal. It encourages the feeling that something magnificently grand but also important, valuable and significant is about to take place. This sense is intensified by the accompanying drum roll and the blare of the trumpets, a call to attention that evokes "a 'looking up' to where the wondrous things are."[2] Cinema has become something of a religious service and experience, and this particular cinematic moment is very much a part of that. There is, after all, a gathering around a text by an audience with a single focus, a liturgical structure to the performance (adverts, trailers, feature), ritualized behavior among the various participants (silence, spectatorship), and an expectation of a form of momentary transcendence (that it will be time and money well-spent). Cinema has proven to be culturally much more significant than any talk of it as a provider of simple "popcorn fare" could ever admit. As a result, it is precisely "because culture matters so much," Ben Agger claims, that "it deserves full critical attention."[3] Speaking specifically of the hegemonic role of the cinema, a particular form of the power of cultural production, Margaret Miles and Brent Plate argue that

> in just over one hundred years, film has become a powerful force in modern life that changes the way we think about, interpret, and live in the world. Because of this alteration of the ways we literally see the world, critical attention to film becomes a vital task for those engaged with issues of religion and ethics, and concerned with more equitable social arrangements.[4]

Following the shimmering appearance of "Lucasfilm" in glorious green letters on the silver screen, the triumphantly full orchestral theme by John Williams resounds. The audience at this point is greeted by the Flash Gordonesque introductory text which begins its fading crawl back into the background. The reference is to civil war, rebel spaceships, an Isaac Asimov–inspired "evil Galactic Empire," an equally Flash Gordon-borrowed notion of an "ultimate weapon," a fairy-tale allusion to a "princess" taken from Akira Kirosawa's *Hidden Fortress* and possibly also providing an allusion to Bruno Bettelheim's work, and an energetic imperial pursuit of stolen plans. It does not take long for the camera to descend and focus on the atmosphere above the desert planet of Tatooine. A very brief moment of silence and calm is shattered by the determined chase of the little Rebel blockade runner Tantive IV by the impressively hulking Imperial Star Destroyer. A dramatic and spectacular space opera like none other before its time has begun. Within a few moments of the curtain drawing back, audiences the world over have been directed to what is promising to be a thrilling ride in the form of an action-packed space fantasy adventure that offers homage to, and blends the style and certain thematic elements of, among other things, older swashbuckler movies, Westerns, Arthurian legend, and Edgar Rice Burroughs' pulp science-fiction literature.

As mentioned above, the movie project simply entitled *Star Wars* at the time (until, that is, the special edition of 1997, although from 1979 it was notionally subtitled "*Episode IV*") was expected to be a disaster. Even after shortening the working title of *The Star Wars*, the Twentieth Century–Fox studio felt that it would be simply unmarketable: "they thought science fiction was a very bad genre, that women didn't like it, although they did no market research on that until after the film was finished."[5] After having experienced the turmoil of box-office failure several years earlier with his avant-garde dystopian work *THX 1138*, a failure that cost his friend Francis Ford Coppola his fledgling company American Zoetrope, *SW*'s visionary, creator, and director George Lucas braced himself for the fall-out. As Peter Biskind admits, "George made plans to be out of town, in Hawaii with Marcia and the Huycks for the opening of *Star Wars*, the way he was when *Graffiti* premiered. He was still afraid the movie was going to be a huge embarrassment."[6] Even the pre-release screenings had not been entirely successful. The limited fan base of science fiction movies at the time makes *SW* a risky project and, at most, Lucas believes it will appeal only to the "$8 million worth of science fiction freaks in the U.S.A."[7] As it transpires, Lucas even forgets the opening night, and spent the evening with his wife in a restaurant near Grauman's Chinese Theatre in Los Angeles. The rest, one might say, "is history...."

In anticipation of this theatrical release, Lucas had issued the novel in order to whet the public appetite. The novel's prologue relates part of the determinative backstory from *The Journal of the Whills*, and reads as a gesture towards a story of political intrigue and democratic decline potentially developable as a tragedy.[8] The Old Republic thrived and grew "under the wise rule of the Senate and the protection of the Jedi Knights," but rotted from within in a fashion that enabled the rise to power of "the ambitious Senator Palpatine," and under his self-declared *imperium* there was instituted "a reign of terror."[9] Later in the story, some further suggestive details from the backstory are offered to Luke Skywalker by the old Jedi Knight Obi-Wan Kenobi when he reveals that one of his very own young Jedi pupils (known in the prequels as "Padawans") had "turned to evil," and this "Darth Vader" had "betrayed and murdered" Luke's father Anakin and "helped the Empire hunt down and destroy the Jedi Knights." "Vader was seduced by the dark side of the Force." This was a significant theme that had been missed by Dale Pollock, however, when he generalized that "Lucas displayed in *Star Wars* a wholesome, naïve faith in the essential goodness of people."[10]

The movie has proven to be controversial among commentators, especially among those attentive to questions of ideology. In fact, the question of the political significance of *SW*'s ideological determinations still remains a live one almost four decades later. This chapter critically tackles what has come close to becoming a dominant account that reads the saga through a Manichaean lens, and suggests that a different reading possibility has been opened up retrospectively by the prequels.

The Politics of the Evil "Other"

Soon after the release of the movie, Martin Scorsese complained "*Star Wars* was in. Spielberg was in. We [the makers of intelligent films] were finished."[11] What is involved in such a claim has been the subject of much comment over the past three and a half decades. According to the post-colonialist study of *SW* by Kevin Wetmore, "*Star Wars* is family entertainment. Its target audience, as stated by Lucas time and again, is children. It is accessible, inspirational, and offers a clear view of the world, unmuddled by complexity. Good is good, evil is evil."[12] What is meant here by "family entertainment," especially when there is so much violence involved in these movies, is a matter for critical reflection. In fact, the use of the term "entertainment" is itself a crucial, and even a misleading, term. Judith Martin's review of the later *Empire Strikes Back* in *The Washington Post* speaks for many when it assumes that "entertainment" is something shallow, intellectually unprovocative, and irrelevant to socio-political matters of induction into ideology and ethical formation:

> This is no monumental artistic work, but a science-fiction movie done more snappily than most, including its own predecessor. A chocolate bar is a marvelous sweet that does not need to pretend to be a chocolate soufflé; musical comedies are wonderful entertainment without trying to compete with opera; blue jeans are a perfect garment that shouldn't be compared with haute couture. There are times when you would much rather have a really good hot dog than any steak, but you can still recognize that one is junk food and the other isn't.[13]

This, of course, is a naïve claim about the ideological significance of the range of cultural products and artifacts, and bears the imprint of an underlying elitist understanding of what is cultural *significance* involves. Movies not only can tell us something of how the cultures from which they arise understand themselves, but they can equally creatively engage with audience members' self-understanding and thus contribute to the shaping of not only what but also *how* they see things.[14] Terry Christensen likewise comments that 1977's *A New Hope* (*ANH*) is one of a class of blockbusters that eschew "politics and analysis in favour of superficial entertainment." What is more interesting in his analysis, however, is the fact that he recognizes that (if this is the case, of course) *SW* thereby becomes conservative *by default*. This can be observed, Christensen maintains, by the viewer reception of the movie. Its "most lasting

impact," he argues, "was to be the persistent preponderance of young
people in audiences, people who were far more interested in entertainment than in serious analytical or political films."[15] This critique verges
on blaming Lucas for the social difficulties Christensen identifies, and
in that regard it is at least important to culturally break open the criticism. In this fashion, James Monaco more generally blames this propensity on the film-student generation, claiming that directors like George
Lucas, Steven Spielberg, and Martin Scorcese "had learned everything
about film and nothing about life," resulting in "a cinema that is formally
(technically) extraordinarily sophisticated at the same time as it is intellectually preadolescent."[16] To return to Martin's account, crucially this
critic simply does not make sense of what Lucas, at least, understood
himself to be doing (or at least claimed to be doing after the event) with
his *SW* movies. Intriguingly and suggestively, in an interview for *American Film* with Stephen Zito, published in April 1977 *before* the theatrical
release of *SW*, Lucas makes a reference not only to "mythologies" but also
to cinematic "education." After Vietnam, Lucas claims, "there was not a
lot of mythology in our society—the kind of stories we tell ourselves
and our children, which is the way our heritage is passed down. Westerns
used to provide that, but there weren't Westerns anymore.... I wanted
it [viz., *Star Wars*] to be traditional moral study, to have palpable precepts
... that children could understand.... Traditionally we get them from
the church, the family, and in the modern world we get them from the
media—from movies."[17] Without any apparent sense of irony, the director declared "I wanted to do a modern fairy tale, a myth."[18] Lucas' claim
here is certainly not an isolated moment in his description of the *SW*
project. On several occasions the moviemaker speaks of the "moral
megaphone" possessed by those like himself who are creatively involved
in the film industry. In his mind, at least, *SW* was specifically designed
to have been broadly educational so as to remind a morally cynical generation in the mid 1970s of the importance of being morally responsible.[19]
"Somebody has to tell young people what we think is a good person. I
mean, we should be doing it all the time. That's what the Iliad and the
Odyssey are about—'This is what a good person is; this is who we aspire
to be.' You need that in a society. It's the basic job of mythology."[20] So
Dale Pollock, Lucas' biographer, claims that "Lucas offers more than just
escapist entertainment; he gives us a vision of what should be."[21]

Of course, the "mythological" reading of *SW* has not only embed-
ded itself as influential and lasting, but also as deeply controversial.[22]

mythological

Where the interesting questions lie instead is in the area of the *SW* saga's ethical and socio-political assumptions and its performance of a particular politics of representation. To return to the second part of Wetmore's claim cited earlier, *SW* apparently "offers a clear view of the world, unmuddled by complexity. Good is good, evil is evil."[23] To put it in religio-philosophical terms, Lucas' cinematically entertaining piece is here understood to be shaped by, and to provide, what might be called a "Manichaean sensibility." In other words, more materially substantive than Christensen's criticism of *ANH*'s conventionalistic form, and even more so Martin, numerous critics observe that *SW* is a "controversial and politically engaged" cinematic text, in Stephen McVeigh's terms.[24] It is what that engagement is seen to involve that has made the saga particularly controversial for commentators who are concerned about egalitarian relations and radical politics. An assessment of a political conservatism running deep within the text has, in fact, become something of a commonplace among commentators on the *SW* saga, and its political place in American cultural life in the mid to late 1970s and 1980s.[25] One does not have to search hard to discover critics who lambaste *SW* for being a fascistic and militaristic movie because of its apparent hierarchies of sex, class, and species, its problematic representation, its politics of identity shaped by a process of "Othering."[26]

The cultural and political context of this is important since commentators identify the Manichaean tendency as being largely the fruit of *ANH*'s political milieu and the type of cultural wistfulness that determines the manner of its ideological performance to its youthful target audience. In a revealing comment, Pollock even claims that in response to the 1970s loss of moral anchorage, "Lucas remembered how protected he had felt growing up in the cocoonlike culture of the 1950s, a feeling he wanted to communicate in Star Wars."[27] *SW*, Booker declares, "is very much a nostalgia film that looks lovingly back to its predecessors in the science fiction serials of the 1930s," and very much "in the mold of Lucas's own *American Graffiti* (1973)."[28] In fact, he continues, "*Star Wars* is, one might say, the sort of science fiction film that filmmakers of the 1930s might have made had they had available to them the special-effects resources (technological and financial) that were available in the late 1970s."[29] What conceptually drives Booker's critique is his identification of the movie's "unpretentious celebration of the kind of simple, straightforward oppositions that had given the pulp fictions of the 1930s their innocent appeal."[30]

"This simplicity and innocence helped the film appeal to children," Booker maintains, "but Star Wars also had a great appeal for adult audiences in the United States in the late 1970s. After the trying times of Vietnam and Watergate, American audiences were eager for the kind of reassurance provided by simple verities and uncomplicated expressions of the ultimate power of good to defeat evil." The conditions for *SW*'s reactionary politics played in to the growing conservative element in American political life. For Booker, then,

> its old-fashioned, nostalgic appeal also marked the beginning of a rightward turn in American politics that would lead to the election of Ronald Reagan to the presidency in 1980. Indeed, looking at the Cold War years of the 1950s, then at the late 1970s and early 1980s, some critics have concluded that science fiction film seems particularly to flourish in conservative times, perhaps because of their escapist appeal to audiences appalled by contemporary reality.[31]

Accordingly, the claim is that both the ethos of Lucas' movies and the cultural reception of them overlap with shifting political sensibilities. As with *SW*, Booker argues, Ronald Reagan appealed "for a return to traditional values, its presentation of international politics as a simple opposition between good and evil, and its belief in the fundamental value of free enterprise." In fact, Booker asserts, "*Star Wars*, perhaps more than any other single science fiction film served as a harbinger of social change in America." Lucas' movies, it would seem, served as something of a touchstone for a new political sensibility after the difficulties of the years towards the end of the Vietnam War and the immediate aftermath. "The success of *Star Wars* announced a new desire for an optimistic, reassuring message that announced the possibility of a better future, a message also delivered by the Reagan campaign and, later, the Reagan presidency."[32] The American voters, in Christensen's words, "wanted a president who was sure of himself and his nation, unbothered by doubt, and unfazed by the complexities of the nation, the world, or human behaviour."[33] The "classic" trilogy creates an evil Empire which the Rebels fight to overthrow, and the legacy of this imagery was famously tapped into for political effect by President Reagan in his rhetorical conflict with the Soviet Union. In Booker's reading at least, the marshaling of *SW* to depict elements of his administration was far from arbitrary or illegitimate.[34] Lucas himself once declared that he felt that he had wanted to use the movies to teach morality during a time of increasing despair and introspection after Vietnam (added to the oil crisis, ecological concerns, and the after-effects of Watergate), but the apparent simplicity of what he "taught" chimed with the mood of Reagan's 1980 presidential victory—the celebratory wave of strong values and confident moral and political self-presentation. As Ian Nathan argues, "*Star Wars* was a universe of innocence," an "infantilising [of the] cinema again" that nostalgically pined for a long-lost age (hence the opening "A long time ago..." reference), for a time when values were understood to be simpler (obvious?).[35] In such a Manichaean political mood, the vague and imminently threatening "Other" has, in a sense, no face (the iconic "Darth Vader" and his "storm troopers" are masked) but is given a name, the "evil Empire." One is encouraged to identify with those who are evidently heroic, and classify the "other" as evil, a projective move of externalizing of evil that creates a mood conducive to a self-secure "us vs. Them" scheme and narcissistic self-perfecting. This evil Empire was stylistically loosely based on various empires—most notably the Roman Imperium and the domination of the Nazi in 1930s and early 1940s central Europe, empires that American television and movie culture have often portrayed negatively as those to be violently opposed. So, Martin Winkler observes with reference to Rome, "the popular American view of the Roman Empire, especially in its reincarnation in the cinema has almost invariably been that of a degenerate totalitarian society characterized by militarism, slavery, religious persecution, bloody games, sexual debauchery, and spiritual emptiness."[36] The visual parallels to the Nazis, for instance, are perhaps even more striking—the officers-class uniforms, for example, and the naming of the shock troops as "storm troopers"; the space battles modeled as they clearly are on World War II aerial dogfights[37]; in *Revenge of the Sith* (*ROTS*) Palpatine's assassination of the Jedi in the event of the Great Jedi Purge with Order 66 bears certain similarities to the Night of the Long Knives; and earlier in *The Phantom Menace* (*TPM*) Palpatine resoundingly declares the need of "a strong Chancellor" who will "bring peace and prosperity back to the Republic," calls for a vote of no confidence in Chancellor Valorum's leadership, and a cleverly manufactured crisis which enables his popularly approved seizing of power (*TPM*), a power that through his engineered war (*Attack of the Clones*; *AOTC*) ingeniously enables his power to become absolute (*ROTS*). The original 1976 novelization of *ANH* has the following claim:

> Aided and abetted by restless, power-hungry individuals within the government, and the massive organs of commerce, the ambitious Senator Palpatine caused himself to be elected President of the Republic. He prom-

ised to reunite the disaffected among the people and restore the remembered glory of the Republic.... Once secure in office [however], he declared himself Emperor ... and the cries of the people for justice did not reach his ears.[38]

According to the macho absolutist political rhetoric and simplistically clear-cut pantomime politics of Reagan's infamous "Evil Empire" speech of March 8, 1983, taking the right side in this conflict (crusade) against evil Soviet Communism was nothing less than the holy Christian duty of the American people. The then president's macho political ideology, and the post–Reagan crusading mentality, did not come out of the blue, but was drawing on a history of American self-understanding, as H.W. Brands observes.[39] It was for that reason that while Reagan was elected with a mere 28 percent of the vote in 1980,[40] not long after was "flush with a sense of power and destiny"[41] and himself came to pronounce the American mission under God:

> The prophet Ezekiel spoke of a new age—when land that was desolate has become like the Garden of Eden and waste and ruined cities are now inhabited.... Our dream, our challenge, and, yes, our mission, is to make the golden age of peace, prosperity, and brotherhood a living reality in all countries of the Middle East. Let us remember that whether we be Christian or Jew or Moslem, we are all children of Abraham, we are all children of the same God. If you take away the dream, you take away the power of the spirit. If you take away the belief in a greater future, you cannot explain America—that we're a people who believed there was a promised land; we were a people who believed we were chosen by God to create a greater world.[42]

This kind of missiological consciousness, deriving from a mythos commonly referred to as "American exceptionalism," demands a sensibility that simplistically sweeps the plenitude of historical evidence that would otherwise challenge its perspective all too easily under the rhetorical carpet, and expresses surprise when others do not recognize just "how good we are."[43] Anything that would reveal and dwell on the significance of brutal episodes and self-interested politics is minimized and discounted from the imagination that is now determined by this sense of unambiguously benign national mission. The hubristic and ambiguous history of the nation is further dishonestly "covered over" (expiated) through refusals to call anything about these brutalizations "waste" and "catastrophe," but instead they are sanitizingly referred to as "collateral damage," "noble sacrifice" or "good" steps on the way to the Good. Thus, subversive knowledge is suppressed and history rewritten in the imagination of the powerful.

In this context, it would seem, *ANH,* in particular, emerges as a product of a particular American politico-cultural environment of the type that Hannah Pok describes as the landscape of "narcissism and fear of the Other."

> The formula for repairing the damage done to the American image and psyche was to target the Other for vilification, and by perceiving in it the external manifestations of all the inner fears and uncertainties of the nation. In the quest to make the self-image perfect, defects had to be dumped elsewhere—conveniently the USSR was at the receiving end, both in Reagan's politics and as the model for the Empire in *SW....* Indeed this wish for the total annihilation of the Other and to ignore the need for the balance of power is a telling one.... [I]n the trilogy the fantasy can be stretched to the limit without fear—the rebels survive to celebrate their victory.[44]

Evil, then, becomes projected onto the "other," and the effect this has is purifying for our sense of "us" in its denial of us being evil as we project it onto a "them." Even if there is any recognition of "our" frailty, occasional error, and so on, the force of this is mitigated by the externalizing of evil and the promise of salvation to the successful.[45] Nationhood in this instance draws heavily not only on the rhetoric of, but the imposing and ultimately legitimating ideology of divine presence in the directing soul of the nation—"God with us," "one nation under God," "in God we trust," and so on. Moreover, this "god" who legitimates those who claim possession of a pure self can brook no rivals—their opposition must be extinguished. In this way, then, claims to national mission sit uncomfortably close to totalitarian politics, in that they, firstly, muscularly secure a refusal to listen to opposing voices; and secondly, they repudiate any possibility that "the Good" might transcend their conceiving and can critically measure their practices. They instead self-assertively impose their own accents on dissenters, and secure the identification of "the Good" with their performance. In other words, they refuse to co-operatively converse or admit the ability to be guided or held accountable by others. It is this sense that contributes to the difficulty the United States frequently has with submitting itself to what it perceives as unwarranted restraint imposed by the United Nations, and instead asserts for itself the right of unilateral action. As Robert Jewett and John Sheldon Lawrence notice, the heart of the spirit of moral and

"Personal crusades against evil, so perfectly exemplified in the American monomyth, hardly qualify as standing within the tradition of democratic sentiment." Instead, they continue, "careful deliberation, knowledge of law, and mastery of book learning [as well as diplomatic conversation] are usually presented in monomythic materials as indicators of impotence or corruption. In the exercise of redemptive power, purity of intention suffices."[46] Later they cite Donald McDonald's complaint about the militarization of foreign policy "when, at critical moments, it is the military who seem to offer the crisp, definite, tangible options—while those who argue for negotiation, diplomacy, and respect for the decent opinion of mankind seem to be offering the unattractive, endlessly prolonged, and inconclusive options."[47] The protracted and least clear of journeys are generally much less appealing than quick and easy solutions (the broad roads, though, that unwittingly lead to destruction).

Has *SW* derived from and been colored by (as well as reminding a more cynical generation of) this sensibility, potentially supportive of "the zealous cult of the nation?"[48] *ANH* undoubtedly works in large measure with America's self-image as a freedom-loving nation which was originally established by rebelling (as an alliance of colonies) against an oppressive British empire; and critics reveal the archetypal American-ness of the Rebel heroes Luke (a frontier farm boy yearning for adventure) and Han (a space-age western-genre loner/adventurer, with his hip-slung blaster and preference for "a straight fight" to "all this sneakin' around").[49] In fact, the "classic trilogy" largely plays—as *Empire Strikes Back* (*ESB*) director Irving Kershner admits—with the American cinematic convention of providing an all–American cast for the trio of heroes (a fourth one with the arrival of Lando in *ESB* and *Return of the Jedi* (*ROTJ*)—Alec Guinness's role as Obi-Wan is significantly minimized midway through *ANH*, thereafter occasionalist and disembodied), with an all–British cast portraying the upper echelons of the Imperial order.[50] This readily plays into self-congratulatory American self-understanding, supporting consciously or not the myth of America perceivably embodied in such post–*SW* movies as *Rambo II* and *III*, *The Patriot*, and *Independence Day*. Thus Peter Lev importantly admits that while "Lucas is not responsible for the uses politicians and governments make of his film ... the ease with which his ideas were put to political and military ends shows something about the Manichaean quality of the story."[51]

As was mentioned in the previous chapter, Lucas once admitted that he offered simpleminded solutions to complex problems, "but if someone would just take one of those simpleminded solutions, the world might be a better place to live."[52] Nevertheless, the complexity of problems, by the very nature of their complexity, *defies* simpleminded solutions. Anything less endangers the usefulness of the proposed solution since distorted patterns of belief generate distorted practices, and the latter assume or shape the former. In fact, if this Manichaean reading can be sustained, the morally nostalgic mood of 1977's *ANH* in particular has arguably ignored the "lessons" of Vietnam and the proper suspicion concerning the political potential for hero-myths within a "righteous us vs. evil them" type ethos. Its depiction of good and evil seems too clear-cut and externalized, and its simplistic moral innocence rides roughshod over proper self-reflection and reasoned skepticism in its "good war" in which everything works out and the good wins out in an anemic happy ending.[53] Although bodies are thrown into the air by explosions, their limbs remain intact. This violence does not resonate "realistically" but as fantasy, and therefore has the emotional feel of dealing death at a distance which cannot adequately explore the horrors of loss. Instead, the dealing of death in this war is evacuated of its complexity, its harrowing emotional resonance, and its forcing of self-questioning. In the end, it is difficult to shake off the nagging sense that the climax of *ROTJ* suggests that the war is justified not only because of the victory of good over evil but also because it eventually leads to the salvation of Anakin. The consumable surface spectacle offers a way of containing and limiting the depth of involvement with issues of war, and invites a kind of awed passivity in the audience. The visceral aesthetics of this cinematic event appears to negate its moral pedagogy. On the other hand, by itself, an appeal to complexity can equally take a conservative turn when by default it is unable to commit itself to a vision of "the good." So *Watchmen*'s Walter Kovacs (a.k.a. Rorschach), according to his actor in Zack Snyder's screened depiction, never loses sight of his victims through an agency deflating sense of the morally grey which, by default, maintains the system of abuse and power. He claims that "we really do live in a complex world, a world of shades of grey. And Walter has just been such a victim of that. For him, that complexity, that bullshit grey, simply justifies the continued victimization of himself and everybody who suffers from someone else's special interest. He had to make the world a place of black and white."[54] For Rorschach, then, an appeal to "complexity" tends to come with inaction, and therefore leads to complicity with irresponsible immorality.

Ending with a New Beginning: Gestures Towards Tragedy

It would appear, then, that, to put it in colloquial terms, in 1977's *SW* the "baddies" were bad and the "goodies" were good, and apart from the ever so slightly more complex roguishness of Han Solo the twain would never meet. George Lucas, the writer and director of the "space opera," expressed on screen something of his own boyhood love of the "good old days" of child-friendly space adventure serials such as *Flash Gordon* and *Buck Rogers*, as well as of westerns, swashbucklers, and war movies. And as Gary Westfahl argues, "space opera is the ... least [intellectually] respected, form of science fiction ... scorned by learned commentators."[55]

There is in marked contrast to this Reaganesque reading, however, the possibility of evaluating *SW*'s "evil empire" in patently different terms. In this revised reading, the "empire" would be the American government, or perhaps a particular period of government, itself. Lucas himself has candidly suggested that the Emperor is a Richard Nixon–type character, and Darth Vader is representative of a Henry Kissinger–type.[56] There may be something in this, and it is certainly true that *SW*, as with any human artifact, reflects a deep cultural resonance. Yet the movies are simply too broad to be read in straightforwardly allegorical terms, and that ambiguity makes singular identifications difficult to sustain. The characters possess too little depth for such unqualified allegorizing specification by virtue of their construction in mythically archetypal ways. Nevertheless, the manner of the ahistorical and archetypal nature of the politics of *SW* can and does encourage one to pay critical attention to even the most self-proclaimed "democratic" and "free" of political environments (and this is one of the main reasons why reductionist complaints of *ROTS* being an anti–Bush allegory cannot be taken too seriously).[57] It is this reading that *AOTC* and more controversially *ROTS* lends some more weight to, particularly in an era when talk of the relation of the U.S. and "empire" is becoming increasingly popular after the post–Second World War post-colonialist aversion to the term.

The frame for a revised reading of the saga comes from the narrative arc of the prequel trilogy as being identifiably one of *tragic drama*. It is important to note what is not being said here. The claim is not that *ROTS*, for example, is as linguistically captivating as is the evident literary quality displayed in William Shakespeare's (1564–1616) Lear raging on the heath against what has befallen him at the hands of his ungrateful and self-aggrandizing daughters. In fact, the claim is equally not that there is the kind of substantive exploration of the complexity of the causes of suffering and wickedness that are enacted to such dramatic effect in Sophocles' (c. 496–406 BCE) protagonist Oedipus who inadvertently creates the tragic situation when attempting to flee them, or Euripides' (c. 480–406 BCE) character Pentheus who becomes the victim of the god whom he offends, Dionysus. In many ways, Lucas' characters and imagery remain a little too archetypally described. The point of the claim is, instead, a *narrative* one, one that has to do with the very thematic framing and material flow of the drama. And in this Lucas is in good company. According to Aristotle's classic and influential definition of tragedy, what makes for tragedy is the *plot*, the *drama*.[58]

The way George Lucas conceives particularly of Anakin as the *tragic protagonist* involves a deconstruction of the myth of the hero, and this opens up substantial political questions with regard to the politics of fear, the politics of Othering, and therefore of the apparently critically perceived and politically significant Manichaean sensibility of the saga. The cultural and political significance of this shift of dramatic structuration is notable. If *ANH* was what Americans emotionally needed during a time of trauma in the mid 1970s, then the events surrounding 9/11 and the Bush administration's march into Afghanistan and Iraq are played out with a subversion of the emotional fervor of patriotism and its national heroes. *SW* was a juvenilization of the cinema, according to critics, most notably the influential film critic Pauline Kael. In her account, *SW* (and Spielberg's *Jaws* 1975) reconstitutes the spectator as child, and then overwhelms her with sound and spectacle, obliterating irony, aesthetic self-consciousness and critical reflection.[59] Nonetheless, the movies subsequent to *ANH* deconstructed the values that many read into and out of it—in particular, and crucially, the simplistic approach to good/evil, to the virtuousness of good characters and the self-aggrandizing megalomania of the wicked, and so on. Of course this tragic perspective should hardly surprise viewers of Episodes V and VI or be terribly controversial among commentators given the numerous significant anti–Manichaean gestures in the classic trilogy itself. Albeit very brief and underdeveloped in *ANH*, the tragic fate of the young Jedi Darth Vader is signaled. Even more important is the shocking revelation of Luke's paternity in Vader's admission to having himself once been Anakin Skywalker which, of course, comes after Obi-Wan in *ANH* had spoken of Anakin in the most glowing of terms. The stage had been firmly set in the "classic trilogy" for revealing *SW* as a kind of tragic drama.

In 1990 Pollock commented that "the audience for *Star Wars* movies seems to have grown up.... Today's movie audiences have also become cynical and jaded; Tim Burton's dark vision of *Batman* is light years from the upbeat morality play Lucas devised for *Star Wars*."[60] The box office success and media hype surrounding the re-release of the special editions of the "classic trilogy" in 1977 and their release in DVD format in 2004 would suggest that Pollock's assessment was wildly premature. Yet when we turn to the prequels there may well be an unwitting truth in his claim. For all its visual delights and its aspirations to Campbellian mythic resonance, and while its sequels were a little more ethically interesting, *ANH* is arguably as morally sophisticated as vintage Saturday morning boys' adventure serials. But the prequel trilogy exhibits much more of a sense not merely of the importance of public systems but of complex political interactions, and these demand readings that are characterized by a more morally sophisticated self-reflexivity. This trilogy of prequel movies comes from a different time, and arguably expresses a distinctly different mood (although there are simultaneously crucial lines of continuity). There is something too wholesome about the violent mood in the classic trilogy, which is why they have proven to be so popular with a young market. In contrast, *ROTS* in particular represents the series relatively politically "all grown up," in many ways the saga at its most mature. It is flush with a distinctly more modern skeptical (albeit not cynical) and perspectival (albeit not relativistic) touch. "Good is a point of view," hisses the reptilian Chancellor Palpatine during his paternalistic pursuing of callow Jedi Knight Anakin Skywalker. Recognizing something of this change in mood, Ian Nathan admits that "for all its childish trappings this [viz. *TPM*] was an adult world threaded with the concerns of the adult Lucas."[61]

The prequels, then, involve a kind of coming of age, both in terms of their political ethos and in terms of the development of their main protagonist. In relation to this movie series itself, this movement of the prequels intensifies the retroactive defamiliarization that occurs already in *ESB* and in *ROTJ*. Each adds not merely a new narrative layer to the saga, but acts as a reading regeneration. There is, then, a real sense in which Nathan's complaint that the "three prequels have added nothing to the original, bar hype and overkill" is seriously misplaced. These movies unsettingly begin to strip some of the pantomime-like ideological readings of the "classic trilogy" from their simplistic dualistic approach to good and evil, and explore in more complex ways causation in human and non-human relations than the earlier movies do. One's whole approach to the saga has to be relearned, although popular readings of the "classic trilogy" itself may themselves be insufficiently nuanced. There can be no simple faith in the democratic order or in the persons who claim to represent it—these can be corrupted, can become complacent, or can even be manipulated in one way or another for the purposes of the self-aggrandizing possession and exercise of power. This, nonetheless, does not call for a simple cynicism over the motives of the moral guardians—for Lucas, the Jedi's motives are indeed virtuous, but they are *ignorant* and complacent in their virtue, having lost touch with the affairs of state.

"I want more": The Tragic Protagonist from Flawed Hero to Faceless Zero

Where the mood and narrative form of the "classic trilogy" is presented as *The Adventures of Luke Skywalker*, those of the prequels appear quite different. *ANH*, and indeed the "classic trilogy" as a whole, follows Luke's journey of maturation from "every [ordinary] man" farmboy, through the stage of Rebel hero, to self-aware Jedi Knight. The mood, moreover, is frequently one of triumph, despite the catastrophic second act of that trilogy, of gain in spite of the losses. This is probably why Lucas was reluctant to develop further his originally very broad plans for Episodes VII–IX. The mood at the close of *ROTJ* is one of hope fulfilled, of an end come, a consummating eschatological *adventus*. Luke's alter ego and nemesis, eventually revealed in one of cinema's great cinematic moments to be his own father, is, of course, Darth Vader. It is of him that Roy Anker claims that "hardly ever has there been a classier, more striking, or more fearsome villain conjured on film."[62] But the significance of this character in the mythology of the saga comes to move well beyond his early manifestation as an iconic screen "baddie." This becomes particularly clear in the prequels when taken together as a whole, which is altogether distinctly more reserved, darker even. It is in and through the deconstruction of this character that Lucas hopes to offer a political sensibility that can be more constructive of human relations but without naiveté. As the credits opening *TPM* ominously announce, "turmoil has engulfed the Republic," and that darkness now comes to cast its sinister shadow back over Episodes IV–VI, darkening their way too in the reassessment that is thereby made necessary. This new emphasis transforms *Star Wars* from the celebratory mood that depicts the heroic adventures of Luke Skywalker into a mood of catastrophism that portrays the *tragedy of Anakin Skywalker*. It is in and through Anakin's personal and domestic tragedy that the narrative provides a thematic microcosm of the macrocosmic tragic fall of the old Galactic Republic.

Tragic dramas come in many shapes and forms, and it can even be misleading to speak of them under a single categorizable heading such as "tragedy" without considerable qualification.[63] In fact, the term "tragedy" (*tragōidia* is Greek for "goat song") itself is such an overburdened word in popular parlance, being used in a range of contexts from the horrors of genocide all the way down to a bad essay grade, or the poorly judged purchase of an underperforming football player, or an eccentric fashion sense. Walter Kaufmann admits that "theories of tragedy always run the risk" of activating Procrustean tendencies to excise those elements which stubbornly refuse to fit.[64] What is particularly important is to distinguish tragic drama from other genres that have "tragic" moments as with, for example, tragicomedies. In *ANH* a tragic *moment* would be the execution of Luke's Uncle Owen and Aunt Beru on their moisture farm on Tatooine; or in *ESB* the freezing of Han Solo in carbonite on Bespin; or in *ROTJ* the vision of the Ewok peoples being slaughtered by Imperial troops; or the death of the repentant Vader. Recalling the preeminent context of "tragedy" in "tragic dramas," and speaking in a distinctly Wittgensteinian vein, Donald MacKinnon remarks that the latter "are inherently complex, and various in emphasis; at best we can discern a family resemblance between them."[65] Even though there is always the danger of "imposing an appearance of similarity of conception where it is at least equally important to stress differences," one account of tragedy has proven to be particularly well-known and enduringly influential. So much has this been the case that it often serves as something of a touchstone for textbook depictions of "tragedy." This is the portrayal offered by the Greek philosopher Aristotle (384–322 BCE) in his *Poetics*. Crucial for him is the identification of tragedy as a serious play that evokes fear (*phobos*) and pity (*eleos*), effecting through them "the *catharsis* of such emotions."[66] While the meaning of this has been much debated and the interpretation disputed, with Terry Eagleton worrying that it involves "a kind of public therapy for a citizenry in danger of emotional flabbiness,"[67] Lucas' use of it to determine the broad shape of the prequels is important. In fact, the depiction here comes in crucial ways to echo the key exemplar of Aristotle's analysis, Sophocles' *Oedipus the King* (and equally, much later, William Shakespeare's *King Lear*). The fleshing out of the Vader character consequently makes him less a figure of audience loathing than one, at least potentially, who is able to provoke fear and pity. It is this transformation that can suitably challenge and purify both our ability to stably identify "evil" as something simply "Other" and our need for vengeance against one who had been characterized too simply as "evil" or "wicked." With the designing of the prequels Lucas frequently admits that this "rehabilitation" of Darth Vader is "really what the story was all about," that in his narrative plans developed in the early 1980s he had already worked out in quite detailed ways the direction his later movies would eventually take. "Darth Vader became such an icon in the first film, *Episode IV*," Lucas admits, "that that icon of evil sort of took over everything, more than I intended. If it had been one movie that wouldn't have happened.... But now by adding *Episodes I, II* and *III* people begin to see the tragedy of Darth Vader as what it was originally intended to be."[68]

Evil does not come from nowhere but is "made," and in this way the tragically plotted prequels offer a considerably more complex response to the nature of moral development and misdevelopment than the depiction of *SW* as evidently constrained by simplistic moral binaries would suggest.

> [*The*] *Phantom Menace* was done really to determine that Anakin was a good person, good heart, nice kid. We're not talking here about an evil little monster child—we're talking about this great kid just like we all start out as, or [we] think we start out as.... The whole reason for going back and doing the back story on *Star Wars* is that there is an evolution from this very good person, very kind person, very loving person into something that one would describe as evil.[69]

Evil is not something that just *happens to* us, or worse to "evil people," but instead has to do with the nature of our relations and complex choices, and the pressures that "conspire" to make people into something other than they can be morally.[70] David Brin recognizes that Lucas upholds "his saga as an agonized Greek tragedy worth of *Oedipus*—an epic tale of a fallen hero, trapped by hubris and fate."[71] The problem for

Brin, however, is that Anakin's fall still appears to come out of nowhere. This would entail that Lucas has been unable to overturn the Manichaeism that many believe dogs Episode IV, but in fact continues to sustain an us-versus-them sensibility.[72] Brin's claim, however, appears to make the problem one largely of style. Lucas does indeed attempt to portray Anakin as a tragic hero, but does so badly. This claim needs to be critically tested.

→ Darth Sidious

"The Chancellor's not a bad man": Machiavelli Manipulations and the Tragedy of the Republic

Palpatine is a Machiavellian figure, manipulating events and people when lurking in the background as Darth Sidious, and is the ultimate image of "evil" in the saga. He, it would seem, is single minded right from the beginning. When in *ROTS* he asserts to Mace Windu "I am the senate," echoing Louis XIV's claim to be the absolute embodiment of the collective will (*"l'état est moi,"* the state is me), the impression is of one very much at home in his position of power. In this Palpatine stands in a certain contrast to Adolf Hitler in that the latter understood himself in the early 1920s, it would seem, as a John the Baptist type figure, preparing the way for a coming great leader, heralding his advent, and attempting to gain the support of the people for him.[73] The impression given by Palpatine in the prequels, in contrast, is of a man with a definite mission, a man with a distinct and unchanging self-consciousness, and this mission is coolly and dispassionately effected. That makes him an even more chilling figure in the context of the politics of the movies than even the distortedly passionate Hitler himself.

Yet the way in which he comes to power is highly suggestive, and harks back to the themes explored in the "classic trilogy" with the revelation of Vader's fall, and particularly of the temptations faced by Luke. So the young Jedi in training's self-recognition scene in the cave on Dagobah could be read in such a way as to provide a warning against becoming the image of the evil "other." This psychologizing moment could offer a cautionary message to the politics of aggressive fear for one's existence (that which is pre-eminently involved in the warring fear for the loss of the nation-state). After all, Luke comes face to face with the fact that his own journey could itself lead to the dark side, and thus he offers himself as a sacrifice to the imperial statesman who ultimately seeks to secure his position. The struggle and turmoil operating at the public and political level in the conflict between Empire and Rebellion has its parallel *within* his very own self here. In this, significantly, Luke as the archetypal hero is an "everyman" kind of figure provides something of a warning against simple externalizing projections of evil onto an "evil other." It is this theme that is unmistakably intensified in the journey of Anakin to the dark side (Episodes I–III). Moreover, in the prequels, the audience is forced to observe that the Empire is not an "alien other," an invading force that conquers by pure assertiveness. Instead, it is a cancerous growth in the very Republic itself, drawing on the commented on tiredness, complacency, vice, and corruption of the senate. It is not insignificant, then, that within the saga the "evil Empire" and the evil that Palpatine/Sidious represents arises from within the crumbling of the good Republic.

When one adds this to the backstory of the "Expanded Universe" advocating that the Lords of the Sith were formed from Jedi who were expelled from the Order who then recruited and trained "dark Jedi," the suggestion is that evil is a growth in and through the good, a distortion and shadow of it, never pre-existing it but feeding off it parasitically. As Sith, the formation and habituation of character is an educative process, an apprenticing in wickedness. This, then, is no simple "evil." In this respect it should be apparent that a rereading of the archetypality of Sidious as evil needs to be offered. The example of Anakin/Vader, for instance, implies that a backstory could be told concerning his fall into the dark side, and which is here not told precisely because his character serves the *story of the fall of Anakin Skywalker* as archetypal wickedness. While the serpent in the Garden promises Eve that if she tastes the forbidden fruit, her eyes would be opened, and she would "be like God, knowing good and evil" (Genesis 3:5), Palpatine promises Anakin that if he dabbles in the forbidden Dark Side, he will "know the full Force." If this reading is correct, then Palpatine's acts of betrayal of Count Dooku (Darth Tyrannus) in *ROTS* and, as Emperor, of Darth Vader in *ROTJ* may well resonate less with Judas' tragic betrayal of Jesus than with the theme of a devilish liar (see John 8:44). Yet it is significant that his temptation of Anakin on General Grievous' *Invisible Hand* and of Luke on the second Death Star echo the role of Satan in tempting Jesus and the serpent in the Garden of Eden. The fact that Vader too becomes satanic tempter, both to Padmé in *ROTS* and Luke in *ESB*, suggests that the Satanic depiction of Sidious and his agency is not unique to him.[74] So in the novelization of *ROTJ* it is revealed that Vader's dream was that "when he'd learned all he could of the dark power from this evil genius [the Emperor], to take that power from him, seize it and keep its cold light at his own core—kill the Emperor and devour his darkness, and rule the universe. Rule with his son at his side."[75] Sidious may be this story's evil archetype, but he cannot be the source of all evil.

Can Palpatine/Sidious be read in the same light as a Vader who has *fallen* from the good? There are certainly numerous hints which suggest that he can and that he should. The difficulty, however, is that this back-story is not narratively demonstrated in the saga, and consequently Lucas leaves an ambiguity in the characterization of Sidious, a man with no background or history (other than the suggestion in *ROTS* that he had been Darth Plagueis' apprentice, betrayer and executioner). By refusing to "redeem" Palpatine/Sidious' character, and by depicting him in Satanic fashion (costume design, and image of the liar and the tempter) the material is pressed too hard. McDiarmid interestingly uses devilish-image to depict his role, announcing that in *ROTS* he is "revealed, finally, in all his satanic glory," although he also suggests something even more sinister: that Sidious "is more evil than the devil. At least Satan fell—he has a history."[76] That comment is highly revealing—in the Christian account of creation there is no dualism in the natural order *as created*, but evil is only introduced into story through a *fall*, and thus the satanic figure of Christian tradition is portrayed as an angelic figure who becomes satiated with the rebelliousness of pride. Bearing that in mind, McDiarmid's comment seems to justify a reading of the *SW* saga in dualistic terms. That would suggest that the various Satan-like images used of Sidious in the saga should be read as ways in which his character is *archetypally* evil, and not as a reference to fallenness as such. He, then, is a character presented without complex motivation and with few redeeming qualities (he does exhibit "patience," "determination," and "devotion to his task"). There is need for concern that there is some jus-tification in the dualistic way in which commentators understand his characterization. Without qualification Hanson and Kay proclaim that "he *is* evil," a remark echoed by Executive Producer Rick McCallum who announces that "the guy who's truly evil is Palpatine. He has manipulated this whole saga."[77] (The only moment which seems to suggest that there is more to him than this is the occasion when he gently lays a hand on the horrendously injured young Vader after the dual on Mustafar, a ten-der moment that suggests real compassion for his young apprentice.)

This is similar in some ways to Christopher Nolan's Joker whose unadulterated presence or intensified momentariness exhausts his meaning as pure meaninglessness, unteleologically ordered violence, and maniacal despair. As Alfred lamentingly admits to Bruce in *The Dark Knight*, "some men aren't looking for anything logical, like money. They can't be bought, bullied, reasoned with or negotiated with. Some men just want to watch the world burn." The echo of Kyle Reese's description of the Terminator is noticeable. ("It can't be bargained with. It can't be reasoned with. It doesn't feel pity, or remorse, or fear. And it absolutely will not stop, ever, until you are dead!") The difference is that Sarah Connor's protector is speaking of a bio-mechanized entity that lacks independent thought beyond its programming.

For years before Hitler was able to finally seize power, his Party had been engaged in a system of mind-preparing propaganda. Combined with the general feeling of shame over the Allies' treatment of Germany through the Treaty of Versailles and disillusionment with the Weimar government, he was able to tap into the dreams, desires, and despair of a significantly large proportion of the German people. Of course, Palpatine, as far as we know, has not played the propaganda game in quite the same way. But his control over the progress of the war (over, in fact, both sides—the Republic forces under the guise of Chancellor Palpatine, and over the Separatist armies under the guise of the Sith lord Darth Sidious), and his control of the reporting of it enables him to create a great swell of popular support both for himself and his political office. These events speak of the operation of "controlling" the range of available public sentiments and affections in a way not too unlike the control-function of propaganda. A good example of how this works is Nazi Reichmarshall Herman Goering's admission at the Nuremburg trials:

> Why, of course the people don't want war.... [B]ut after all it is the leaders of the country who determine the policy, and it is always a simple matter to drag the people along whether it is a democracy, a fascist dictatorship, or a parliament, or a communist dictatorship. Voice or no voice, the people can always be brought to the bidding of the leaders. That is easy. All you have to do is tell them they are being attacked, and denounce the pacifists for lack of patriotism, and exposing the country to greater danger. It works the same in any country.[78]

In this way Palpatine is able to create for himself the position of popular heroic-leader, a strong and reliable authority who could be seen on numerous occasions to be winning the Republic's war against the Separatists (a war that, unbeknown to all but his Sith apprentice Count Dooku, he had manufactured). He seems to be someone, along with the popular war hero Anakin, who is able to become the very embodiment of the projected hopes and dreams for peace and security of the Republic. He *is*, indeed, winning the war (a war, however, that is the fruit of his diseased maneuverings) and thus bringing a peace and stability to the galaxy, *just as he promises*. In so doing he encourages a state of childlike dependence upon his paternal ability to secure his subjects, and this has several significant facets. As French thinker Jacques Ellul claimed in the 1960s,

> The cult of the hero is the absolutely necessary complement of the massification of society…. He feels, thinks, and acts through the hero. He is under the guardianship and protection of his living god; he accepts being a child; he ceases to defend his own interests, for he knows his hero loves him and everything his hero decides is for the propagandee's own good…. For this reason every regime that demands a certain amount of heroism must develop this propaganda of projection onto the hero (leader).[79]

Firstly, there is an uncritical trust which stimulates a generous reading of the attitudes and actions of the hero that may be less than virtuous in other situations. The citizens of Corsucant and the Galactic Senate generally seem to approve of his abnormal actions—the initial militarization of the Galaxy (the creation of a Grand Army of the Republic to counter the separatist threat); the retention of power long after the term has expired; their condoning of emergency powers executively bequeathed to the Chancellor on several occasions; the further militarization of what is then renamed the "Galactic Empire" with the formation of regional governors to oversee the administration of the Empire.

Secondly, in that movement of trust there is blindness to what might otherwise be seen and disapproved of, an inability to think otherwise than through the operation of this projection of hope. Propaganda circumvents the normal processes of deliberating, testing and thinking. There is little way of critically interrogating the message. The relational autonomy or moral subjectivity is sacrificed for the comforting feeling of protective care, or, as is usually the case with propaganda, is taken away from one by the nature of the appeal of propaganda. As Gore Vidal observes, it is difficult for "a nation [or, indeed, any group we could add] that sees itself as close to perfection as any human society can come" to hear criticism of itself.[80]

Palpatine's politically self-aggrandizing tactics take the form of var-

Palpatine's power

ious ways of inducing and maintaining fear. In a totalitarian regime run on the lines of domination, he instills a fear that he can shape and direct to his own ends. So in the guise of Palpatine he initiated and sustained the Republic's Civil War (better known as "the Clone Wars") by playing on the citizens of the Republic's fears for their own existence at the hands of their fear of a threatening enemy. In this "emergency" situation Palpatine is granted "emergency powers" that are understood to be temporary, granted for the duration of the conflict. However, through Sidious' careful management of the conflict (Sidious, of course, being able to directly manage in the persona of Palpatine the Republic's forces and military strategy, and indirectly through Dooku the Separatist Confederacy's military services and war tactics) the moment drags on into a protracted war. His subsequent successes considerably enhance his political and military reputation among the majority of the Republic's populace. In addition, his abduction at the hands of "the fiendish droid leader, General Grievous" (which Sidious had, without Grievous' knowledge, carefully staged), improve his general popularity further among his concerned people. Moreover, the cessation of the Clone Wars slip into the emergency situation of resistance to the new "terrorism" caused by the newly formed Rebellion against Palpatine's self-named "Galactic Empire."[81] In those ways the "fear of the other" is effectively used for political effect. Another form of muting the message of resistance and circumventing the potential for critical opposition is procured through inducing fear by using tactics of intimidation, isolating those who resist into a minority, and also by buying off others with promises of power and prestige. The fear of Palpatine's power secures his position. As Chancellor he introduces a way of checking much potential political dissension through a surveillance system, the intrusive use of hovercams and the deactivation of Privacy Screens in the Senate. Furthermore, there is the obvious ideological function of labeling opponents "treasonous" in _ROTS_ and Palpatine's patriotic reference to loving the Republic, tactics that cannot be lost on American audiences who themselves are frequently accused of having no patriotism and being treasonous when they critique the values, and beliefs that supposedly make America and her government. Therefore, even if criticism is offered the socio-political machinery ensures that it is muted, unheard, or if heard done so only as the ranting's of the mad, the unpatriotic, and so on. Dissenting mischief that cannot be managed and kept safely at bay, then, can be crushed. And this threat is enough to prevent much otherwise potential sedition from arising and gaining a foothold sufficiently threatening to Palpatine's political arrangement. Significantly in *ANH* Grand Moff Tarkin announces to an assembled group of leading military personal that the Emperor has dissolved the senate but will be able to keep rebelling star systems in line through *fear of* "this battle station." While Jedi Master Mace Windu explains in the novelized version of *ROTS* that "the *real* treason would be a failure to *act*," echoing a claim made by President Theodore Roosevelt in 1918, he is a good example of what happens to the seditious just as Alderaan is in *ANH*.[82]

To blame the violent imperial turn in the Republic's history wholly on the insidiousness of the evil Palpatine is, therefore, an excuse that significantly blinds one to a point closer to home. The preconditions for Palpatine's rise lie deep within the greed that was beginning to tire the Republic out *from inside*, and the Republic's attraction to the war-mongering tactics in order to secure its own existence as it is, and thinks it always was. It is, through its own disposition, susceptible to the flattering projection of problems onto others. Hence, one is unable to discuss the evil of Palpatine's absolute rule without understanding the elements that enable and support its birth, progression and maintenance. As Mon Mothma declares, in a scene filmed for *ROTS* but eventually deleted, "the Chancellor has played the Senate as well. They know where the power lies and they will do whatever it takes to share in it." It is the citizens of the Republic who desire to defend their way of life, their prosperity and sense of self-righteousness at all costs; it is they who reinforce their sense of security by projecting their fears onto "threatening others," demonizing those who oppose them, imposing on them an identity designed simply to shore up their own. Padmé, the great supporter of the Republic's democracy, admits that "popular rule is not democracy, Anni. It gives the people what they want, not what they need" (*AOTC*, a cinematically deleted scene). Palpatine, seemingly, has played the typical political game by appealing to popular instincts while offering that which is deeply destructive of the good of the Republic. This is the instinct that V in *V for Vendetta* criticizes when he makes his television appearance to "have a little chat," as he puts it.

Even the Jedi Order is unwittingly complicit in the process that eventuates in its destruction. While admitting concerns with Palpatine's growing power, the creation of the Grand Army of the Republic (an instrumentalization of life as bio-mechanoids), and the beginning and progress of the Galactic Civil War, the Order is blind to its own place in the ensuing tragedy. An illustration of this can be found in a double scene towards the end of *AOTC*. Obi-Wan avers that "without the clones we would not have won this victory." In a tone of surprise Master Yoda criticizes this as a glib perspective: "Victory! Victory you say! Master Obi-Wan, not victory. The shroud of the dark side has fallen. Begun the Clone War has." Nonetheless, Yoda too is implicated in the unfolding doom. He is unable to see what is really occurring, and the scene that immediately succeeds this one depicts the clone troopers marching off to war with the Imperial March, largely reserved for Vader in *ESB*, theme resounding. Understanding this depiction of the Jedi Order's ultimately self-destructive complicity in the tragedy is badly missed by Rohan Gowland's review of *TPM*. He argues that Episode I, at least, is still ideologically continuous with the "classic trilogy" in retaining the simplistic "us-vs.-them" mood. The "Western-style democracy, the Senate, ... is portrayed as bureaucratic and intrinsically corrupt. The only hope rests on the religious order of Jedi knights to intervene and take direct action as the righteous saviours of all that is morally good."[83] This problem, he declares, is that "religious fundamentalist groups would be rejoicing at this portrayal of a righteous group by-passing an elected democracy and taking justice into their own hands." This morally vulgar vigilantist "mythology" of the righteous interventionists Gowland sees as being played out at the time of his writing in the NATO military intervention in the Balkan conflict at a time of perceived bureaucratic incapacitating of "the United Nations, the democratic body," to act effectively. "The ones taking action, in this case NATO, by bypassing the bureaucracy, are seen as 'people of action,' the good guys on a supposedly moral crusade." Of course this very political perspective had been intensively expressed later in the crusading interventionism of U.S. president George W. Bush and British Prime Minister Tony Blair in the Middle East, with the projection of "evil" firmly onto others, and the attendant rhetoric of euphoric self-righteousness. Nevertheless it is difficult to interpret *TPM* in this way. Primarily Episode I is concerned with Naboo's *self-defense* against the pre-emptive strike of the a conquistador-like Trade Federation that is seeking "gold" (in this case, a trade franchise agreement). Chancellor Valorum does not send the Jedi to engage in military intervention but for diplomacy on behalf of the *Pax Republica*. Significantly, what Gowland also misses is the Hitler-Reich connection of the saga to that point, and the notion that the Rebellion begins against an elected and relatively popular government that is nonetheless *pushing its hold on power to a level that prevents challenge level*. This could as easily be applied *against* western interventionist governments as much as in support of them. There is a large and complex set of moral questions in the saga to this point that cannot be pushed unambiguously in one direction or another.

The climatic image of the movement towards Galactic tragedy is encapsulated by a comment, the political resonance of which reverberates around recent American political history. "So this is how liberty dies. With thunderous applause," bemoans Padmé Amidala as the Galactic Senate cheers dictator-in-waiting Palpatine while he announces a crusade against the Jedi. In this case, Hanson and Kay's following comment is odd, anachronistic and utterly displaced from the saga's own terms: "After September 11, 2001, as America comes to grip with the losses of freedom after the tragedy of the terrorist attacks, the ... archetypal characters ... help us to sort out mentally who is good and who is bad, and they provide a loose instruction for how to combat fear and oppression.... The evil faction is out there, and we need a rebellion."[84] They have badly missed the point, possibly because of some prevailing guiding patriotic/nationalistic assumptions that subsequently prevent them from reading the saga on its own terms.

The evident echoes of conditions following September 11 have themselves received heated comment. Several within the American political right have denounced *ROTS* as an anti–Bush diatribe, as was mentioned above. The parallels may well be intended, but they are also more general. Joseph Campbell once claimed about the "classic" saga that "the fact that the evil power is not identified with any specific nation on this earth means you've got an abstract power, which represents a principle, not a specific historic situation. The story has to do with an operation of principles not of this nation against that." Similarly, Lucas himself, elsewhere claiming his story's conception during the Vietnam War, appeals to the more general:

> All democracies turn into dictatorships—but not by coup. The people give their democracy to a dictator, whether it's Julius Caesar or Napoleon or Adolf Hitler. Ultimately, the general population goes along with the idea.... That's the issue that I've been exploring: How did the Republic turn into the Empire ... and how does a democracy become a dictatorship?[85]

However, the criticism also drastically misses the point in that even if George W. Bush (and to a lesser degree Tony Blair), or in fact any political leader is perceived as falling foul of Lucas' presentation of the principles underlying the "evil empire," then so much the worse for him and his way with the American people. How far people can continue to follow charismatic and self-professed divinely-guided figures depends on whether they will be able to learn the difficult task of thoughtfully interrogating their own ideological formation.

Of course one could attempt to propose the beneficence of the American imperial project, what Michael Ignatieff calls an "empire lite, hegemony without colonies, a global sphere of influence without the burden of direct administration and the risks of daily policing."[86] So Ignatieff argues that this "empire lite" commendably refuses to possess territories directly through annexation, colonization and direct central-ized governance, and is to be celebrated and maintained on the grounds that it is necessary for "bringing order to the barbarian zones."[87] Accord-ing to Deepak Lal, the U.S. can take "over from the British the burden of maintaining a Pax to allow free trade and commerce to flourish."[88] Given this kind of reasoning it is not wholly surprising to discover a critic who asserts that "Lucas confused the good guys with the bad" in that he missed the point that "the Empire is good."[89]

The example of Anakin, however, should give one pause for critical reflection here. He seems to have taken on face value Palpatine's appear-ance as a wise ruler ultimately interested in peace. Anakin too was con-vinced by Palpatine, as were many others. In an important sense it would be a mistake to speak of Anakin *blindly* following Palpatine, as if he does not have reasons for doing so. Nevertheless, he is *blind to the truth* of Palpatine, and therefore his reasons are only partially sensible but ulti-mately misguided. It is only the "reader" of the movies, transcending involvement in the partiality of perception within the complexities of the fray, who can feel safe in making moral declarations on Palpatine. It is only they, with a God's eye perspective, who can see that the one in whom Anakin has placed his faith is the dark character who instrumen-talizes the lives of others, and constantly himself lives in fear of a coup from his own disciple (hence he has no qualms about sacrificing Darths Maul and Tyrannus). The trouble is that in his naïve and trusting opti-mism the young Jedi Knight never tests the meaning of "peace" and mis-judges the *oppressive* nature of Palpatine's peace, which is that of the victors' self-interestedly imposed peace (for their self-securing and self-protecting), a "peace" that spells calamity for the losers. Moreover, what the "author" encourages the audience to think of as evil (the destruction of the Jedi Order) is perceived by Anakin to be little more than radical surgery for the health of the body, collateral damage necessary in the cause of the greater good—"peace" and stability. As Claes G. Ryn maintains, "desire for power rarely shows itself in its own tawdry voraciousness.... They feel the need to dress up their striving in appealing garb. Hence the will to power almost always presents itself as benevolent concern for others, as an unselfish wish to improve society or the world."[90] Moreover, even had a ruler like Palpatine been motivated by what one might call more benevolent purposes could the shape of his rule and his policies have been wholly free of the distorting influences of those motivated by ends less benevolent? Perhaps that is the significance of the mention of the bureaucracy and corruption that were weighing down Finis Valorum's term as Chancellor, a situation that enabled Palpatine, with his promise of strong leadership, to be propelled into the Chancellor's political office (*TPM*). According to Christensen, "American political films tell us that politics is corrupt."[91] This claim might be overly simplistic if applied to the *SW* prequels in that there is no blackening of the political *qua* political. The prequels, one could argue, do seem to imply that governance is a complex matter. However, even more crucially they reiterate the classic trilogies' sense not only that there is something very sinister about the imperial project, but they do so in a way that subtly forces self-critical attention to American ideology itself. In the context of *AOTC* the economically self-interested Separatists (the Confederacy of Independent Systems) are opposed by a Republic that increasingly becomes tinted with an imperial hue, and it falls into becoming an empire driven by self-interest and enforced by a "grand army of the Republic" (the post–Civil War reference in Palpatine's language here is clear).[92] In the wake of Palpatine's rise to dictatorial power, lives are wasted, horrendous evils are perpetrated, and those who suffer them would seem to have little hope left. Darth Sidious worships the "god" or idol of self-interest, of personal prowess which is expressed as a lust for domination over and brutally securing of his self against the threat of others, the fear of loss and death rather of the serving self-giving and concern for others' well-being.

Ignorance of the Flaw of Fear Is the Path to the Darkside

According to Aristotle, largely following the pattern of *Oedipus the King* rather than other quite different tragedies, the tragic protagonist is to be no ordinary personage but rather someone of significant social or political standing. This classical pattern was largely the norm until the thought of Italian Renaissance philosopher Pico della Mirandola (1463–94) and the more recent "domestic tragedies."[93] The protagonist is to be some eminent person, and frequently this has taken the form of a royal or some other high noble figuration. The "fall" is therefore more significant than the disruption that is caused for the protagonist and/or her closest relations alone (actually, *King Lear* has two "falls," that of Lear himself and also Gloucester). In fact, unlike *Oedipus, Macbeth, King Lear*, and other plays for whom a macrocosmic political importance of the main character is only implied, Lucas draws the personal fate of Anakin more directly into the tragic political story of the fall of the Republic. In many ways the political story is not only inextricably linked to the fate of Anakin, the one who enables Sidious to defeat the Jedi and bring an end to the civil war (the Clone Wars) with his slaughter of the leaders of the Separatists, but the narrated tragedy of Anakin is at the same time a focal microcosm of the larger collapse of the democratic Galactic Republic.

Unmistakably, Anakin is no ordinary character, and film critic Peter T. Chattaway entirely misses the point of the connection with classical tragic drama when he complains that "for all the talk of 'democracy,' … (*ROTS*) is actually less interested than any of the others in the lives of ordinary people."[94] Not merely is Anakin one of the Force-conscious minority from the ranks of which the revered icons of peace and justice are selected and trained, but the very nature of his *conception* and birth play a vital symbolic function in the narrative. In an earlier conversation between Jedi Master Qui-Gon Jinn and Anakin's mother Shmi Skywalker, a "virginal conception" is suggested, and the Jedi Master later makes the connection with the boy's identifiably high concentration of midi-chlorians.[95] The hero, in Carl Jung's terms, is a "greater man … semi-divine by nature,"[96] and it is highly likely that Lucas contrived his story here under Campbell's claim that the story of a virgin birth is a key part of the heroic monomyth. Nevertheless, the echoes of the messianic materials in the New Testament are also striking—so Qui-Gon believes that Anakin is "the Chosen One" whose coming to bring balance to "the Force" was prophesied long before [*TPM*]. The nobility required for the fall of the tragic hero type is secured here in the grandest of terms. Given the immense power at his disposal, his fall cannot but have the most catastrophic consequences for even the galaxy itself.

Aristotle unpacks the character of the tragic protagonist by refusing two options, which would fail to provoke fear and pity in the audience.[97] Firstly, he claims, justifiably or not, that a wicked person's fall would not evoke the responses characteristic of a tragedy, presumably since the audience would consider this to be just recompense for the wicked acts. Secondly, and perhaps most controversially, the fall of a good person would simply shock the audience since an "innocent's" fall is merely traumatic and not tragic. (Readers of Cordelia's terrible demise in *King Lear* will indeed be shocked, but may disagree that it is not tragic.)[98] Tragedy, instead, involves someone good who suffers a calamitous reversal of fortune by a *hamartia* (Greek, "error"), and falls into catastrophe (*nemesis*—Greek, "retribution").[99] *Hamartia* is often considered by commentators on Aristotle to involve a flaw that expresses a certain lack of virtue—Lear's *hubris* or pride, for instance, demands the flattery of his daughters before he hands over the rule of his kingdom. In contrast, the nine-year-old slave boy of *TPM* is, critics argue, presented in too neatly and unambiguously good terms to be a believable Vader-in-the-making. Anakin's fall seems to come out of nowhere.[100] Reading *SW* as a dualistic set of filmic texts seems to have been one of the principal reasons (and therefore a more interesting one than the complaints leveled at young actor Jake Lloyd's screen performance) why many find it difficult to watch and take seriously the portrayal of Anakin in *TPM*. Of course, when this movie was released in 1999 the audience was well aware of the fact that he was going to become Vader. Yet as a child he is portrayed in the brightest and least morally suspect of terms. So, for instance, in the slave quarters of Mos Espa in Tatooine his mother Shmi agrees categorically with Qui-Gon's positive assessment of the quite remarkable ethical virtue of the boy, that "He [always] gives without any thought of reward," by recognizing that "he knows nothing of greed." It thus proves just too shocking for many viewers to imagine this boy becoming the Dark Lord of the Sith known as Darth Vader. That, perhaps, says more about American, perhaps even Western, culture's ideological horizons of expectation than the quality of Lucas' storytelling. Perhaps, like Aristotle, critics like David Brin find the fall of the innocent youth too scandalous to be tragic, and therefore too deplorable to watch. The just providential conditions of the universe simply cannot allow for such a catastrophe. Lucas' reflections are, however, instructive as to how he refuses to define "evil" according to "the Othering" habits of the Manichaean imagination:

[*The*] *Phantom Menace* was done really to determine that Anakin was a good person, good heart, nice kid. We're not talking here about an evil little monster child—we're talking about this great kid just like we all start out as, or [we] think we start out as.... What brought me back to finish the whole thing off was the question of why, and how, Darth Vader became evil. The whole reason for going back and doing the back story on *Star Wars* is that there is an evolution from this very good person, very kind person, very loving person into something that one would describe as evil.[101]

However, there is something vital to the meaning of *hamartia* that is important to Aristotle's account of tragic drama. It specifically bears the sense of ignorance and unwitting fall, in other words of tragic irony. As Chris Baldick argues, "Aristotle's emphasis was ... upon the protagonist's *action*, which could be brought about by misjudgement, ignorance or some other cause" rather than deliberately wicked willfulness as such.[102] After all, although Oedipus in *Oedipus at Colonus* comes to recognize and admit his "pollution" in the murder of his father and marriage to his mother, he denies that he had erred since he had done both deeds inadvertently.[103] The tragic situation had been caused in *Oedipus the King* by his attempting to flee the oracle's prophecy that he would accomplish just such heinous deeds.

Yet, in spite of his technical resilience, evident Jedi potential (as Qui-Gon reveals to Shmi, "the Force is unusually strong with him"), distinct moral qualities, and innocence of wickedly self-aggrandizing desires, Anakin's flaws are not far from the surface of the text of Episode I, and "flawed" is exactly the language that Lucas uses when describing him.[104] This shocked and puzzled form of criticism of *TPM* probably has more to do with untested popular metaphysical assumptions that bear the imprint of an ontological Manichaeism than with the quality of Lucas' characterization. Certainly it has to do with a Western illiteracy that has no time for classic tragic dramas, a hangover of the Platonic banishment of the tragedians from the *polis*. Why some of us become as dark as Anakin while others do not has no simple answer. Suggestively Lucas comments that "most of them [viz., those who are wicked] think they're good people doing what they do for a good reason." This, of course, takes one into claims made concerning "the banality of evil" by Hannah Arendt, well articulated by John Doe in David Fincher's *Se7en*, and it is this that tragic dramas can and do often present in the most disturbing of ways.

Ultimately, Anakin is like a young Hitler, who is just trying to find his proper place in the world. Anakin goes on to kill countless billions of people just like Stalin. With *Revenge of the Sith*, I'm trying to show that the human butchers like Hitler and Stalin may have been misunderstood. I don't condone what Hitler and Stalin did, but I do think that Anakin proves that some things are decided by fate.[105]

But what are his flaws? An illuminating scene in *ROTS* portrays the main protagonist, now a young Jedi Knight and poster-boy hero of the Republic's war effort, rushing into the Galaxies Opera House on the planet Coruscant after having been summoned by Chancellor Palpatine. While it would be too speculative to attempt to connect the setting of the Mon Calamari balletic performance and the commentary on the drama provided by the chorus in Attic tragedies, it is nonetheless interesting to note the importance of this scene to the tragic performance— it offers (commentary-like) insight into the unfolding tragedy as well as contributes to its development. Here Anakin displays something of his moral intentionality, reflecting the *good* but flawed character depicted by Aristotle. For instance, on the one hand he defends against Palpatine's criticism of the Jedi Order by appealing to the latter as good and selfless, and on the other hand, directed both by loyalty to a mentor and intense personal moral integrity, he refuses to fulfill the Council's order to spy on the Chancellor. Nonetheless, Anakin can be seen here to suffer from at least three types of tragic "flaw," difficulties that Lucas claims are far from unique to him. Everyone faces certain pressures, temptations and strains, but we all have to find ways of coping and dealing with those constructively. As Lucas suggestively comments: "The issue that he's confronting is that a good Jedi overcomes those flaws and ... goes above the normal human tragedy that most people have to experience."[106] The adolescent, however, fails to develop the kind of capacity for restraint and good judgment that is required of a Jedi, and it is this that makes his fall possible (perhaps even inevitable). The childhood trauma of, for instance, Bruce Wayne creates the shadowy dark alter ego, the heroic dark knight Batman; Anakin's trauma, in contrast, induces him on to a path towards "the darkside," a life of ordered or governmentally sanctioned "crime." The difference in their pathways has, in large measure, to do with the guidance they receive in making their choices in becoming the moral characters they finally grow to be.

Firstly, with his flattery of the young Jedi the wily politician is able to appeal to Anakin's pride. Pride, Chaucer's nun's priest famously summarizes in his cautionary tale, comes before a fall. Despite the Jedi code, Yoda admits arrogance is "a flaw more and more common among Jedi. Too sure of themselves they are, even the older more experienced ones." Over the past decade Anakin has grown up with the memory of Qui-Gon's belief that he is "the one who will bring balance to the Force" whose coming an ancient prophecy had foretold [Mace Windu, *TPM*]. Anakin is not just any boy, and he has not been just any Jedi Padawan. He has had to carry the claim made about his potential in the history of "the Force" since his reception into the Jedi Order. He has been led to believe that he "*is* the Chosen One" [Qui-Gon], the key to life, the universe and all things, and this undoubtedly weighs heavily on his young and emotionally developing shoulders. The pressure on the maturation of a humble and wise Jedi that comes with such awareness is incalculable. It is this which accounts for his immense self-confidence— indeed overconfidence. He is reckless, as his disastrous lightsaber challenge with Count Dooku demonstrates [*AOTC*]. Hayden Christensen, the actor portraying Anakin, comments that "he has ... this unhealthy sense of grandeur."[107] In his unleashed torrent of uncontrollable and spiteful abuse of his mentor's name, Obi-Wan Kenobi, Anakin alleges that his Master "is jealous," and this is why he is holding the Padawan back from realizing his full potential [*AOTC*]. "I'm not the Jedi I should be. I want more." This sounds like the stereotypically ill-tempered and whinny reaction of a sullen, headstrong adolescent to authority, particularly parental authority, as Henry Sheehan recognizes. "This is simple adolescent moral narcissism, an obnoxious period we all pass through.... Emotionally, this narcissism looms as Anakin's primary resentment.... Once you become alert to this side of Revenge of the Sith, then the whole Star Wars project begins to seem like a study of adolescent narcissism."[108] Critics who comment that Anakin has become an unlikeable character in *AOTC* and *ROTS* miss the point entirely, and fail to notice the link with the sullen, sulky and whiny Luke of the first half of *ANH*. He expressly is a type, a *recognizable* type of teenager. In that sense he is average, ordinary, an everyboy-type figure.

Yet one cannot bypass the unhealthy exploitation of Anakin's ambitions by Palpatine. In a gentle moment reminiscent of a father-like conversation with a respectful son, the elder statesman instructs, "you don't need guidance, Anakin. In time you will learn to trust your feelings. Then you will be invincible. I have said it many times, you are the most gifted Jedi I have ever met.... I see you are becoming the greatest of all

the Jedi, Anakin, even more powerful than Master Yoda." [*AOTC*] Of
course, all this is true—Anakin has indeed a midi-chlorian concentration far surpassing even that of the great Yoda. Moreover, it is significant
that the next scene contains a compliment by the highly renowned Jedi
Master Mace Windu to the effect that "the boy has exceptional skill."
The problem is what such complimentary feeding does to Anakin's ego,
and it is this which simultaneously fuels his resentment of Obi-Wan's
more restraining guidance.

It is worth spending some time reflecting on the relationship between
Anakin and Obi-Wan in this context. Significantly the Tatooine grief
scene indicates the flaws in the relationship between the Jedi Master and
his Padawan most intensively, and this echoes an earlier scene in *AOTC*
in which the Jedi-in-training petulantly demonstrates an intense resentment of his Jedi tutor. "It's all Obi-Wan's fault! ... He's holding me back!"
On the one hand this outburst has something of the ill-tempered reaction of headstrong adolescence to authority about it, particularly parental authority—and this is manifest in their regular bickering. Anakin is
19 at this point, and he exhibits all the arrogance and whinny sullen
peevishness of the stereotypical teenager, and the description of Obi-
Wan in paternal terms on several occasions accentuates the stereotypical
antipathy to parental authority. So while Anakin on one occasion claims
that Obi-Wan is "like a father to me" or "you're the closest thing I have
to a father," an irritated Obi-Wan has on another occasion to proclaim
that the youth "will pay attention to my lead.... And you will learn your
place young one."

However, this is only one layer of a multilayered story—not only
is Anakin's behavior the expression of an unhealthy instinct, but Obi-
Wan himself has apparently contributed substantially to the way their
relationship has developed. There is no secret in the fact that the Jedi
Master in his own way resents Anakin too, and regrets the promise that
he was pressured into making by the dying Qui-Gon to train the boy.
In *TPM* Obi-Wan even confronts his Master in a rare moment of dissent
over his blind faith in the chosenness of the youngster from Tatooine.
Thus he always harbors suspicions of the Padawan he has been forced
to instruct. Later, of course, he acknowledges to an apparently dying
young Darth Vader in the hell of Mustafar, "I have failed you Anakin, I
have failed you"; and later again, in *ROTJ* he admits his own failings in
the process of training Anakin: "I thought I could instruct him just as
well as Yoda. I was wrong." Anakin himself reveals his Master's short-

comings to Padmé: "he feels I'm too unpredictable. He won't let me move on.... He's overly critical; he never listens; he, he doesn't understand. It's not fair!" Padmé, of course, wisely responds by recognizing that although that must be frustrating for Anakin, "all mentors have a way of seeing more of our faults than we would like. It's the only way we grow." Put starkly, Obi-Wan is not the best person to guide someone like Anakin, and this gives both potency and poignancy to Qui-Gon's instruction to the nine-year-old Anakin: "Stay close to me and you'll be safe." [*TPM*] Recognizing this, an accusatory outburst in the 2005 animated shorts entitled *Clone Wars* records Anakin barking at his mentor, "you're no Qui-Gon Jinn!"

As mentioned earlier, into that messy and emotionally charged relationship insidiously slithers Palpatine. His work is fundamental to the ensuing and overlapping tragedies, those of the political tragedy of the fall of the Republic, of the personal tragedy with the fall of Anakin, and of the domestic tragedy with the death of Padmé and the separation of the infant twins.

The Tragedy of Fathers and Sons

Where Palpatine's role is most significant in the Skywalker narrative is in his paternal positioning. Ian McDiarmid, Palpatine's actor, comments that "If you wanted a subtitle for these movies it could be 'Fathers and Sons.'... Palpatine ... is certainly a father-figure for him."[109] He comes to act where he can as a surrogate father-figure, watching, guiding, advising, and supporting this young Jedi, and it is to him rather than Obi-Wan that Anakin wholeheartedly devotes his obedient trust. Lucas explains also that Darth Vader feels indebted to Sidious even after learning of the death of his wife: "Vader is very thankful to Sidious. If not for Sidious, then Vader would have died on Mustafar at the end of *Revenge of the Sith*. So, essentially Vader owes his life to Sidious. Vader is bound to Sidious in a very psychological way. It seems beyond thought for Vader to betray the one person who really understands and supports him. It takes Luke to be on the brink of death for Vader to finally turn on and destroy Sidious."[110] In a scene from *ROTS*, Mace Windu ominously reveals that "it's very dangerous putting them together. I don't think the boy can handle it. I don't trust him." By this time Mace and Yoda both doubt the faith they had put in the young Jedi Knight and his significant place in the history of the Jedi. So when Obi-Wan asks, "With all due respect, Master, is he not the chosen one? Is he not to destroy the Sith and bring balance to the Force?," Mace responds with a skeptical "So the prophecy says," and Yoda pointedly adds "A prophecy that misread could have been." At this comment Mace nods in agreement.

As mentioned above, the statesman is integral to "feeding" or guiding Anakin's unhealthy self-consciousness, both feeding the rising Jedi star's ultimately detrimental feelings of ego-filled self-importance, and glorying in the flattery of Anakin's Force and military prowess. Palpatine subtly fans into a great conflagration Anakin's sparks of narcissism.

Secondly, Palpatine even more insidiously appeals to Anakin's fears—his paranoia over how the Jedi Council regards him, his concerns that the virtues of the Jedi Council had been compromised by self-regard and misdirection, and, as we will see below in the third point, his anxiety over the future of Padmé. Importantly, with regard to the second of these fears, by the time of *ROTS* the Jedi Order itself has become generally feared and distrusted, suspected in many circles of plotting to seize political power, manipulating the military hostilities for their own ends. An expression of this mistrust can be seen in a deleted scene from *ROTS* in which Senator Mon Mothma worries about Padmé's desire to tell a Jedi of the Loyalist's "plot" and of the Petition of the Two Thousand—"We don't know where the Jedi fit into all this." And in Stover's novelization of *ROTS*, Yoda reveals of the Jedi that "Lost the trust of the public, we have already."[111] Palpatine successfully intensifies Anakin's own worries about the Jedi by interfering inappropriately in internal Jedi matters when appointing Anakin to the Jedi Council. This deed is calculated to both accentuate the Council's suspicions of Anakin and that, in turn, has a spiraling effect on the youth's already burgeoning paranoia and feeling of personal insult. (There are suggestions that Anakin is already deeply wary of Mace.)[112] His feeling of insult explodes in a rash outburst against Mace when the latter announces "we do not grant you the rank of Master." [*ROTS*] At this point the camera pans around the faces of several of the seated Council members, who by now are looking rather embarrassed for Anakin. Anakin's eruption is greeted by the camera with the faces of several embarrassed Jedi, and Obi-Wan shakes his head disappointedly at the evident lack of maturity displayed by his former Padawan. Anakin's complaint that "it's unfair" echoes his earlier adolescent bemoaning of Obi-Wan's restrictive tutelage, and the latter is a scene in which the seeds of darkness are seen to be firmly flourishing in the young man's soul [*AOTC*]. This moment equally echoes Luke's similar outburst against Uncle Owen's restricting him to farm-chores-before-fun [*ANH*].

Palpatine successfully plays on these fears and Anakin's own growing distrust of the Order when attempting to persuade the young man of the Jedi Council's untrustworthiness. In the first place, Anakin has been appointed by Palpatine to the Jedi Council, a move that intensifies the Council's suspicions of the youth, and that in turn has a spiraling effect on his already burgeoning paranoia. The expression of this lack of complete faith in him accentuates the pressure on Anakin of his own suspicions of the motives and wisdom of the Jedi Council itself, and of a feeling of deliberate personal insult as well as resentment of their deliberate retraining of him. Part of the backstory is that Anakin is especially distrusted by many senior Jedi because of his prosthetic right arm that had replaced his limb lost in combat with Count Dooku on Geonosis (*AOTC*). Stover's dramatization records Anakin asserting that "it has to do with them all being *against* me. They always *have* been—most of them didn't even want me to *be* a Jedi."[113]

Again, Palpatine's move is carefully calculated, fully anticipating just such a clash of mutual suspicions, while both playing into Anakin's own ambitious desires for promotion and, by flattering him with such a promotion, augmenting Anakin's trust of Palpatine further. The Chancellor admits: "I hope you trust me, Anakin.... I need your help, son.... I'm depending on you ... to be the eyes, ears, and voice of the Republic. Anakin, I'm appointing you to be my personal representative on the Jedi Council." The young man is aware that "the Council elects its own members. It will never accept this," but is reassured by the elder statesman's determinative "I think they will. They need you more than you know." When the young Jedi Knight is asked by the Council to "spy" on Palpatine, a man the Jedi Council is now suspicious of, his worst fears over the Order are seemingly being realized by Jedi duplicity. Anakin's sense of Jedi double standards is displayed in the novelization: "'What I understand,' Anakin said grimly [to Obi-Wan], 'is that you are trying to turn me against Palpatine. You're trying to make me keep *secrets* from him— you want to make me *lie* to him."[114] Anakin's loyalty to Palpatine is unqualified, and the movie portrays him admitting that "the Chancellor is not a bad man, Obi-Wan. He befriended me, he's watched over me ever since I arrived here.... You're asking me to do something against the Jedi code, against the Republic, against a mentor and a friend, that's what's out of place here." Stover depicts Obi-Wan's realization of the magnitude of asking Anakin to perform such an act. First he reveals "that abstractions like *peace* don't mean much to him. He's loyal to *people*, not to principles. And he expects loyalty in return."[115] Then he bewails the task: "I am firmly convinced that Anakin can do anything. Except betray a friend. What we have done to him today.... That's why I don't think he will ever trust us again.... And I am not entirely sure he should."[116] Anakin has been encouraged to assert himself *against* the Jedi Council, as he reveals to Padmé: "Obi-Wan and the Council don't trust me.... Something's happening—I'm not the Jedi I should be. I want more. And I know I shouldn't." Anakin refuses to abuse his position of trust with the Chancellor, which is why he equally refuses Padmé's advance to encourage the legislator to favor diplomacy over military strategy for ending the war: "Don't ask me to do that. Make a motion in the Senate where that kind of request belongs."

In the opera house box Palpatine, after providing some attention-grabbing flattering of the young Jedi, speaks of a treasonable Jedi "plot." To an incredulous Anakin the Chancellor responds with a clever tapping into the youth's conscience: "They asked you [to] do something that made you feel dishonest, didn't they? They asked you to spy on me, didn't they?" Espionage directed against the Chancellor, Anakin had earlier complained to Obi-Wan, is itself treasonous, and the acutely honest younger man senses that the Council's request of him to engage in such a treacherous act conveys serious moral duplicity on the Jedi leadership's part. Cleverly, the manipulator here taps into Anakin's own affected conscience. But a Jedi plot? Even Anakin is unprepared for this charge, although the earlier conversation with Obi-Wan would have been ringing in his ears. Of course, events would soon conspire to look as if a coup d'état is exactly what is occurring, and Mace's refusing that Anakin be present at Palpatine/Sidious' arrest only waters the seed of his suspicions. For now the politician has to turn his persuasive rhetoric in a more general direction, and the seed of mistrust is well and truly sown.

Thirdly, in the opera house scene Palpatine also simply but effectively exploits Anakin's fears for Padmé with his telling of the Sith legend of "the tragedy of Darth Plagueis the Wise," and tempts him by suggesting that there is a vague and distant possibility of learning how to prevent his loved one from dying through the Darkside of the Force. To understand this particular fear requires an appreciation of the appearance of a particular identifiable anxiety in *TPM* and its amplification in *AOTC*—the separation-from-mother complex. *TPM* does not focus attention on any possible psychological effects on Anakin in having been a *slave*—he is later haunted by visions of his slave-mother's sufferings rather than his own. Nonetheless, the young boy's asking if Jedi Master Qui-Gon Jinn has come to Tatooine to "free" the slaves may possibly hint at the kind of desire for freedom that will feed Anakin's adolescent resentment of authority later while Padawan to Obi-Wan [*AOTC*]. Whatever the truth of this, it is clearly the case that when Anakin is first presented to the Council the Jedi are particularly concerned about this anxiety, and it initially costs him a position as a Jedi Padawan. To Jedi Master Ki Adi Mundi's observation that the boy's "thoughts dwell on your mother," Yoda announces, "Afraid to lose her, I think." After all, when departing his home Anakin, in a move filled with symbolic value as well as dramatic poignancy, looked back at his mother and ran toward her with an embrace that anxiously wept, "I can't do it, mom, I just can't do it!" It was Shmi who painfully and gently counseled, "now, be brave and don't look back, don't look back." In his initial meeting with the Jedi Council Anakin somewhat justifiably puzzles over the relevance of such an insight, but Yoda's admonishing response illuminates the difference between the Jedi and the Sith: "Everything! Fear is the path to the dark side. Fear leads to anger, anger leads to hate, hate leads to suffering," the astute Master Yoda admonishes. Attachments to people and things induce fear over their loss, and this in turn moves us to attempt to secure their possession—this is what Jedi training constantly teaches is the path to "the darkside." "The fear of loss is a path to the dark side.... Attachment leads to jealousy. The shadow of greed that is.... Train to let go of everything you fear to lose" (Yoda, *ROTS*). It is for that reason that Yoda's concluding declaration in the Jedi Council Chambers in *TPM*—"I sense much fear in you"—is another portentous warning that reverberates like a death knell through the succeeding two *Episodes*. Even when the Council does eventually agree with the proposal for training him, largely out of respect for the memory of the slain Qui-Gon and the abundance of faith he had in Anakin as being "the chosen one," Yoda strongly registers his dissent from the decision: "The chosen one the boy may be. Nevertheless, grave danger I fear in his training." Dwelling on the past, or inordinately looking back, is what Qui-Gon's counsel to his young Padawan at the beginning of this movie would rule out: "Don't centre on your anxieties, Obi-Wan. Keep your concentration on the here and now where it belongs ... [and] not at the expense of the moment." The occasion was over talk of "mindfulness of the *future*" rather than the past, but the logic works in this case too. Later to Anakin he enjoins, "always remember, your focus determines your reality." Anakin insufficiently learns how to practice this wisdom, and his reality-determining focus wanders off in unhealthy directions.

The fear that hardens into anger and hate is viciously displayed in a scene in the 2005 *Clone War* short animations depicting his ferocious duel with the Sith-want-to-be Asajj Ventress. Anakin demonstrates an inability to control his anger—encouraged, against the Jedi way, as he has been by Palpatine to act on his feelings, especially his anger. Ominously, however, in his eventual victorious rage the images of the dark side are cast upon the scene—the red glow of Ventress' lightsaber that he used to destroy her with is cast upon him, and the "Dual of the Fates" music is portentously sounded. Brin's claim about Anakin's untragic characterization is, therefore, distinctly exaggerated and inattentive to an evident emotional difficulty. It appears to miss the substantial hints as to what is ordering Anakin's soul and directing his problematic judgments. Anakin's fall has indeed been a long time in the making.

Stover's novelization of *ROTS* puts the matter like this with respect to Anakin's dread of Padmé's death haunting his dreams: "Palpatine had somehow seen into his secret heart, and had chosen to offer him the one thing he most desired in all the galaxy. He didn't care about the Council, not really—that was a childish dream. He didn't need the Council. He didn't need the recognition, and he didn't need the respect. What he needed was the rank itself. All that mattered was Mastery. All that mattered was Padmé. This was a gift beyond gifts: as a Master, he could access those forbidden holocrons in the restricted vault. He could find a way to save her from his dream."[117] Anakin is now hoping to be able to have some sense of control of his destiny, a promised gift which encourages the deepening of his trust in a Palpatine for whom he has the most reverential regard.

That, then, encourages one to ask whether Qui-Gon was wrong in his judgment concerning Anakin, forcing by sheer blind faith a terrible tragedy on Obi-Wan, the Jedi Order, and ultimately the galaxy by insisting with his dying breath that his own Padawan train the boy. Does wisdom lie in this situation instead with the most hesitant of the Jedi Masters, the iconic Yoda? Lucas wades into this arena by claiming that

I think it is obvious that [Qui-Gon] was wrong in Episode 1 and made a dangerous decision, but ultimately this decision may be correct. The Phantom Menace refers to the force of the dark side of the Universe. Anakin will be taken over by dark forces which in turn destroy the balance of the Galaxy, but the individual who kills the Emperor is Darth Vader— also Anakin. The tale meanders and both the prediction, and Qui-Gon are correct—Anakin is the chosen one, and he did bring peace at last with his own sacrifice. Luke couldn't kill the Emperor himself, but he could make Anakin reflect on his life and kill the Emperor.[118]

This set of claims somewhat trivializes the situation, though. The evil inflicted on the galaxy in the form of Darth Vader, and the dreadful carnage and waste that occurred cannot and should not be covered over by a thin netting of dangerous utilitarian-sounding rhetoric—"oh, well, it all worked out alright in the end." So Hanson and Kay, for instance, glibly deny Anakin's story its tragic quality by proclaiming that his "strange and incomprehensible journey" is "one of success" in *ROTJ*.[119] To refer to Shakespearean tragedy, certainly the kingdom could be stronger after the deaths of Lear's two self-serving daughters, Gonerill and Regan, and the agent of the Earl of Gloucester's misfortune, his bastard son Edmund. But this would by no means be a simple providential restoration of justice. The murdered Cordelia, an unwitting victim of her own honest but loving silence to a father deludedly bathing in the dishonest flattery of her two sisters, remains dead.[120] Gloucester's gouged out eyes will never return; his friend Lear has died of heartache; and he will always harbor the guilt of his earlier carnal sin, wherein he tragically bore the agent of his destruction. Both Cordelia and Gloucester have paid the price of loyalty to their self-deposed king. Moreover, it is an interesting, albeit speculative, question as to how the scars of remembrance will impact Edgar's reign. Indeed, albeit without any explicit revision of his theology, Edgar's emotions force him to conclude with a partial recognition of the loss.[121] What we encounter in this play, therefore, as A.C. Bradley describes, is "the most terrible picture that Shakespeare painted of the world."[122] It is distinctly arguable that what the emotionally troubling display of a near incinerated and limbless Anakin pathetically attempting to claw his way up the bank by a cybernetic hand, of the Frankenstein resurrection of iron-lung besuited Anakin by the death-like Sidious, of Padmé's funeral, and of the poignantly scored recapitulation of Leia's theme and the new hope theme, do is disturb the very glibness of the utilitarian sensibility. The Jedi Temple has been destroyed, the tremendous potential of many Younglings' has been ruth-lessly annihilated by Vader's ruthless enactment of the Emperor's Order 66; the great Yoda has to flee into exile; and the Wookies are about to face a perilous existence under the Empire. *ROTS* may offer hope, but its narrative movement refuses to provide the viewer's gaze with easy consolation or neat resolution. As George Steiner observes, in tragic drama there is no "compensation" or adequate healing of wounds, only "irreparable" damage.[123] For example, in contrast with Steiner's detection of a "liturgical-grace note" in *King Lear*, one could note that Lear's joy in the "dream scene," albeit pervaded with shame in the acquired recog-nition of his folly, is quickly shattered by subsequent events which are all the more "dark and comfortless" *because of* the hint of redemption that has preceded it.[124] Likewise, even in *ROTJ* Anakin's "redemption" is now rendered particularly poignant when the shadow of *ROTS* is cast over it. While he finally gets to see Luke face to face as his "true" self (Anakin), as with Lear and his youngest daughter Cordelia, the recon-ciling gaze is all too brief. He dies, as do Lear and his beloved offspring. Anakin's becoming one with "the Force," despite what Yoda argues with respect to not grieving but rather celebrating this event (*ROTS*), cannot "compensate" for that brevity and for the fact that he never is able to embrace his daughter. This has the character of a too-little-too-late moment even if *ROTJ* prevents the audience from gazing on it for too long. Certainly the galaxy can now be stronger because of Vader's redemptive intervention, but this is by no means a simple restoration of providential justice. Whatever readers want to argue with regard to Vader's redemptive "end" or the sense of "eternal justice" in the galactic "Force," there remains a disturbing tragic quality in his salvation that cannot be undone: the consequences of Vader's evil, in spite of personal repentance, remain and stain his legacy—Padmé remains dead; Luke and Leia are raised apart for 19 years; the Jedi Order is almost wholly obliterated, and all but two of its greatest Jedi are massacred; the stores of recorded Jedi wisdom stay irretrievably destroyed or utterly corrupted; and Anakin's own great potential in "the Force" was never realized. The symbolic value of Qui-Gon's death is similarly important: "This is a hor-rific, post-modern notion that Lucas has conjured. The hero *cannot* overcome all circumstances, prevail against all odds, good does not always win over evil ... the hero is as mortal as the villain."[125]

Also, one must bear in mind the deliberate parallelism of the Anakin-Luke cycles. In *ESB* Yoda initially is highly reluctant to train Luke

because "he is too old," and when Luke informs the Jedi Master a little later that he is not afraid (fear being a primary driving force in Anakin's succumbing to "the dark side"), Yoda forebodingly warns "You will be, you will be!" Perhaps most important, however, is the fact that the ability to say whose belief was *eventually* fulfilled in Anakin is only something that can be said *after the event* with a considerable degree of hindsight. But at the time, this is not something that can be pronounced. In fact, given the nature of knowledge and the flow of time, unless one wants lazily to promote a deterministic frame of reference, it is a category mistake by virtue of the fact that this approach drastically misses the important contingent factors that contribute to the tragedy of Anakin Skywalker, factors that had they been arranged differently, purely absent, or even learned to be handled differently by the young man could have produced markedly dissimilar results.[126] As Qui-Gon argues against a skeptical Obi-Wan, "his fate is uncertain, but he's *not* dangerous." That faith seems to be borne out in Anakin's morally commendable and self-less apology: "Qui-Gon, sir, I don't wanna be a problem." It may be spec-ulation to suggest that Yoda's reference to the danger in Anakin's "training" could involve the processes and activities involved in the training by the trainers as much as by the boy's being trained, but it would fit the realities involved.

By the time of *AOTC* Anakin has become a more complex figure than the boy of 10 years earlier, although he is now crucially the neu-rotically intensified product of the loves, desires and neuroses of that child. The flaws lie deep within his person-forming soul. Significantly he is even rather ominously wearing darker colored robes than his Jedi kin. Speaking of the 19-year-old Anakin Lucas claims,

> In this film, you begin to see that he has a fear of losing things, a fear of losing his mother, and as a result, he wants to begin to control things, he wants to become powerful, and these are not Jedi traits. And part of these are because he was starting to be trained so late in life, that he'd already formed these attachments. And for a Jedi, attachment is forbidden.[127]

Understandably, the young man bears deeply the wounds of leaving the mother to whom he was profoundly attached, and he is now visibly tortured by nightmares of her suffering severe pain. On initially leaving her a decade earlier he had promised, "I will come back and free you mom" [*TPM*]. However, he had been unable to keep this pledge, and the resultant feeling of culpability weighs heavy on him. Rightly or wrongly, he blames and gradually resents the Jedi Order itself for preventing him from rescuing her. He finally goes searching for his mother only to watch her die in his arms, and in that moment the Jedi trainee's own guilt in having abandoned her and even his bitterness against the Jedi are considerably intensified. His guilt is further deepened by his actions in the immediate aftermath of his mother's death. Losing emotional self-control, his seething fury is destructively unleashed against the captors, the Tuskan Raiders. As he remorsefully admits to Padmé a little later, he massacred not merely the men, but the women and children as well. He has become, in that moment, as primitively savage as the way those sand dwelling nomads are archetypally presented as being.[128] "They're like animals and I slaughtered them like animals." And, of course, it is this shame that Palpatine noticeably exploits so effectively for his own ends in *ROTS* on *The Invisible Hand*.

What we witness in the succeeding grief scene on Tatooine is the way Anakin's anger, guilt, resentment and sorrow, all growing out of his attachment to his mother, take on a new form. Padmé consoles an Anakin grieving over the death of his mother in the captivity of the Tuskan Raiders, "to be angry is to be human." But her hearer rightly recognizes that controlling this properly is vital: "I'm a Jedi—I know I'm better than this." It is the theme of an attachment to people and things that induces fear over their loss and a consequent move to secure their possession that Jedi training constantly instills as being the path to "the dark side." As the diminutive Jedi Master declares to the emotionally troubled young man in *ROTS*, "the fear of loss is a path to the dark side.... Attachment leads to jealousy. The shadow of greed that is.... Train to let go of everything you fear to lose." To return to the grief scene in *AOTC*, the themes of a vicious rage fuelled by guilt and grief, and arrogant adolescent resentment of his mentor literally combine melodiously as John Williams' musical leitmotifs associated with Darths Sidious and Vader play. In his anguish he claims to desire the power over life and death, the power to be able to "fix" life in the same way that he can exercise technical expertise over machinery. He refuses to hear Padmé's claim that "sometimes there are things that no-one can fix," and here is an early indication of Anakin mechanistically reducing others' lives to the status of *things*, notably echoing the Siths' instrumentalizing disregard for the independent lives of others. Anakin's pain verbalizes that he "should be" all-powerful, and threateningly expresses a new-found determination "that some day I will be. I will be the most powerful Jedi ever. I promise you. I will even learn to stop people from dying." This is not merely his "grief talking" since a little later, when in a calmer frame of mind, he promises at his mother's graveside: "I wasn't strong enough to save you, mom.… But I promise I won't fail again." He imagines that the solution is one of sheer power and brute force. The spirit of the Sith-way is already determining what he values and is now shaping his judg-ments, and is dramatically fulfilled later when—after dreaming of Padmé dying in childbirth—without any sense of "cost" he moves to secure the *power* he thinks is necessary for her safety from the scheming Palpa-tine/Sidious [*ROTS*]. The young man's self-deception is exhibited most impressively in his proclamation to Padmé that "love won't save you, Padmé, only my new powers can do that." His wife despairingly asks, "But at what cost?" Anakin has not given much consideration to that. Instead, his response is to possessively assert his power: "I won't lose you the way I lost my mother. I am becoming more powerful than any Jedi has ever dreamed of, and I'm doing it for you, to protect you." This is not love but a narcissistic possessivism, a self-projective attachment. As Eagleton observes, "there are none so blind as those who only see themselves."[129]

Anakin's possessive fears for Padmé take a considerably more sin-ister direction in *ROTS*, and in this the statesman is even able to encour-age Anakin to become suspicious of his wife. In one deleted scene the young Jedi significantly refuses to meet his wife's look with his own dur-ing Padmé's confrontation of Palpatine on behalf of the Delegation of Two Thousand. The Chancellor sinisterly announces that the Delegation and those they represent have another agenda: "I sense there is more to their request than they're telling us.… They are not to be trusted." The obvious protestations are made by the young Jedi over Padmé's trust-worthiness, at which point Palpatine returns a gentle look and the claim that "these are unstable times for the Republic, Anakin. Some see insta-bility as an opportunity. Senator Amidala is hiding something, I can see it in her eyes." Palpatine's cynical approach to "truth" entails that truth is only the truth of power, and it is power that all are seeking. Despite Anakin on this occasion concluding with a note of faithfulness to his beloved, the suspicion has been sown, and to this is added a final chal-lenge to Anakin's Jedi ego and to his well-developed sense of honesty: "I'm surprised your Jedi instincts are not more sensitive to such things.… [Y]ou don't seem to want to admit it."

An Anakin overwhelmed by emotional and ideological turmoil later has cause to doubt the integrity of Padmé further. In the privacy of their home his wife reveals her concern that the very "democracy we thought we were serving no longer exists, and ... the Republic has become the very evil we've been fighting to destroy." Anakin's political faith is, however, considerably more simplistic and unintuitive precisely because he associates the Republic with the Chancellor, and in Palpatine he has enormous faith. (Later he proclaims, "I will not betray the Republic. My loyalties lie with the Chancellor, and with the Senate, and with you.") Anakin turns on his wife, spitting "you're sounding like a Separatist." He is unwilling to hear criticism of his beliefs but instead deflects critical attention with an assertion of patriotic responsibility. The Loyalist attempt to *purify what is beloved*, as Bail Organa depicts his untreasonous loyalist work with Mon Mothma in a deleted scene, is no more patriotic to Anakin's mind than Dooku's Separatist rebellion. The Jedi's tumultuous anxieties come to be fixed on Padmé to be in the process of betraying him in league with Obi-Wan, a paranoia that comes to its uxoricidal breaking point on Mustafar.[130] Anakin, now reborn as Darth Vader, rants "You're with him! You brought him here to kill me!" And to Obi-Wan he raves, unable to see how his change has changed his relations, "you turned her against me! ... You will not take her from me!" In an early scene in Stover's novelization of *ROTS*, Padmé greets her returning husband with the words that things between them have changed, words which Anakin promptly misunderstands. He forcefully grabs her by the shoulders and accuses her in a thunderous rage of having *someone else*.[131] In the movie version, despite his evident love for Obi-Wan earlier, the second dream of Anakin's that is shown onscreen depicts Padmé suffering. But what is important about this occasion is that the dream contains an image of Obi-Wan sitting by her urging her not to give up. At this point Anakin announces to his wife that "Obi-Wan and the Council don't trust me."

Fourthly, and highly significantly, the Chancellor even subtly undermines the Jedi philosophy of the virtuous life in Anakin's mind, and this plays into the youth's un–Jedi-like instincts. So when the persuasive voice of the shackled Palpatine demands that Anakin execute the defeated Dooku, Anakin responds by announcing, "I shouldn't have done that. It's not the Jedi way." But the voice is too overwhelming and the war hero eventually succumbs. The blood of Dooku now weighs as heavily on his mind as does the blood of the Tuskan Raiders, the nomads on Tatooine. In the most fateful of all the scenes in *ROTS*, Mace Windu announces that he needs to summarily execute justice on Palpatine, now revealed as the Sith Lord Darth Sidious, and Anakin refuses to allow the same moral mistake to be made as on Grievous' flagship with Dooku. Hence the young man intervenes merely to prevent Mace's effecting his planned punishment, thus allowing Palpatine/Sidious to recover his strength and dispatch Mace from the window of the Chancellor's chambers high in the skyscraper. There is actually the possible reading that Palpatine feigned defeat against Mace in order to provoke Anakin's intervention, and therefore force the young Jedi to be morally implicated in the betrayal and death of one of the most eminent Jedi, thus adding to Anakin's own psychological turmoil.[132] Anakin has acted out of the best motives on two occasions, but on both he has momentously made the wrong choice, and these problematic judgments disastrously contribute deeply to his already excessive and morally debilitating sense of shame and guilt. The power that the distorting influence of Palpatine has over Anakin is central to this ignorance in judgment. It is the involvement in the execution of Mace that is the most immediate of numerous longer term causes that results in his bending his knee fatefully to Sidious, and effecting annihilating action against all the Jedi present at the Jedi Temple.[133] These flaws and the misjudgments caused by ignorance make him particularly impressionable and malleable by Palpatine, who now creates him as Vader.

To return a little earlier to the scene in the opera house, the Chancellor is heard to gently instruct Anakin in political philosophy: "Remember back to your early teachings, all who gain power are afraid to lose it—even the Jedi." It is significant that Anakin does not turn this principle back on Palpatine and on his achievement of power. Obi-Wan had already suggested that this man was deliberatively and manipulatively clinging on to power after his term in office had expired. Instead, Anakin, compelled by Palpatine's charm, responds with an appeal to Jedi altruism: "The Jedi use their power for good."

Palpatine's approach now takes a slightly different tack, confusing Anakin about the very nature of moral reasoning itself: "Good is a point of view, Anakin." This might sound like moral relativism, but Palpatine is instead trying to encourage his immature conversant to appreciate that everyone associates their own values with "the Good," after which he attempts to persuade that the Jedi's definition of good and evil may not be the best (dare I say it, the "true") one. He does this, of course, not in order to provoke Anakin into imagining there to be some *equally valid* moral consciousness in *both* Sith and Jedi, but rather to take him further towards decoupling him from his commitment to the Jedi and to believing in the ultimate rightness of the Sith *against* the Jedi. That is why the statesman is ultimately attempting to instill Sith values in Anakin, and also why he moves on to announce the similarity of the Jedi and Sith in "their quest for greater power." Anakin's response is that the Sith "think inwards only about themselves." Palpatine's statement "and the Jedi don't?" is a chilling deconstruction of moral endeavor, reducing it to power (that which the Sith appreciate and celebrate, while the Jedi openly deny but secretly practice). Stover's novelization makes this even clearer: the Sith are only evil "From a Jedi's point of view.... *Evil* is a label we put on those who threaten us, isn't it? Yet the Sith and the Jedi are similar in almost every way...."[134] Later, of course, Anakin (now known as Darth Vader) announces this newly learned perspective when dueling with Obi-Wan: "From my point of view the Jedi are evil." That certainly does not suggest that he has become a moral relativist. On the contrary, his sense of absolute right could not be more pronounced. At this point it is Obi-Wan who casts suspicion on anyone's ability to make such absolutist claims for their own perspective: "Only a Sith deals in absolutes." This, too, is not moral relativism, but is rather an admission of the fragility of goodness and of anyone's knowledge of it.

These observations on power and the exclusion of threatening others by associating them with "evil," and so on, are ethically astute, but nonetheless function as little more than a cover for Palpatine's method of persuasion, which is at heart one of accusation and suggestion. He does not allow Anakin to entertain the possibility that the Sith's way may truly be evil. Instead, he reduces the difference between Sith and Jedi down to a sound-bite (against the "narrow dogmatic view of the Jedi"), and to a difference in degree (they differ only in method) rather than admit a qualitative difference (the very ends that determine their different methods radically differ). In fact, from Palpatine's apparently Machiavellian point of view there is no good or evil, in a sense, there is only power. Power is his good, or at least his good when he is not on the receiving end of another's assertion of power, one would imagine. Hanson and Kay claim that "that is why he is a politician," although this both lends itself to suggesting something of the evil *of* politics and misplaces the importance of Padmé as the inverted image of Palpatine, the (even of Bail Organa and Mon Mothma) politician of the Republic.[135] These commentators continue by announcing that "he is motivated not by evil, but by the absence of feeling and emotion," but this too is notably misleading. It imagines that Palpatine is emotionless whereas, in fact, in the guise of Darth Sidious he reveals himself to be deeply passionately driven (demonstrating anger and impatience, for example, with the Neimoidians in *TPM*). The real question is what the motivations for his passions are, and here is where Hanson and Kay's comment could prove to be somewhat disingenuous. Their distinction between evil and emotionlessness unwittingly suggests that evil is some substance, something other than the way Palpatine behaves, something other than his desire and drive for power and the way that he treats others in the gaining and wielding of that power. These commentators' talk of Palpatine being "the ultimate evil in the universe" does not help matters.[136] Not only is such talk distinctly theologically problematic, it does not, as this chapter is arguing, make sense of the *SW* prequels in particular. Certainly Palpatine does not understand himself to be doing evil—but, then again, evil is not a substance as such but a distorted way of relating to, and treating, others and the world around. That is why he imagines that good and evil are irrelevant to him and that only power matters, in the end. The way he conceives life is through inventing his own values, values that serve his, and only ultimately his, well-being. In the logic of this he is not that radically different from the leaders of the Trade Federation, the voracious Jabba the Hutt, or Han Solo, for all of whom financial gain is the seeming motivation for living. (Han announces to Leia, "I expect to be well paid, I'm in it for the money," to which Leia sneers, "If money is all that you love, then that's what you'll receive.") Likewise, his values are not far removed from those of the callow Luke of *ANH* and much of *ESB*, for whom self-interested adventure and excitement are the key values. Luke's training with Yoda has the effect of deconstructing his notion of heroism—so Yoda critically tuts, "a Jedi must have the most deepest commitment, the most serious commitment…. Adventure, huh! Excitement, huh! A Jedi craves not these things." As Christensen notes about the Sith, "usually lust for power or personal ambition is their motivation but sometimes ambition is supplemented or even subsumed by greed."[137] Palpatine's is a greedy ambition, a greed for control of others, while the type of greed that Han represents is a greed for wealth, and presumably what wealth can buy. It is significant in this respect, then, that Sidious' rise to power was substantially directly aided by the greed of the Trade Federation.[138] This is the theme that pervades the backstory of the cult of the Sith lords. As Lucas reveals in interview with Moyers,

One of the themes throughout the films is that the Sith Lords, when they started out thousands of years ago, embraced the Dark Side. They were greedy and self-centered and they all wanted to take over, so they killed each other. Eventually there was only one left, and that one took on an apprentice.... But there could never be any more than two of them, because if there were, they would try to get rid of the leader, which is exactly what Vader was trying to do [with the Emperor], and that's exactly what the Emperor was trying to do [with Vader].... And that it is the antithesis of a symbiotic relationship, in which if you do that, you become cancer, and you eventually kill the host, and everything dies.[139]

This self-serving instinct construes "power" in terms of that which serves the promotion of the one seeking it—and therefore has connotations of domination, control, oppression. Thus, the Empire seeks to control its star systems through the use of military coercion and the regional control of the governors (the Grand Moffs). The contrast between this style of the uniformity of centralized rule and that of the Republic, with its space for partial regional autonomy, is notable. The difference between Palpatine and both Luke and even, to a lesser extent, Han are that he possesses no sense of loyalty to, or respect for, any others—all without any exception are there to serve his well-being. (As mentioned earlier, the only contradiction to this rule is his seeming moment of compassion for the injured Anakin.) In this Palpatine seems to be an unambiguous instance of the drive for power, power unleashed from the end of general social and political well-being. Even Count Dooku, a type of Palpatine, and who at one point in *AOTC* seems to have more moral ambiguity and is believed to be an elegant idealist who departed the Jedi Order in disillusionment with the increasing corruption in the Senate, becomes revealed as one who greatly desires power. He is someone who is at heart more a self-serving pragmatist than political idealist. Therefore, it is significant that his very name has been adapted from *doku*, a Buddhist term meaning "to govern" or "to poison."

Lucas, therefore, connects "evil" and the menacing power over others. The novelization of *ANH* explains of Vader that "the cloud of evil which clung tight about this particular one was intense enough to cause hardened Imperial troops to back away, menacing enough to set them muttering nervously among themselves. Once-resolute crew members ceased resisting, broke and ran in panic at the sight of the black armor—armor which, as black as it was, was not nearly as dark as the thoughts drifting through the mind within."[140] The effect of Palpatine's self-understanding then entails that others, in their relation to him, become stained by his dark dye. The fruit of Sidious' prideful ambitions is determinative of the identities of others. His aggressive will to power creates victims among those who have been forced to yield to his dominating for of his lordship. These oppressed peoples (the enslaved Wookies, for instance) are caught in the *vicious* circle of Sidious' wickedness, and are forced to participate in it in their own way. They are rendered wholly passive, puppets of his control, and denied the equity of being creative agents in their own right. Power, as controlled by a Spencerian form of Darwinism that operates from the ideology of the "survival of the fittest," becomes expressed in Palpatine as the power for self-assertion in a way that entails that it seeks to make others do one's will, whatever their own wills otherwise may be. This is the great evil, so injurious and destructive of others as it is, of the way he negotiates his relations with other beings. The peaceful co-existence with other masters, other co-creators, is foreclosed. All that is left is violence—the violating of other's agency either by making them slaves, or the violence against other agents by removing the possibility of their acting agentially. Thus those who will not bow the knee (Luke) will die. In this Palpatine is closer to Western liberal values than many would like to admit, following something of the pressure of the logic of Thomas Hobbes' influential claim that society is but the contractual ordering of otherwise conflictual relations, the free consent to be bound by the rule of "public" law, and the threat of punishment for law-breakers, in order that the potential for conflict between self-interested parties be restrained.[141] As Walter Wink explains, Western mythologies are shaped by the dynamics inducing violence, "Life is combat.... [I]t is a theatre of perpetual conflict in which the prize goes to the strong. Peace through war; security through strength."[142]

The Sith Lords, then, take this self-interested individualism to its logical conclusion, and as such there is something deeply significant about the fact that they cannot make the kind of peace that involves good relations—in fact the only peace available to the Sith is the peace that comes from the silence of those living in fear for their lives at the hands of this Order and the silencing of those who dissent. Relations shaped by the possessive grasping for dominating power, however, are ultimately unstable. Unless secured in some way, they are necessarily self-devouring. The Sith can create no intrinsic loyalty or friendship, but they suffer the anxiety that comes with the mutual suspicion that plagues all non-graceful relations. The Sith, by their very nature, cannot cooperate, unlike the Jedi, since all things are there to serve one's own self-promotion. All the Sith can generate is fear, suspicion, malicious tyranny and betrayal, and it is for this reason that the backstory to the Lords of the Sith emphasizes their engagement in several near self-annihilating power struggles. In the aftermath of "the New Sith War" (c 1032 BBY), the sole Sith survivor Darth Bane, himself betrayed at the end by Darth Kaan, instituted the "rule of two." This is something of an echo of the Jedi order of relations, but is even more limited in its singularity in that there are only ever to be two Sith at any one time, "a Master and an apprentice," as Yoda makes reference to in *TPM*, and not *multiple* pedagogic pairs. This line of two successfully served to prevent strife in "the modern era of the Sith" and better hid their existence from the Jedi. On saying that, however, the line does not prevent the betrayal of Darth Plagueis by his pupil. That seems to be something that Darth Tyrannus (Count Dooku) forgets when he looks genuinely surprised and horri-fied by Palpatine's order for Anakin to execute him aboard *The Invisible Hand*. In fact, the whole incident involving Palpatine's abduction by Grievous and his Magna Guards, imprisonment aboard the starship, and the dual between Dooku and both Obi-Wan and Anakin are carefully and elaborately staged by Palpatine/Sidious in order to investigate whether Anakin could be turned to the dark side. The execution of the defeated and unarmed Dooku is Anakin's pre-eminent test. According to James Luceno, "Sidious had promised to intervene in the dual, in the unlikely event that Anakin gained the upper hand. But intervention, too, was never part of the real plan. Blinded by pride, Dooku had failed to grasp that, like Darth Maul before him, he is little more than a place-holder for the apprentice Sidious has sought from the beginning: Sky-walker himself."[143] As Sidious, via hologram, informs Grievous on Utapau, "his [viz., Dooku's] death was a necessary loss. Soon I will have a new apprentice, one far younger and more powerful." "Sidious may have even feigned losing to Windu at the right moment [later] to cast a difficult impression on Anakin when he arrives at the Chancellor's office."[144] In the weeks leading up to the events portrayed in the opening of *ROTS*, Anakin and Obi-Wan have been sent off on a mission to the Outer Rim in order to set up the apparent abduction of Palpatine from Coruscant by Grievous. In the novelization Anakin comments to Padmé on what he imagines to be coincidental, and therefore unaware of the truth in his talk: "If the Chancellor hadn't been kidnapped, I'd still be out there [fighting the war in the Outer Rim].... It's like it was all arranged just to bring me home again."[145] Moreover, a little later Obi-Wan is ordered to Separatist-occupied Utapau to confront Grievous, so that with him absent there is less potential for Anakin to be restrained in being suscept-ible to Palpatine's wiles.[146]

To continue with this thought concerning the instrumentality of others' (*all* others') lives for Sith self-aggrandizement, it is telling that in *TPM* Palpatine *uses* an ultimately disposable assassin, Darth Maul. The Zabrak Maul had been kidnapped from Iridonia as an infant in order to be trained in the ways of the "dark side of the Force," but his function was simply to quietly assassinate the early political enemies of Palpatine. It is this instrumentalized existence (imbibing its determin-ing ideology) that results in the rendering of Maul as such a flat mono-dimensional and thin character alongside the more complex Sidious. He is evil's assassin pure and simple, physically portrayed as a rather obvious and unsophisticated incarnation of evil in a way that is remi-niscent of the bestial and demonic. Moreover, as mentioned earlier, it is this theme of the instrumentalization of the life of others that arguably constitutes the main moral problem behind the issue of both the Grand (Clone) Army of the Republic and the hideous monstrosity of the bio-technological recreation as a cybernetic organism of the near fatally injured Grievous (and even more so, later, of Darth Vader).

But perhaps there is even more to the Anakin-Palpatine relationship than this, something still more deeply sinister. There is some ambiguity, a quite deliberate one Lucas claims, in the relation of Anakin's forth-coming tragedy and his "virginal conception." The point at issue arises with Palpatine's recounting to Anakin of the Sith legend of "the tragedy of Darth Plagueis the Wise" in *ROTS*, and the possibility is suggested even more strongly in the novelization. Plagueis became so powerful that he could even manipulate the midi-chlorians in order to create life. This, of course, is a reference to the God-like desires of the Sith, but the audience's mind is cast back to Anakin's apparent birth in "the Force," to what Qui-Gon described as a "vergence in the Force." Is this a coin-cidental overlap of stories? The Chancellor reveals that Plagueis' pupil learned all that his Sith Master knew and then betrayed and murdered the teacher. In other words, the knowledge of how to manipulate the midi-chlorians to create life was possessed by another. The climax to this revelation comes in the Chancellor's chambers a few scenes later when he reveals his true *Sith* self—Darth Sidious—and tempts Anakin to become his pupil so as to learn how to prevent Padmé's foreseen death in co-operation, since Sidious had himself been the pupil of Darth Plagueis. There may well be more of the hand of the "gods" in Anakin's fall than might otherwise have been thought. This would give new, and even more ominous, significance to Palpatine's friendly remark to young Anakin after the Battle of Naboo: "we will watch your career with great interest." Even the reference by Yoda that "clouded this boy's future is" may well be a metaphor for the covering over, the shroud or masking of the Sith that envelops Anakin's future development. After all, early in *AOTC* Yoda reveals that "the dark side clouds everything. Impossible to see the future is." Again, later in that same movie he castigates a Obi-Wan for a lazy comment and announces that "the shroud of the dark side has fallen."[147] Stover presents Palpatine urging: "understand who you truly are, and your true place in the history of the galaxy.... You *are* the chosen one.... Chosen by *me*." The ambiguity remains, but the suggestion of a sense of determination involved in Anakin's being, learning, and falling to the Dark Side is difficult to completely ignore.[148]

Anakin, "a Man More Sinned Against Than Sinning" [Lear][149]

While tragedy may be "an unfashionable subject these days," the two sets of *SW* trilogies offer a marked difference in mood largely because of the shift from the core mythic or Jungian archetypes of the adventures of Luke Skywalker[150] to the plotting of the tragedy of Anakin Skywalker which then comes to have a more Freudian feel.[151] For instance, in an echo of the Oedipus tragedy, immortalized by the Greek tragedian Sophocles and formulated by Aristotle, Anakin becomes a tragic figure who attempts to escape "destiny" by taking his future into his own hands, but who nonetheless is fated to kill (here his surrogate father) Obi-Wan (although Padmé, of course, functions differently from Oedipus' mother). The *SW* universe is now not conceived as a simple good-overcoming-evil scheme. In fact, it is questionable that *ESB* and *ROTJ* were as simple in this regard either, and there is an important question concerning how receptions of Episodes V–VI have been dominated by the simplistic impressions received from *ANH*. Lucas seems to conceive of the nature of things as being particularly messy, and as a result no obviously harmoniously neat and glibly untragic story about it can be told. Thus, to narrate the saga as tragedy is both to ask for a vastly different light to be cast on the movies as a unity than would occur if they were "Manichaean," and also to unmask the deeply "sentimental humanitarianism" pervading Anglophone culture.[152]

As Anakin attempts to crawl free from the lava on Mustafar, the monstrous picture of warped personhood is a profoundly tragic one of fall, loss and waste (of self-control, limbs, friendship, family, the good counsel of the Jedi, potential for greatness, his own name, and of the Republic's freedom), of brutal dehumanization [*ROTS*]. "Here is a guy who has lost everything,"[153] who is "cursed by the same flaws and issues … that … everybody struggles with,"[154] and who has done irreparable damage to the lives of many. (Padmé and the Temple's younglings lie slaughtered, the Republic has fallen into the hegemony of the Galactic Empire, Anakin's twins are raised by others worlds apart from each other.) The young man even loses the capacity to live without his mechanical aid. (He even loses his name, so as he tells Luke in *ROTJ* when the Jedi calls Vader "Anakin," "that name no longer has any meaning for me." Luke's response is: "It is the name of your true self. You've only forgotten.") Vader's garb, inasmuch as it hides his "humanness," reveals a darkness that functions as a visual metaphor for a loss of self, and this is depicted by the fact that his helmet prevents him from having a visible face and therefore face to face relations. This is both a deliberate hiding and a faceless dehumanization. According to Jerold J. Abrams,

> Vader's enframing is, to be sure, all but complete. His being-in-the-world is so artificially mediated, so incredibly distorted, that he no longer fully *understands* what it is he's doing—or *why*. No longer human, he has entirely lost touch with himself.… He has, at the very least, forgotten the man he used to be. And beyond that, in a very Heideggerian sense, he has equally forgotten his own original being-in-the-world—indeed he has even forgotten his own name.[155]

According to Terry Christensen, it is invariably the case in American movies that when action is taken by the heroic protagonists it can be seen clearly that "the bad guys act out of greed or ambition, and the good guys act to stop the bad guys."[156] This is not easily the case in *ROTS*. Here the archetypal icon of evil from the "classic trilogy" is portrayed as falling into the dark side while trying to pursue lofty ideals, and while the Jedi are not as such portrayed in darker colors they are plagued by ignorance and partiality just as much as Anakin is. Certainly Anakin is flawed and his fall involves his actions (his intervention in Mace Windu's attempted execution of Palpatine/Sidious, his bowing to the Sith Lord, his brutal march into the Jedi Temple at the head of the 501st, and his murderous rage against Padmé and Obi-Wan). Yet Anakin's action against Mace and eventual backing of Palpatine/Sidious against the Jedi has been determined by some complex events. More particularly, he can be seen to act badly, ironically, for the very best of reasons. Admittedly he desires power, but out of a desire for "peace" and Padmé's safety. Yet the very pathway to "power," coming from making a Faustian pact to save Padmé, is itself tragically the direction that actually destroys her. He even acts out of a conservative loyalty to the Republic, and he naively and blindly trusts Palpatine to do what is right. As Anakin promises in *ROTS*, "I will not betray the Republic," the Republic that he has profound (blind) faith in. In this he has been skillfully manipulated. Anakin thus comes to perceive the Darkside not as evil but rather (wrongly) as a different/better way of achieving his *good* purposes for bring peace to the galaxy. He attempts to prevent arbitrary and summary justice without trial being exacted on Palpatine/Sidious (having regretted his execution of Dooku), and yet in that moment of moral anxiety he unwittingly helps to destroy Mace in an act that finally leads him into the arms of Sidious and the obliteration of the Jedi Order. As Lucas suggestively comments, "Most of ... [those who are wicked] think they're good people doing what they do for a good reason." And so the director instructs Hayden Christensen in his performance in *ROTS* by informing him that "there's always this good in you at this point. The good part is always saying 'what am I doing?' And the bad part is saying 'I'm doing this for Padmé, I'm doing this for us, it'll be better for the universe, it'll be better for everybody....'"[157] So Obi-Wan can accurately lament to Padmé, "he was deceived by a lie, we all were." [*ROTS*] The tragic conflict bears the scars of a bewildering array of moral antinomies for Anakin—he possesses all the best intentions but without the guidance of the requisite wisdom. So as *AOTC* reveals, for instance, he imagines a "power" separated in a crucial sense from wisdom, and this is something Stover's novelization of *ROTS* reaffirms. So we read of Anakin petulantly announcing to his former Jedi Master "I have the power of any five Masters. Any *ten*. You know it, and so do they [viz., the Jedi Council]." With more wisdom Obi-Wan warns, "Power alone is no credit to you."[158] The pathway to the "power" to save Padmé is itself the direction that destroys her.

And it is that *lack* of wisdom, a lack of understanding of "the Good," that is crucial in his succumbing to the seduction of the one who has carefully engineered politically and personally favorable events over the past couple of decades, including the very apprenticeship of Anakin himself in the way of the Sith. Anakin is a victim because not only because he is unable to control his emotions, but because he lacks the understanding of "the Good" that would enable him to discern that which is truly wicked in Palpatine's insidious machinations. In tragedies, good may be produced by evil, and may, conversely, lead to it as dramatically it is here. Even the Jedi Council, with their initial war support, their blindness to the Sith in their midst, and the way they treated Anakin, are similarly complicit in the tragedy of their destruction. The disturbing consequences demonstrate the possibility that those who honestly believe themselves to be doing the right thing may, in the end, be deluded.

What happens to the tragic hero is often called *nemesis* ("punishment"), and Anakin's "punishing" *metabole* ("reversal of fortune") has many layers, each taking him deeper in his fall. But it is very clear that this *nemesis* is not the same as the receiving of some "poetic justice." Thus while tragedy embodies something of the notion of moral responsibility, and therefore of a concordance between the moral character of the tragic personage and his destiny, this "concordance" is usually exceedingly difficult to make out.[159] Like Oedipus and Lear, Anakin's sufferings are disproportionately greater in scale than his vices. Something uncontrollable and overwhelmingly calamitous has been unleashed by his tragic mistakes. What he is indeed guilty of is of being *blind to the truth of the situation*, of being a bad judge of the terrible reality being played out behind his back as well as in and through him. (This theme of distorted vision is symbolized by the fallen Anakin's eye-color change and his eventual looking through the armored mask.) His is, as Jeffrey Overstreet sympathetically remarks, something of an understandable fall into wickedness: "Lo and behold, Darth Vader did not strive to be a heartless villain. He became one by trying to protect the one he loved, going blind to the greater good in the process. The stakes are finally high enough to earn gasps, and the ensuing tragedy is almost Shakespearean."[160] The depth of the tragedy is that not only does this profoundly great potential, and that of the wise senator Padmé in a *Romeo and Juliet*–type doubling of the waste (Padmé gives up her will to live after realizing that Anakin has, in a sense, died), become wasted, but that so much that is good in the galaxy is distorted and destroyed as a consequence.

Conclusion

One of the complaints frequently voiced concerning the second trilogy of *SW* movies is that they are too political. After all, even the romance that is vitally important to the generation of the twins who will be the focus of the drama in the "classic trilogy" is occasionally itself subordinated to the lovers' political conversations and significant disagreements. In one specific scene in *AOTC*, set on particularly idyllic spot on Naboo with a field of flowers surrounded by cliffs and waterfalls, Anakin's appeal to a strong leader who would do what is right is given a visual context of allusion to the coming of German Nazi annexation of Austria in *The Sound of Music* (1965).[161]

There is quite a lot going on here in this criticism, however. In the first place, it assumes that the earlier films were not political—meaning that they did not contain any political message. In the second place, the fact that it is put as a *criticism* (that they are *too* political) entails that the earlier films were read and enjoyed, at least, *as pure entertainment* (which usually means "privately and passively entertaining") and, at most, as *personally inspiring*.[162] Campbell's "psychologizing" of mythology can unwittingly contribute to this "personalizing" or "individualizing" of the enjoyment value of these movies. But there is a highly significant sense in which this assessment is deeply shallow and problematic, suggesting that these critics are projecting themselves by failing to listen closely to the texts' concrete particularities. They especially fail to perceive the politics of Empire (which critically includes an imposed racial and gender hygiene in the Imperial forces) and emancipatory anti-colonialism (which includes more expansive forms of inter-species and gender co-operation) performed even at the narrative level of the classic trilogy. In fact, Peter Krämer observes, in a poll conducted by Michael Ryan and Douglas Kellner in 1986, about half of the respondents understood *SW*'s Empire in general terms "as an embodiment of evil," as opposed to 24 percent who viewed it as representing right-wing dictators, and 12 percent who read it as representing communism. Krämer comments, "This poll suggests, then, that audiences were not only willing to attach political meanings to this science-fiction fairy tale but did so according to their own political beliefs, drawing on both historical precedents and current events."[163] Booker, however, despite his intensive (if largely derivative) criticism of *SW* offers one possible form of political significance: "the very fact that the rebels do employ terrorist tactics in the interest of a presumably virtuous cause asks us to reconsider some of our own recent demonization of terrorists and to remember that they may have a point of view that is more complex than the mere pursuit of evil for its own sake."[164] Moreover, the apolitical fan-reading misunderstands the pedagogic intentionality of Lucas. After all, he designs these stories in order to help form personal and social (i.e., political) identity, and this means that his "texts" operate at the metaphoric level Lucas' comment on the Vietnam conflict and the presidency of Richard Nixon. In relation to the "texts" themselves, the impulse currents of *SW* run deeper than these given its notable potential for symbolic significance.[165]

Nonetheless, that *SW*'s classic trilogy had been read and received as politically reactionary and nostalgically by a large body of cultural commentators and fans not only cannot be underestimated, but suggests that something significant is being done with the seemingly "more (radically) political" prequels. The latter can be read precisely as a commentary on, and political clarification of, the earlier trilogy of cinematic texts in the saga. The "bad guys" were largely single dimensional icons of evil in the 1977 blockbuster, placed on screen as the vehicle for the celebration of heroic endeavor, the heroism of several fledgling Rebels whose deaths are distinguished in a moment of the audience's cathartic release. Wink explains the process involved: "The psychodynamics of the television cartoon or comic book are marvellously simple: children identify with the good guy so that they can think of themselves as good. This enables them to project onto the bad guy their own repressed anger, violence, rebelliousness, or lust, and then vicariously to enjoy their own evil by watching the bad guy initially prevail.... When the good guy finally wins [and he always has to win otherwise the basic system will not work], viewers are then able to reassert control over their own inner tendencies, repress them, and re-establish a sense of goodness. Salvation is guaranteed through identification with the hero."[166] The succeeding *SW* movies, however, complicate this Manichaean portrayal through the complicating the characterization of Vader. Of course, there still remain vital and complex issues of race and gender representation that this chapter has hardly even touched on, but at least the tragedy of *evil from within* provides a pre-eminent disruption of the so-called *realpolitik* emerging from a politics of fear, a fear that demands a process of "Othering" of the kind that critics have read out of Episodes IV–VI. Because of the retroactive defamiliarization that has come from the five movies in the saga made since *ANH*, and particularly with the prequel trilogy, commentators should now be considerably more careful in speaking of *SW* generally as a politically nostalgic text borne out of a Manichaean sensibility. To tell the story of the *SW* saga as tragedy (albeit tragedy with a certain sense of restoration, as occurs when Episodes I–III are brought into conversation with Episodes IV–VI) is to ask that a vastly different light be cast on the movies as a mythological unity than that commonly applied through a darkening dualistic filter.

To suggest that evil has a history is itself not particularly radical, especially when one considers the Christian doctrine of original sin in its flourishing Augustinianism. But, one should remember, *SW* is supposedly a "popcorn movie" series, and popcorn movies are, by nature, generally averse to painting moral shades of grey. After all, the thesis of Jewett and Lawrence, among others, is that American consciousness is largely driven by the generally rather morally unambiguous myth of the hero. This assumes, in Eagleton's terms, the notion of "monsters [who] are other people."[167] In contrast, however, as Lyden recognizes, evident in the *SW* prequels in particular is the notion that "the 'enemy' is not a political 'other,' but ourselves, or at least the threat that we will lose our humanity to greed and a selfish quest for power—symbolized by the Dark side."[168] Taking this seriously will require quite an upheaval of cultural and political consciousness. *SW* has the capacity to interrogate our political practices. By naming the shape of "evil" in the way it does, it can engender further self-reflection that at least can thwart complacency, and the temptations to sentimental understandings of ourselves and our nations, and also has the potential for creative suggestions of what may be wrong with human relations. In contrast to the delicate balance between the externalization and internationalization of evil in the *SW* saga, if we continue to interpret evil individualistically in subjectivist terms as either "personal sin" or corporately in objectivist terms as the "demonic others," then we will have lost the hopeful capacity for being able not only to identify evil but to resist it, since both options trade on an evil themselves (the first misplaces the social and structural dimension which in turn can lead to neglect of the evils imposed on us and others; the second negates the place of evil in the self ... and of one's responsibilities). This means, in the end, that evil is not easily or obviously discernible, and the relationship between good and evil can be very messy indeed, lacking in hermetically sealable and policeable borders. According to Adrian Poole, tragedy expresses "that we are connected, even interconnected, by complex systems of cause and consequence, in which questions of innocence and guilt are all caught up and embroiled, and from which no one should expect to be exempted."[169] While tragic drama raises the most potent ethical questions, it removes the license for making claims regarding moral self-righteousness in a fallen and tragic world so potent in common popular moral and political discourse. Those who display such moral smugness deflect critical attention being paid to themselves, the ideologies they inhabit, and the effects of their actions. When read well, then, tragedies can present a kind of perpetual moral wakefulness that enables one to continually ask about the complexity of motives, the wisdom in decisions, the characters we develop, and the importance of external factors in shaping events, to name a few features of our narrative identities. Goodness (even when we think we know what that means) is fragile, all moves toward human self-control and self-possession (be they psychological, economic, political, intellectual, etc.) are conspicuously hazardous, and human beings are vulnerable to evil. "Tragedy," Peter Ahrensdorf argues, "should not offend the just hope that the good will be rewarded and the wicked punished, but it should beware of lulling us into a thoughtlessly complacent belief that justice is always done in the world and that the human condition is free from [unjust] suffering."[170] Consequently, in suggesting something of the density involved in speaking well about "evil," Lucas' nuanced and complex portrayal is more authentic than, for example, the superficial dualisms of the mythos of much recent political rhetoric.

In being remade as "more machine ... than man" [Obi-Wan, *ROTJ*] the eyes of the descending mask in which he becomes imprisoned invite us to view the world (through the camera underneath) with him. (It is this symbolism of Vader's distorted vision that is further recorded in one of his last requests of Luke in *ROTJ*: "Luke, help me take this mask off.... Just for once, let me look on you with my own eyes.") As Eagleton argues, the tragic protagonists are "not men travestied, dehumanized, violently disfigured, but signs of the violent disfiguration that is humanity itself."[171] In this way, the story of Anakin is one to be feared. It is a story displaying the fragility of judgment, the vulnerability and deformability of the good life, depths of ignorance over the conditions that will harm rather than heal, of lives destroyed by a world uncontrollably "out of joint, that ... [the world] is fundamentally indifferent or hostile to our efforts to achieve happiness, justice, and understanding, and hence that it is at odds with our deepest desires,"[172] and unmasking the irreparable shallowness and cheapness of doctrines of humanitarian progress.[173]

Anakin, the tragic figure who loses everything, is pitiable, a kind of every-person even with his midi-chlorian nobility. Taking tragic dramas seri-ously in moral reflection, consequently, highlights the fragility of good-ness, the difficulty of good moral deliberation, and the messiness of situations that create conditions of intensive blindness to the destructive potential and problems of damage to oneself and others caused by one's own ways of being and acting. There can be no room for complacency of an outlook determined by various types of "realized eschatology." The story of Anakin is construed as a contemporary tragedy, and thus a warn-ing about the irresponsibility of such blindness: irresponsibility to both the society of which we are a part, and even to ourselves.

So asking honestly about the *complex* causes of wickedness does not absolve us of the difficult task of reflecting seriously on how to deal with certain (more obvious?) manifestations of "evil" when they surface. Anakin may, to a large degree, have been the victim of circumstances, bad relations, and insidious scheming, but Obi-Wan is still painfully and tragically forced to confront him in a battle to the death—otherwise, the threat that Anakin poses to the peoples and worlds of the now shat-tered Republic will be even more catastrophic. But what all this does suggest, nevertheless, is that the whole predication of power and response to threats to power in a "politics of blame" (one that wants to blame and does so by self-flatteringly *faulting others*) is wholly misplaced.

> Bombast about evil individuals doesn't help in understanding anything. Even vile and murderous actions tend to come from somewhere, and if they are extreme in character we are not wrong to look for extreme situ-ations. It does not mean that those who do them had no choice, are not answerable, far from it. But there is sentimentality too in ascribing what we don't understand to "evil"; it lets us off the hook, it allows us to avoid the question of what, if anything, we can *recognize* in the destructive act of another.... If we act without questioning, we change nothing. It is not true to say, "We are all guilty"; but perhaps it is true to say, "We are all able to understand *something* as we look into ourselves."[174]

John Kekes claims that in such a world "the best we can do is to plan our lives so as to minimize their [i.e., the conditions that create tragedies] influence," assuming, of course, that we can adequately iden-tify them all.[175] But with their deconstructions of the stable subjectivity of the humanistic hero, tragedies are not without hope, even if optimisms (or the securing of the future to sight) are precluded, and in this regard the intercutting of the mechanized "rebirth of Vader" (which is a form of death, both a living death without hope for Anakin, and his deathly presence to the Imperial enemies) and the birth of the twins, followed by the symphonic rendition of the "New Hope" theme as an infant Luke is delivered to his new family on Tatooine. In this regard, there is a politically significant contrast with Zack Snyder's *Watchmen*, or at least in Iain Thomson's reading of it. His argument is that Alan Moore's award-winning graphic novel deconstructs the very idea of a hero, but in the process assumes a determinative nihilism:

> *Watchmen* deconstructs the hero by developing its heroes—extending traditional hero fantasies beyond their limits—to the point where the reader comes to understand that these fantasies, realized, become nightmares.... By suggesting that all such paths may be either hopeless or horrific, and that the heroes' motives for seeking them are either dangerous or else unworthy of our admiration, *Watchmen* develops its heroes precisely in order to ask us if we would not in fact be better off without heroes.[176]

For Thomson, "although *Watchmen's* heroes all subscribe to the nihilistic belief that reality is ultimately meaningless, they are *heroes* precisely in so far as they embrace this nihilism and nevertheless seek a path leading beyond it."[177] However, this claim does not make sense for several reasons: it does not take seriously Rorschach's embrace of an absolutist ethic; in the face of the joke that existence is the Comedian embraces a brutal will-to-power; or the fact that Dr. Manhattan's "beyond" is that of apathy for the well-being of others; and finally, Thomson's conclusion is glib in the teeth of arbitrary action, action that has no ground or meaning other than its having been chosen.

Anakin is the answer to the question of what if the Jedi were real? What would we, who displace our vices in our self-idealizations, look like if we were placed in the position of the Jedi? His power in the Force is generous even when compared to the likes of Mace Windu and Yoda, which is why Sidious tells the diminutively wizened Jedi Master that "Darth Vader will become more powerful [than] either of us." And it is the power in the Force and spectacularly destructive control of a lightsaber that appeals to the audience. Yet *ROTS* is asking deeper questions, questions about character, about morality, about what instincts drive us away from even the best in our moral reasoning. That is what many have missed in the characterization of Luke, and even of the redeemed Anakin—they are culturally valuable for a mass of fans precisely because of their *power*, their Force-technical prowess, rather than for their moral exemplarism. And here is the irony of the merchandizing in which Luke becomes an important figure in child's role-playing because he comes complete with both a laser-pistol and a lightsaber. What if the immense power of the Force was available to someone whose emotional instincts and psychological condition was less than virtuous and well self-controlled? The prequels move closer to stripping away the mask of moral distance by graphically brutalizing the body of Anakin as a visual representation of the moral disrepair that has overcome him. The young man cannot cope with the demands of moral knowledge and the development of virtuous character when he is denied positively appropriate emotional and moral support. Anakin, then, is not to be idolized as hero, but he is to serve as a mirror to our own moral disrepair. In this regard, the tragedy of Anakin Skywalker can function to interrogate the process of idolization in which heroes are chosen, without interrogating us and thus leaving us morally in a state of blithe spectatorial existence unencumbered by the depth of mutual commitment. However, unlike Moore's *Watchmen* Lucas does not offer a disenchanted universe that cannot but slip into nihilism. While his depiction of the Force is certainly theologically thin, involving an eclecticism characteristic of decontextualized and detraditioned western liberal pluralism, it at least offers a grounding of immanence in a sense of Otherness and therefore of responsible interrelations or moral mutuality. To put it another way, it offers a witness to the possibility of hope even in catastrophic conditions.

3

DYSTOPIAN POLYVALENCE
Emancipating the Mediated
Life from *The Matrix*

Philosophers in particular have long been concerned with the nature of the "real," the type of metaphysical issue that demands consideration of the knowing (that which one can metaphorically depict as intellectual in*sight*) and understanding of it, and the mediating frames of reference that distort it. And for a period during the 1990s philosophers were provided with numerous cinematic texts useful for philosophical illustration, one feature of which was a prominent concern over the nature of the real and its perception. Reality is not as it appears, according to *Total Recall, The Truman Show, The Matrix, Fight Club, 12 Monkeys, Equilibrium, V for Vendetta, Dark City*, as well as the earlier movies *1984*, and *Soylent Green*, and in the 2000s *Inception, Moon, Source Code*, and *The Adjustment Bureau*. Of course, several of these movies are built less around the possibilities for socio-political and economic comment provided by the dystopian form than around the spectacle of an audience-pleasing violence. Perhaps the most culturally interesting of these are *The Truman Show, Moon*, and the somewhat different *Branded*, and it is in the first of this trio, for example, that there appears suggestions not merely about the contingency or the simulated nature of the American Dream but about modern anxieties over the screening of reality, and the pervasive system of surveillance in what amounts to an enrichment of the dystopian imagination. The reality television program's creator and executive producer Christof in *The Truman Show* reveals that "we accept the reality of the world with which we are presented," although in Truman's case at least Christof makes the mistake of remarking that "ultimately, Truman prefers his cell."

According to Frederic Jameson, however, American science fiction has a particular affinity with the dystopian rather than the utopian imagination, resulting from a cultural atrophy in which the future cannot be constructively imagined.[1] This does not, or at least cannot, mean that all dystopian movies can be "dismissed as trashy infatuations with an equally trashy future.... [T]here are others which try to point to present tendencies that seem likely to result in corporate totalitarianism, apocalypse, or both."[2] Dystopian movies, when done in a particular fashion, can function as mediating lenses through which to critically interrogate beliefs, values and decisions that are deemed to have catastrophic consequences for the nature of human identity. In other words, they can function as sites for the formation of what J.P. Telotte calls "a kind of cultural unease."[3] As such, dystopian movies play into cultural concerns about dehumanizing conditions in late modernity, as the self and society become problematically mediated in and through cultural regulations of the bureaucratizing, homogenizing, and commodifying of social life. It is in this critical process that possibilities for the critical re-imagining of the political conditions, relations and their control of the flow of power can operate, according to Raffaella Baccolini and Tom Moylan. Accordingly, they maintain, "the dystopian imagination has served as a prophetic vehicle, the canary in the cage, for writers with an ethical and political concern for warning us of terrible socio-political tendencies that could, if continued, turn our contemporary world into the iron cages portrayed in the realm of utopia's underside."[4]

This chapter presses the socio-political critique of the dystopian imagination, but does so by assuming that there are varieties of dystopianisms. Not all dystopianly charged texts can function as effective critical aids to what Baccolini and Moylan call the "emancipatory utopian imagination."[5] Some slip, in fact, into forms of anti-utopian nihilism, while others provide what Peter Fitting describes as "false utopian solutions to the dystopia of the present."[6] Specifically, the chapter will focus on the Wachowski brothers' *The Matrix*, arguing that it subverts its own critical dystopian potential, to use Jameson's terms, "of making us more aware of our mental and ideological imprisonment," and thereby utopianly slides back into the mode of celebrating the simulated realities it attempts to criticize.[7] Its sequels serve to disrupt the Idealist subjectivity that sustains the first movie in the trilogy, pushing the series towards a flashy nihilism only to restrain it through offering a fragilistic and contingent form of transcendence of systemic determinism.

Cinema and the Mediated Life

In *The End of Education* cultural theorist Neil Postman turns his attention to the nature of language in relation to learning. Ringing in the background is the defamation of language in *1984*'s "Newspeak," a revisionism that curtails not merely the ability to develop an expansive vocabulary, but equally the ability of the imagination to envisage alternatives. According to Postman, "a metaphor is not an ornament. It is an organ of perception. Through metaphors, we see the world as one thing or another."[8] What Postman has in mind is the way in which language and perception are bound up together. Language is not merely an afterthought, literally, as in the Cartesian dualistic system whereby the subject's consciousness grounds and essentializes one's being as thinker in advance of any form of linguistic mediation. Instead, "language creates a worldview," and so Postman wants to indicate that the so-called "turn to the subject" requires complication by the so-called "turn to language."[9] Metaphors are not merely cerebral matters of verbally offered linguistics, but forms of representation that envision matters in complex ways. In that case, "the real" can only arrive through metaphoric mediation, a deferred presence or self-presentation of "the real." Consequently, Postman articulates in his *Amusing Ourselves to Death*, "We do not see nature or intelligence or human motivation or ideology as 'it' is but only as our languages are. And our languages are our media. Our media are our metaphors. Our metaphors create the content of our culture."[10]

Mediation is a prominent theme in cinema, particularly in science fiction film. After all, the visual narration provides representational imagery in an intelligibly structured fashion. Cinema is involved in a *mimesis* that screens and mediates "the real." Often attention to optical metaphorics serves to induce paranoia over surveillance culture, and thereby asks questions concerning the nature of human liberty, privacy, and the intrusions of a big brother political culture. In one set of cases, this is distinctly focused on political surveillance, such as in *Equilibrium*, the deterministic *The Adjustment Bureau*, and the controlling socio-constructivism involved in the sinister psychological and social experiment being conducted in *Dark City*. A different type of political use of optical imagery occurs in *12 Monkeys*, with the visualization of the imprisoning scientists' eyes being exaggerated by magnifying lenses in order to suggest not insight but blindness, ignorance and misjudgment.

In another set of cases, the questions take a more socio-cultural form. For instance, F. Scott Fitzgerald's use of eyes as a metaphor for judgment on a decadent high-society culture whose self-concern uses Jay Gatsby for its own hedonistic whims appears in the recent filmic depiction of his *Great Gatsby*. The somewhat undervalued *Surrogates* explores the theme of mediation as itself dehumanizing, disconnecting people from each other out of fear of their own bio-fragility, a theme picked up in a different fashion by Pixar's *Wall-E*. In *Surrogates* experience itself is dematerialized in an echo of philosophical concerns with Cartesian anthropological dualism. While not invoking "the visual" as the controlling theme, it is worthwhile noticing the determinative Cartesianism in a scene in the all-too abruptly aborted and short-lived rebooting of the alien-invasion television series *V*. The invading Queen instructs her medics to find the human soul from within the captured human subjects. The determinative assumption is that this is the seat of human life, of identity and character, a perspective that problematically reduces the "soul" to an aspect of biomechanics. The Queen's task, then, is an indication of the struggle in contemporary Western (especially American) society to understand "the human," and perhaps her search for the soul is a cultural hangover of the continuing influence of a Cartesian "ghost-in-the-machine" type anthropology. It has, in fact, been a common science-fiction project to imaginatively involve the transferal of consciousness to other bodies (or shells)—something comically presented in *A Man with Two Brains*, for instance—or even dispensing with bodies altogether with the development of post-human cyber-consciousness— as in the exploitation of fears of the digital era in the cyber-thriller *The Lawnmower Man*. Unlike the occasional desire for the post-material form of this Cartesian existence, James Cameron's *Avatar* at least depicts the trans-materialization of Jake Sully's identity-determining consciousness. Christopher Nolan's clever thriller *Memento* further refuses the body-loss so that the bio-graphologized body now is the site of memory and consequently of human identity itself. To return to consideration of *Surrogates*, the political subtext invokes cultural revolutionaries as the occasion for the eventual overthrow of the techno-lives in a privileged materiality that approaches a form of technophobia. An echo of this occurs in the graphically brutal *Gamer* which involves concerns with a hedonistic culture's instrumentalization of the bodies of others (the bodies of the prisoners locked into the Game "Slayers," and the bodies of those forced into a form of cyber-slavery to a host of cyber-controllers—the ability of both groups to consciously determine their bio-actions as autonomous agents is replaced).

A different form of life dehumanized in the process of its being instrumentalized by the spectatorial gaze, and of the forms of displaced maturation of the observers themselves, drives the "big-brother-as-entertainment" premise of *The Truman Show*. It comes as a humanizing relief when Truman Burbank discovers the exit. And what results? In a curtailing of the utopian imagination, the program's addicts finally switch off their televisions, but they, and even Truman, do not contest in any politically meaningful sense the abuse of a manufactured life for the sake of televisual ratings. As the protagonist is about to exit the dome he delivers his catchphrase, "In case I don't see you, good afternoon, good evening, and good night," and he subsequently bows to the show's viewers. The opportunity for Truman to fulfill his long-time romantic fantasy provides a cathartic purging of any potential political outrage.

The movie *God Bless America* could be construed as a revenge tragedy depicting the shadowside of the socio-political culture characterized by aestheticized spectatorial existence. The main protagonist, Frank Murdoch, slips into despair over the way deformed versions of contemporary American popular culture shapes and constrains performances of civility. To one of his colleagues' questions, "What about you, Frank, did you see that freak on *American Superstarz* last night?" and the comment that it was "funny," Frank retorts,

> It is not nice to laugh at someone who's not all there. It's the same type of freak show distraction that comes along every time a mighty empire starts collapsing. *American Superstarz* is the new colosseum. I won't participate in a show where the weak are torn apart every week for our entertainment. I don't really. Everything is so cruel now. I just want it all to stop. I mean, nobody talks about anything anymore. They just regurgitate everything they see on TV or hear on the radio or watch on the web.... [T]his is the "oh no, you didn't say that" generation where shocking comment has more weight than the truth. No one has any shame any more. And we're supposed to celebrate it.... Why have a civilization any more if we're no longer interested in being civilized?

It is not an ideologically subtle movie, and unlike the interrogation of the American dream involved in the tragic addiction movie *Requiem for a Dream*, for instance, it succumbs to a lengthy homiletic exposition at various points, as does Derrick Borte's 2009 movie *The Joneses* with the guilt-stricken Steve Jones' honest and revealing admission following the death of Larry Symonds. Nonetheless, its movement is rendered tragic by the murderous depths its emotionally exhausted and socio-cynical protagonist feels he has to resort to in order to enact the only possible form of agency that he regards open to him, the brutally violent form of justice inflicted on a sham atomized culture. In the climactic scene, Frank announces to the camera,

> America has become a cruel and vicious place. We reward the shallowest, the dumbest, the meanest and the loudest. We no longer have any commonsense or decency, no sense of shame. There's no right and wrong. The worst qualities of people are looked up to and celebrated. Lying, spreading fear are fine as long as you make money while doing it. We've become a nation of slogan saying, bile spewing hate mongers. We've lost our kindness. We've lost our soul. What have we become when we take the weakest in our society and hold them up to be ridiculed, laughed at for our sport and our entertainment?

In contrast to *Falling Down*, which somewhat mitigates audience feeling for the protagonist in turmoil by jeopardizing the protagonist's ex-wife and child in what appears as a relationship of abuse, *God Bless America* still enables a sympathetic treatment of the central character in spite of his gusts of homicidal rage. In this regard, it offers a similarly sympathetic treatment of its judge, jury and executioner for a late modern age as *Assault on Wall Street*, which also falls under the *Dredd*-like category of retributive justice that pleasures audiences caught in the ideological web of the myth of redemptive violence and retributive justice. How far is this ideological mood removed from the emotionally purging delight determinative of the "torture porn" spectacle of the *Saw* franchise and its offshoots? What results is a violent voyeurism that itself depends on the moment of injustice in order to cathartically revel in its brand of antagonistic authenticity, as with the "John Doe" character in *Se7en*.

An interestingly stylized and formalistic take on mediation was launched by Eduardo Sanchez's and Daniel Myrik's original and intelligently designed low-budget *The Blair Witch Project* with its framing of spectatorial affections. The viewers' very ability to see what is transpiring is technically mediated by a video-camera, and it effectively uses this to generate terror over the most primal of fears (fear of the dark, of the threatening stranger, of being lost and alone) without ever having to resort to the shocks and gore of the schlock-fest slasher movies. This first-person camcorder style of cinematically regulating the audience's experience has, of course, been copied less effectively by not only the

horror crossover movies *Cloverfield* and *Apollo 18*, and the tragic adolescent superhero tragedy *Chronicle*, but it has taken in a slightly different direction through the use of the home surveillance system in the
increasingly self-duplicating and banally repetitive *Paranormal Activity*
series. One of the reasons for the success of *The Blair Witch Project* was
its freshness in enabling the intensity of the primal drive to fear to be
evoked so successfully. By perceiving events through the eyes of the protagonists, through their use of video equipment, the audience is invited
to see what the three students from Burkittsville see, hear what they
hear, and, most impressively, feel what they feel as they become lost and
terrified, and thereby participate in the drama by becoming a part of its
imaginative portrayal. The sense of horror is mediated through first person participation rather than third person distancing. The confusion,
fear, and the building to an eventual crescendo of absolute terror of the
person with the camera, through whose "eyes" the audience is entreated
to the drama, become the spectators' own. What is significant about the
setting of the film, paralleling numerous other movies in the horror
genre, is that the dramatic and unruly events, or rather the reign of terror, occur during the night. Darkness, with its mother the night, plays
a central role in maintaining the audience's primal fear. Sanchez and
Myrik's movie turned on the fact of being *lost* in the dark, exhibiting
loss of control, nescience, fragility, insecurity, and vulnerability to
unknown and unseen forces and predators beyond the protagonists'
capacities to shape and direct events. As Julius Caesar once remarked,
"The invisible dangers are always the worst." In the dark this statement
can take on new intensity.

The Matrix *Beyond the Surface Depth of Dystopian Matrices?*

Noetics, ethics and ocular metaphorics are interconnected in crucial ways in *The Matrix* and its two sequels, and are so in such an evident
fashion that philosophers have been encouraged to ransack the movie
for the purposes of illustrating Plato's Cave allegory and the epistemic
project involved in René Descartes' method of doubt (or, at least, two
forms of it—the dream and evil deceiver arguments). Thomas Wartenberg, for one, appears to suggest that the movie involves a philosophical
investigation of the knowing of the Real. So he argues that "*The Matrix*

can be seen as doing something distinctively philosophical, namely unsettling our established habits of belief and action, getting us to call into question our taken-for-granted assumptions."[11] "This," he declares, "is what Descartes is doing in the first chapter of the *Meditations* through the dream and evil demon arguments." A similar perspective can be found in the analysis of Christopher Grau, among others, who eulogizes that "*The Matrix* is a film that astounds not only with action and special effects but also with ideas."[12] Such a potential for "getting ... [an] audience to *think* [is] something that is far too uncommon in the conventional Hollywood product," Dino Felluga observes, apparently setting the Wachowskis' movie apart from other science fiction spectaculars.[13] The problem, however, is that the types of questions it tends to have provoked in the critical literature have largely been metaphysical ones, and this has left the political ideology of the individuated subject versus the "evil other" intact by default. Suggestively, the first moment we encounter Thomas A. Anderson, whose computer hacker handle "Neo" is an anagram of the "One" (the grand depiction offered throughout by Morpheus), he is awoken by a message on his computer: "Wake up Neo. The Matrix has you." In his introduction to *The Matrix and Philosophy*, William Irwin admits that "after watching *The Matrix* we are impressed by the action and special effects, and also besieged by questions.... Despite the multitude of questions, there is but one imperative: WAKE UP!"[14] The epistemic limit condition provided by Descartes' argument from the possibility of dream also provides the dramatic moment of irresolution in Christopher Nolan's *Inception*. However, what is important with these concerns over the nature of knowledge of "the real" in *The Matrix* is the context that shapes them. In fact, there is considerable disagreement among commentators as to how far the movie realizes its philosophico-political potential, makes authentically promising suggestions concerning the questions it asks, and effectively offers a waking life or whether it is restrained by slipping back into and consequently reinforces the gravitational pull of its own philosophical slumbers.

THE ESSENCE OF A SIMULATED CULTURE: WELCOME TO THE DESERT OF THE HYPER-REAL

Much hangs on the movie's reference to Jean Baurillard—Neo's fake copy of *Simulacra and Simulation* is visible early in the movie. Felluga is one who regards this as enabling a socio-political concern that is only masked by the reduction of reflection on the movie to matters of epistemology. He reads *The Matrix* utilizing Baudrillard's critique of postmodernism, and thereby emphasizes the movie's theme that persons are batteries powering the capitalist system. Accordingly, Felluga maintains, the movie offers a "commentary on the way each member of the audience is itself a coppertop, whose own fantasies are being manipulated by and thus feed capital."[15] On the other hand, it is highly suggestive that Felluga resists making any grand claim about the effectiveness of this critique, and even leaves open the prospect of a critical reading: "the use of theories that are themselves highly critical of multinational capitalism [may be] just a way for the Wachowskis to have their cake and critique it too." This is a crucial gap to leave in the evaluation given the distinct possibility that the use of the cultural philosopher is largely a skin-deep reference that actually distorts Baudrillard's thought. For him, the proliferation of different media forms has meant that what has been understood as reality and experience is so mediated that the real and the simulacrum have slipped into an indistinguishability between the real and the hyperreal. In this regard, the Wachowskis' suggestion that our experienceable or phenomenal reality is itself a construction is evident from the opening moment of the movie with the recoloration of the production companies' logos that precede the dripping computer code. Visual effects supervisor on *The Matrix*, John Gaeta, in his DVD commentary asserts that "we felt they [the studios' logos] were an evil empire bent on breaking the creative juices of the average director or writer, so we felt that desecrating the studio symbols was an important message to the audience, that we basically reject the system." On this Keith Booker observes that "the film suggests in a number of ways that our own reality is a media-produced illusion, to which the film industry itself makes crucial contributions."[16] In fact, Booker continues,

> *The Matrix* also includes television in its media critique. Morpheus, for example, specifically mentions television in his description of institutions that contribute to the illusions of the Matrix, along with work, church, and taxes. Televisions and video screens are prominently displayed at several points in the film, and one of the favorite devices employed by the Wachowskis involves a seamless transition from viewing a scene on a video screen to being inside the scene itself—suggesting the way in which, in our own world, television plays a major role in the postmodern blurring of the boundary between reality and fiction.

However, the film, by continuing not to offer a consistent simulacrum at all, presents a "reality" that lies beyond the very technologically simulated illusion of the Matrix.[17] In other words, not all is unreal, and through Morpheus' guidance Neo, or Thomas Anderson, comes to *know* this, a direction that likewise broadly shapes the dramatic climax of *The Thirteenth Floor* (1999) as well.[18] To draw on the Platonic imagery, Neo is freed from the cave and, like Plato's philosopher, he observes the very Truth and Form of things, reality in its ontological depths. So when the reawakened Neo meets his guide after his liberation from the pod he is greeted with the unambiguous statement, "Welcome to the real world." In a mood suggestive of a form of Gnostic metaphysical essentialism, the movie portrays Morpheus as being able to perceive and comprehend this situation through a panoptic gaze, an omniscient look into the heart or reality of things in the phantasmic or simulated world. In this regard, Morpheus expresses a freedom from simulations, from ideological capture in the enclosing system, and this conceptual move corresponds less to the liquid selves of Baudrillardian hyperreality than to a stabilized ontological gesture with the essentialized modern self as the intensified continuity underlying all appearances. So Andrew Gordon argues that the movie "plays on Baudrillard's ideas about simulation, but without Baudrillard's pessimism, because *The Matrix* offers a solution to the problem of simulation whereas Baudrillard believes there is none…. *The Matrix* is not faithful to Baudrillard's conclusions, because it creates a world in which the unreal is forced on people (whereas in our contemporary world we are doing it to ourselves) and because it offers the hope of returning to the real, which Baudrillard claims is no longer possible."[19] The fact that it is a *fake* copy of Baudrillard's book that Neo is seen to possess might serve as a metaphor warning commentators away from reading the movie at the imagistically mediated level of its surface representation.

Morpheus importantly asks, "How would you know the dream world from the real world?" The cinematic text of *The Matrix*, however, actually does not answer the question of how the characters know that what they take to be reality is not another simulated setting. Mark Conrad's account offers an interesting evaluation of what is being assumed.[20] He addresses the question of how the knowledge of the real works in the movie by suggesting that the Wachowskis rely on an unsophisticated and naïve kind of post–Romantic affective (dogmatically maintained) hunch.[21] Morpheus and those whom he persuades to take the red pill have to rely ultimately not on an intellectual and reasonable intuition but something more akin to simple affectivity, to little more than "gut-feeling, … like being in love, … completely subjective. And of course subjective states are proof enough of our own feelings, thoughts, or conditions but don't necessarily say anything at all about reality."[22] A sense of this is provided by the Oracle who explains that knowing that one is the One is like knowing one is in love—no one can tell one that it is love, one simply "knows" it. As Booker observes, "Morpheus and his crew certainly believe that their reality is 'real,' and most viewers of the film seem to accept that premise as well."[23]

The contrast between Larry and Andy Wachowski's *The Matrix* and movies like David Cronenberg's *eXistenZ* and Christopher Nolan's *Inception* is revealing at this point. While *The Matrix* offers the audience a perception of "reality," and the protagonists liberated from the system's grip can slip in and out of the illusory field of perception at will, Cronenberg's and Nolan's versions continue to offer the audience the tease that all may not be well, or rather the reality at the end may not be "real" at all. Cynthia Freeland observes that "at the end of *eXistenZ*, we feel unable to tell the difference between reality and illusion, since we have learned, in a surprising coda, that the entire film we just watched was itself an illusion, the testing of a virtual game. Many aspects of this 'outer' game mimic the inner game, and so viewers might well be perplexed about what was real and what an illusion. This confusion is epitomized when one frightened character asks, 'tell me, are we still in the game?'"[24] In fact, *eXistenZ* refuses to pull up short by succumbing to the consoling demand for the action spectacle in the way both *The Matrix* and *Inception* do. It would seem that in *The Matrix* the rabbit hole is not as deep, and its terminus is seen to offer stable ground on which the action can be given a secure footing.

KNOWLEDGE IS POWER

Politically this reading-perspective generates an intensely significant set of critical observations. In the first place, the movie's very epistemic sensibility involves for Booker a readily detectable sensibility shaped by a political nostalgia, a celebration of "traditional values" that "look to the past for solutions to our contemporary malaise."[25] "The structural opposition of the real world versus the simulated world of the Matrix," Booker argues, "is very much an opposition between past authenticity and present fakery, based on the assumption that a legitimate and genuine reality does exist, even if that reality may be difficult to access through the web of representations that now cloak it."

In this regard, the movies emerge from a worry about the mediating effects of digital technologies while a confused response in terms of, on the one hand, a yearning for authentic connection beyond the digital system (Neo and Trinity's growing affection, for instance), while, on the other hand, overplaying a technophiliac's appeal to choice to make use of the seductive constructions of the digital image. So Patricia Melzer observes "an ambivalent relationship to technology that shapes the notions of identity, body, and reality that run through the film."[26] One might respond that the narrative's requirement for return to the Matrix, of course, is a politically responsible act, and yet something disruptive will be argued a little later in this chapter, a hint of which is provided by Melzer: "It is here, in the film's representations of technology as *medium* and the pleasure it evokes is more relevant in its construction of meaning than is the narrative content."[27]

Questions of power are further raised by the assertive agency involved in Morpheus' ability to control the flow of knowledge to those being offered the choice between the red and blue pills. Even if it is the case that he only remains the herald for the coming One, the utterly convinced channel of revelation engages in an evangelistic performance that is characteristically reducible to out-narration (the story he tells Neo of the scorched sky and the subsequently constructed Matrix) and assertive rhetoric. It is significant in this context that in *The Matrix Reloaded* he responds to a criticism that "not everyone believes what you believe" with what looks like a fundamentalist proclamation of unquestionable faith and an unconversationally self-reflexive dismissal of the critic; "My beliefs don't require them to." Of course, there may be a more modest way of understanding Morpheus given that his unshakable faith in the One is able to be demonstrated by Neo's spectacular performance in the final action scene of *The Matrix*. Moreover, the fact that he gives the evangelized a *choice* does at least mitigate the sense of imposing confessional power. On the other hand, that someone so utterly convinced of his message as Morpheus is, firstly, accompanied by a small group of believers (strength of conviction "by numbers"); who, secondly, offers an alternative to someone increasingly disillusioned with "reality experienced" (which proves, in the end, to be the Matrix); but who, thirdly, rhetorically weights the offer of the choice, is already exerting a significant presence of power. So when he claims that "All I'm offering is the truth, nothing more," unless one contests the perspective, the choice is distinctly weighted—who wants to deliberately choose a "lie" instead? (Cypher is not a counter-example to this since it is precisely from a perspective of "knowledge" that he chooses to return to ignorance—for him, the "truth" is not all it should or could be.)

It is nonetheless important to see Felluga's intertextual contestation of such a reading at this point since it might provoke a reading that is more hesitant over making grand accusations of metaphysical essentialism. Firstly, he observes that the Wachowskis situate Morpheus' revelation to Neo in "the construct" rather than in the ruins of the "real world." Yet this could be explained as a device for breaking Neo in more gently, visually displaying the artificiality of the Matrix as a simulated environment populated by digitalized selves. Secondly, and more interestingly, Felluga notes that the Babylonian king Nebuchadnezzar, after whom Morpheus' ship is named, had troubling dreams. Thirdly, Morpheus' name itself derives from the god of dreams and a master of counterfeiting humans in Greek mythology. "The heroes of the real in the film," Felluga maintains, "are thus made ambivalent, suggesting that all may not be right with the (real) world."[28] These ambiguities are too little and underdeveloped, however, and are further suppressed by the overwhelming sense of "the real world" that the movie provides. Arguably, that is intensified in the sequels, particularly the third installment which largely descends into a simplistic science fiction war movie. Despite Felluga's hope that "the Wachowskis leave open … [the] disturbing possibility for the next two installments of *The Matrix* saga … [that] there is no way for the human rebels to be sure that their entire rebellion is not itself being generated by a yet more sophisticated Matrix," the way the third movie in the trilogy's sequence does indeed realize the possibility is in a quite different manner—not the inescapability of hyperreality, but rather ideology as false consciousness underlying which remains the real that the audience is, with a God's eye, invited to observe.

BECOMING SOMEONE IN MEDIATED SPACE

It has been suggested above that *The Matrix* assumes a stable notion of the subject's identifiability and materiality. In this connection it offers a marked differentiation between real self and mediated self that expresses the individuation of late modern models of freedom. It is instructive here to observe first the attractiveness of the cyber-self, and secondly the consumptive instantaneity, both of which arise from culturally idealized patterns of the formation of subjectivity.

Early in his dealings with Neo, Morpheus taps into his generalized but ill-formed sense of dissatisfaction by admitting that "there's something wrong with the world." The 1999 movie belongs to a late twentieth century cultural mood of anxiety over the frustrating conditions experienced within the context of personally unsatisfying and monotonously unstimulating work. These conditions for Thomas Anderson involve a form of dehumanizing corporate conformism and the routinization of working life by day. He works in a sterile office cubicle environment designed in a symmetrical fashion, equally suggesting heavy management, for the software company Metacortex Corporation. The attendant feeling of isolation and alienation is suggested by the space of the working conditions, and he is forced to seek meaningful or authentic exchange at the subcultural level in the form of a consoling anti-authoritarian hacking by night. The movie taps here into concerns with the superficial culture in late modernity, operating from the suggestion that there must be more to life than this, and with paranoia over increasing surveillance technologies pervading everyday life. (The ocular corporate name of Meta*cortex* Corporation suggests the mediating of perspective and of the surveillance of those whose reality is mediated.)[29] As the movie cleverly comes to reveal, a compliant workforce in the Matrix that is dependent upon a docile and slumbering population is literally the source of the machines' system's power. Consequently Morpheus speaks in terms of bondage and liberation, revealing to Neo that the Matrix is "a prison for your mind" and that in the Matrix "you are a slave." However, in this context, then, it would appear that Neo's problem is largely the late modern one of simple boredom, and the consequent desire is to be able to escape from the mundane conditions of his stultifying working life. The fact that Cypher later reduces his frustrations with "the real" to terms of it being less pleasurable than the Matrix may well support such a reading.

It is difficult to overcome the sense that Neo's life of dissatisfaction and disappointment is validated only by the violent turn in his aggressive *resentment* against authority and the projected desire to become an autonomous agent and take control of his life. When Agent Smith announces, "You have a problem with authority, Mr. Anderson," Neo suggestively admits, "I don't like the thought that I'm not in control of my life." The ontological assumptions in this statement are significant, and are echoed in Neo's reiterated use of language of personal "choice" to the Marovingian, and of the humans' "control" of machinery to the Council Elder in *The Matrix Reloaded* (on both occasions he is somewhat sarcastically brought up short by his interlocutor). In fact, it would seem, with a speech of Neo the first movie in the trilogy ends with what looks like a claim about being liberated but, in fact, it appeals instead to the most privileged values of a late modern society. As Conrad observes, in this vein the first movie in the trilogy abandons "any notion of transcendence and any concept of the a priori and is thus contrary to the spirit of Cartesian or Platonic metaphysics and epistemology."[30] Neo concludes the movie by asserting: "I know that you're afraid … afraid of us. You're afraid of change…. I'm going to hang up this phone, and then show these people what you don't want them to see. I'm going to show them a world without you. A world without rules or controls, borders or boundaries. A world where anything is possible. Where we go from there is a choice I leave to you." In this context Neo's concluding promise of revealing "a world … without rules or controls, without borders or boundaries, a world where anything is possible" is especially appealing to a late modern society in which many suffer from wearisome boredom of the tedium and therefore from dissatisfaction and unease with their lot. This is a significant revelation of the movie's underlying socio-political philosophy, a suggestion of self-possessive and indeterministic subjectivity. For Booker, not only does this involve a significant cultural cliché but its commended individuation of human subjectivity and agency itself can offer no real resistance to capitalism, and therefore at its best sustains it.[31] "[F]ar from touting socialism as an alternative to capitalism, *The Matrix* advocates individualism, failing to see that it thereby endorses one of the principal tenets of capitalist ideology, thus reinforcing the very system it seems to want to criticize."[32] On the one hand, the system is self-perpetuating, a carefully constructed way of keeping human beings in their slumbers, and that consoling slumber is the product of mediating human identities conducive of their being productive (producing energy for the machines). Yet, the notion that it is capitalism that generates the consumptive subjectivity is conspicuously understated in the narrative. Gregory Grieve, for instance, maintains insightfully that "all that is left is the lone reified individual—no longer trapped in Weber's iron cage, but quagmire in an infinite swamp of convenient but empty commodities, all available at the click of a mouse."[33]

Echoing Adorno's theses on the culture industry, Melzer argues that this means that *The Matrix* belongs firmly in "the Hollywood tradition of appropriating subversive cultural elements and absorbing them into the liberal, profit-oriented industry."[34]

In this regard, the pressure of cultural immediacy and the consumerist intensity of the moment shapes the processes of "learning" that are integral to the Zionists' ability to survive on re-entry into the Matrix. In an instant, knowledge of weaponry and helicopter flight controls are "downloaded" into the digital avatars who are preparing to enter the simulated world to rescue Morpheus from Agent Smith and his two compatriots. Without the pain of patient endurance, and even simply the pain resulting from the effort required, Neo and his companions are thereby able to master martial arts and any other feature of human culture in a matter of seconds. (Following the operator's downloading of a martial arts program into Neo's cortex, Neo announces, "I know kung fu.") Of course, this is possible only in their avatarial existence in the digital projection, but nonetheless, the cultural desire for instantaneity (provided by the speed of access to information in cyberspace) becomes the longing of the movie at this point. In fact, one can connect this to the fascination with the body of the virtual projection itself. According to Cynthia Freeland, "*The Matrix* creates a naive fantasy of overcoming human flesh."[35] This reading might appear to be subverted by the materiality of "the real" as the staging point for identity *apart from* the bio-transcendence available to existence in the Matrix.[36] After all, those who are liberated from the digital prison have consciousness and corporeal existence reconciled. On the other hand, in many ways the enhanced capabilities available to the digital self provide a considerably more authentic indication of the movies' abiding aesthetic interests. To cite Freeland again, "the hero moves from being 'penetrated' and connected to others to being self-controlling and intact—even immune to bullets."[37] In that regard, she continues, "*The Matrix* reveals an adolescent fear of the body as something that can veer out of control (something true of a real, changing, flesh-and-blood body). This fantasy suits geeky young males who yearn for autonomy and mental powers." For Freeland, in contrast, David Cronenberg's movie of bio-technology is more committed to the vulnerability of embodiedness, to its sheer visceralness with all its messiness and sensuality. In fact, she argues, the movie celebrates the eroticism of bodies, a feature played out through frequent images of penetration. *The Matrix Revolutions* intensifies this supercharged bodily identity with Neo's capabilities in "the real" coming to echo those of the One inside the digital program.

The Matrix might appear to depict bodied materiality in particularly positive terms given the desire to escape from the prison of the Matrix into the real. But the desert is deserted of many redeeming qualities. Authentic existence for those who are "free" takes on a particular visual hue (and by this I do not merely mean the sharper differentiation of color from the green tonality of the Matrix), expressing a further form of the mundane for which the moments of engagement within the Matrix appear to be a welcome relief. This time the mundane takes the form of unappetizing cuisine, ragged clothing, the impoverishment of the aesthetic forms, and the continual fight for what seems to be the barest forms of life as survival during severe military conflict. In this regard jacking into the Matrix offers not only the viewer respite from these constraints but disrupts the liberationist ideology by offering the cyber-self as an *alluring* expression of selfhood in considerably more interesting ways. The gaze distraction provided by the design of the woman in the red dress, for instance, is an illustration of the possibilities for constructing and managing a more enthralling and gaze-focusing environment. A comparison of this with *Elysium* or *Wall-E*, for instance, serves to illustrate the point by recognizing a commonplace aesthetic contrast that defines the narrative's thematic. The contrast is marked between the earthly dilapidation and the glamorous and sedate conditions of life on the space station/craft. *In Time*, on the other hand, provides a broadly similar contrast only this time with the self-segregated and self-protectively gated rich occupying the same planetary space as the working poor. With *Blade Runner* the off-world colonies (presumably populated by rich *whites*)[38] are never utopianly visualized, but the aesthetic design of the polluted and decaying city, identified as Los Angeles, is rich for the movie's visual metaphorics. Whereas George Lucas' *THX 1138* stylistically echoes Stanley Kubrick's masterpiece *2001: A Space Odyssey* by utilizing intense light and severely clean and white spaces to depict the sterility of a system that dehumanizes, Ridley Scott returns to the darkened settings that so effectively managed the dread-inducing atmosphere of the Nostromo in *Alien*. With the Los Angeles of *Blade Runner*'s 2019 it is difficult to know whether it is day- or night-time since all is dark, one long night. In the opening scene flames burst into the air from towering stacks, a visual reference to a hellish environment, and perhaps another allusion to a Holocaust scenario of dehumanization.

The mood, as well as the dystopian conception of the setting, is darkened by dismally unremitting rain and perennial absence of sunshine, which, given that this is Los Angeles, itself suggests something is wrong with the ecosphere. These visual elements are "constant reminders of a planet out of balance."[39] However, by refusing to envisage the alternative abodes of the wealthy the movie refuses to offer a consoling escapism, whether in terms of the central protagonists in *The Island* literally sailing away from the cities that would constrain them, or in terms of *Elysium*'s ability to imagine the collapse of the controlling system. To return to *The Matrix*, while the directors provide numerous visual clues as to the system of the Matrix being a distorting dystopian space (for instance, through the off-kilter hue and the dilapidated environment the resistance group utilizes for offering the emancipatory choice), certain critics still complain that "reality" is considerably less interesting and attractive than the relish taken in the aesthetic excesses of the Matrix (as fetishized space). Gilmore, for instance, argues that "if part of what haunts Neo is the thinness of the world of hypermarkets, that message is complicated by the glamor of life for the heroes within the Matrix as compared with life outside the Matrix."[40] Gilmore continues, "The movie cannot be about how superficial cool clothes are because cool clothes are so clearly glamorized in the movie." In this regard, *The Matrix* is pervaded by the ambiguity that allows not only for the liberating escape from the system but the seductive possibility of the digital self as enabling an escape from the unattractively mundane.

This criticism is somewhat exaggerated, at least at a conceptual level, given the function that Cypher plays. The movie itself is well aware of the problem caused by the gap between the digitally simulated world of the Matrix and an identified "real world." Accordingly, it depicts Cypher's lethal betrayal of his friends in order to escape reality for a more palatable dose of life in the Matrix. Of course, Cypher is described in an unappealing form as a character for whom the audience will find it difficult to sympathize—but the reason for this has less to do with his desire for escape from the banality and drudgery of everyday life (which, after all, is what consumer culture depends upon and reinforces), however, than for the lack of moral qualities given the purely *hedonistic* form of his desires. Such a hedonistic perspective is often set in movies in characteristically sharp relief with the privileging of more responsible relations and friendships with others. This is the nature of the Han Solo portrayal in *SW*'s *ANH*, for instance. George Lucas, as much as Larry and Andy Wachowski, suggests that a certain form of hedonism is not only morally irresponsible but is what it is precisely because it is evacuated of meaningful human contact and is therefore, *The Matrix* would advocate, an illusory happiness. Both *The Matrix Reloaded* and *The Matrix Revolutions*, in fact, develop the sense of intensive relationality in the desire of One for Another. The Neo and Trinity relation of mutual care functions as a type of all the interconnections suggested by the erotically charged, and equally hedonistic, moment of Temple frenzy that has echoes of the religious passion of Dionysian exuberance. A different critical take on contested capitalist hedonism appears, of course, in David Fincher's *Se7en*, with "John Doe" contesting it not so much from a perspective of its isolating human beings from meaningful relations as from a perceived performance of the seven deadly sins.

The point that a Cypher-character can raise, if nothing else, is that illusions are indeed attractive and that it is their appealing form that continues to sustain them. They appeal to desires for consolation, for security, and for power. As the titular V from the Wachowski's adaptation of Alan Moore's critically acclaimed graphic novel *V for Vendetta* reveals to his television audience when lamenting the state of totalitarian England (it is not clear what has become of the Union) under High Chancellor Adam Sutler:

> there is something terribly wrong with this country.... But, again, truth be told, if you are looking for the guilty, you need only look into a mirror. I know why you did it. I know you were afraid. Who wouldn't be? War, terror, disease, there were a myriad of problems which conspired to corrupt your reason and rob you of your commonsense. Fear got the best of you, and in your panic you turned to the now High Chancellor Adam Sutler.

V's effort is to unmask what has since become a naturalized way of governance and socio-political life within the undemocratic nation-state. This is to strip away the mask of the illusion, and presumably expose the country again to the wounds that led to the landslide electoral victory for Sutler in the first place. (As it transpires, unlike in Moore's version of the story, the V of the Wachowskis is aided in this regard by exposing Sutler's involvement in events—the disaster of the "St. Mary's virus"—not unlike the National Socialist disturbances of the peace which enabled the party to sweep into power with the promise of providing a strong government that would deal with the social unrest, among other things.) On the other hand, and this is a crucial difficulty, it is awkward to avoid the implications involved in recognizing that *The Matrix* spends so much time lavishing its visual love on the environment of the Matrix that it renders reality too uninteresting to even sustain the argument that "it is real, it is not an illusion." The "physical" possibilities for the self-aware in the simulated environment are so attractively portrayed that the Matrix itself can become a fixating space and the real is evacuated of lasting significance. As mentioned earlier, one of the training exercises even comes complete with the fetishized object of the eye-catching out-of-place woman in the red dress. So Freeland claims that "the movie celebrates not freedom from the matrix, but the indulgence in exciting film simulations."[41] Likewise, Dawson argues that "*The Matrix* is arguably a critique of the image-saturated postmodern world where the 'real' has lost all meaning.... In the 'real' world, characters wear shapeless grey jumpers and outfits, with the clothes appearing entirely functional and without fashion." Dawson continues by contrasting this situation with that of the world of the Matrix: "This world is without the image-consciousness of the postmodern matrix. However, one of the [many] ironies of the film is that whilst the destruction of the matrix will lead to freedom and a permanent state of the 'real'..., the vast majority of the pleasure for the audience is in witnessing events within the witness itself. It is there that the excess—from the bullet time photography to the leather-clad Trinity—can be exploited and where the 'cool' look of the film is set."[42]

In order to offset some of those concerns, *The Matrix Reloaded*'s scene of erotic festivity, aligned with an intercut depiction of the sensual connection of Neo and Trinity, suggests the satisfying of the operations of desire even in "the desert of the real." "This is apparently supposed to suggest the primal 'authenticity' of these humans, in contrast to the repressed, passionless uniformity of machine-agents like Smith."[43] In fact, the way the relational responsibility operates through even the stabilized forms of material subjectivity in *The Matrix* at least allows for the possibility of a politics that is circumvented by the kind of Romantic escapology that one finds in *The Truman Show* or in *Dark City*.

Dark City opens with John Murdoch awakening in a hotel bathtub with no memory of how he arrived there. There are few clues in the room to help solve the mystery—an odd medical instrument, the dead body of a woman, and newspaper clippings in his overcoat pocket detailing the murders of several prostitutes. None of these make any sense either to him or to the audience, and only as the film-noir style movie

unfolds does the audience's understanding of what has occurred progress. The climax does offer a catharsis of double resolution: the revelation of the experiment that has been taking place all along that constrains
and shapes the lives of all those present in the city; and the escape to
Shell Beach from where Murdoch can begin to woo his love, now devoid
of memory of him and their time together. In this regard, then, the
movie parallels the reality description of *The Matrix*, and its use of "the
other" as threat. It is suggestive of the *Dark City*'s sensibility that its "others" are named "the Strangers." Politically, though, even more than *The
Matrix*, Proyas' piece operates on the level of a nihilistic constraining of
the imagination dystopian, an anti-utopia, within which a resistant solution is largely the fruit of a form of escape. According to Peter Fitting,
therefore, this movie serves to "reflect the confusion and helplessness
of people frustrated and discouraged with the political system today. In
the film ... the only way offered out of this gloomy prison is strictly an
individual one, as Murdoch sets out to create the Shell Beach of his memories."[44] The audience is left without any sense of what will happen to the
others or whether Murdoch will find solace in "his own solipsistic utopia."

On saying that, however, *The Matrix Revolutions* takes a distinctive
nihilistic turn with the revelation of Neo's identity and the necessity of
the conflictual circle, with only the One's intensive relational commitment only momentarily breaking the causal determination. The Marovingian's pompously delivered exposition of the necessity of cause and
effect in *The Matrix Reloaded* comes to appear well substantiated by the
revelations of the relationship of Zion and the Matrix system in *The
Matrix Revolutions*—Neo's late modern assertion of freedom of *choice*,
which already sounded hollow at the time of its delivery, is unmasked
as being itself a conformity-making delusion of the controlling system.
As the Architect claims in *The Matrix Reloaded*, the sixth version of the
One is distinguishable from its predecessors only because of the specific
attachment he has developed. Yet, even this commitment to Trinity is
curtailed by his beloved's death. In the end, there appears to be nothing
outside of the system, not because the simulations go all the way down
but because the conflictuality demands a balance of forces. Commenting
on the irony involved in the title *The Matrix Revolutions* ("is there such
a thing as revolution within a pre-programmed system?"), Catherine
Constable speaks of "revolution as an endless, revolving cycle.... The
One is not free to do whatever he chooses. Neo's actions result in the
fulfilment of the function of the One in that they serve to regenerate the

system."[45] It would seem, then, that the only possibility of any kind of freedom beyond the system's control is the hiding that is opted for by several programs.

While offering a partial echo, there is considerably less noetic and moral resolution in the little known movie *Cube*, and the possibilities of a nihilistic reading offer themselves even more obviously. Drawing on the theme of sleep and consciousness prominent in the dystopian movies *The Matrix* and *Dark City*, six people awaken to find themselves trapped in a strange prison but without any knowledge of how they arrived there. Thus it echoes *Dark City* and contravenes the waking moment in *The Matrix* for which the arousing into consciousness signals the emancipation of the subject. The prison in *Cube* is geometrically designed like something that might come from the imagination of Escher, a maze of seemingly endless and interlocking cubic chambers. However, many of the rooms are fitted with sensors integrated into the walls that set off destructive booby traps that kill in the most gruesome of ways, ways that reflect many of the torture-porn elements that characterize the brutal imagery of the *Saw* series and *Hostel*. There are various interpretations of what is going on. An early suspicion offered by Helen Holloway, one of the older of the two female protagonists, is that it is the work of the government. She later claims that "only the military industrial complex is rich enough" to stage such an experiment. But these suggestions are immediately shot down by one of the other characters, Quentin, a man who identifies himself as a policeman. He argues that it is too complex and big to be a government product. On the other hand, he does not want to speculate on the construction as being the work of aliens either: "You can't see the big picture from in here." His own theory articulated later is that it is the work of a superrich James Bond–type villain who has created his own psychopathic form of entertainment. While the group suffers mutual suspicion even in the act of negotiating the cubic environment together, it becomes clear that each of the prisoners has something to contribute to solving the terrifying puzzle of their current incarceration facility and aid in their escape—a prison escapologist, a policeman, a medical doctor, and a high school maths genius—which seems to suggest that the selection of imprisoned personnel was not random, and that there is some purposefulness in the events. One of the prisoners, David Worth, is revealed to have been "contracted to design a hollow shell of a cube," even though he was unable to specify who was responsible for the project since contractors had been hired independently to work on only small parts of the cube. "This may be hard for you to understand, but there is no conspiracy. Nobody is in charge. It's a headless blunder operating under the illusion of a masterplan.... Big brother is not watching you.... I looked, and the only conclusion I could come to is that there is nobody up there." As he comes to ask, "Do you think anybody wants to ask questions? All they want is a clear conscience and a fat paycheck." The problem is that as the questions pile up, so too do the difficulties in providing any concrete answers. What emerges is an ominous reality that emerges from a confused postmodernity, a culture suffering from bewilderment and a sense of purposelessness to the point of nihilism other than a simple will to live, but that fears the claustrophobia of being trapped in the constructions of others.[46] Holloway appeals to the group's humanity in order not to leave Kazam behind: "we're still human beings. That's all we've got left." And yet the term "pointless" is used several times with regard to the cubic complex and their presence in it, and very soon Quentin turns murderously against the others.

The One and the Many

Power is equally mediated in the way that the One is construed in the first of the *Matrix* trilogy, according to a number of critical readers. Andrew Gordon, for instance, suggests that the movie circumvents possibilities for political agency since it necessitates the *deus ex machina*, a messianic savior.[47] It is not insignificant, then, that the movie ends with Neo rocketing into the sky in a moment reminiscent of a Superman configuration of his newfound power. Anna Dawson, noting the Wachowskis' professional origins as comic book writers, explains that "Neo is a glamorised 'hacker' come saviour rather than computer nerd, in a sense a superhero in the making, as powerful as Spider- or Superman blended with the spiritual angst of Luke Skywalker."[48] And in this Neo is unique in the narrative, "the Chosen One" as Morpheus continues to believe even in the teeth of multiple appearances to the contrary. According to Booker, "even within the Matrix it is only Neo who seems to have unlimited freedom from boundaries and restraints. He cannot serve as a model of liberation for others because, as the One, he is literally one of a kind whose example cannot be duplicated."[49] However, Booker's claim is considerably less effective as a critical argument than Gordon's. The former's argument would not make sense of the *moral* exemplarism that the superhero mythology would suggest is appropriate. After all, *The Dark Knight* speaks about the Batman as the symbol Gotham City deserves, and while he himself complains of copy-cats wearing "hockey-pads" he pushes Harvey Dent as the symbol Gotham needs. Moreover, it is at least arguable that while Neo is the central and super- (or rather hyper-) powered protagonist, there is no circumvention of his dependence on his friends, at least in the environment of "the real," and these themselves have thematically political potential if pressed in ways that depict the self, life, and agency as a performance of the mutuality and interdependence. Gordon's criticism, instead, is that there is no significant and lasting challenge to the simulated system of the Matrix until Neo's arrival, and this messianic *adventus* renders viewers expectant and therefore politically passive. Neo stands as agent in their place.

Crucially then, *The Matrix* trilogy depends upon a sense of what might be called "the grand men of history," that history is written as the story not of complex movements of persons and events, but of significant actors lying behind the grandly narratable events in a Hegelian fashion. This dystopian type also includes movies such as *Equilibrium* and *V for Vendetta*, even the series of *Terminator* movies, the *SW* saga (with its Sith puppet master manipulator, Darth Sidious), and *Tron Legacy* (with its megalomaniac C.L.U.). Alex Royas' *Dark City*, less politically colonialistically, portrays the city's manipulators as performing a social experiment. As Morpheus informs Neo in one of the most significant ideologically demystifying moments of the Wachowskis trilogy, "the Matrix is the world that has been pulled over your eyes to blind you to the truth that you are a slave, Neo. Like everyone else you were born into bondage, born into a prison that you cannot smell, or taste, or touch. A prison for your mind." In this regard, its form of dystopianism echoes that of the Owellian manipulations by the grand imperialists, although in Orwell's text it is not clear whether there is truly anyone who transcends the system and therefore is not dehumanized by it (this is likewise the case with Lucas' *THX 1138*).

A quite different sense is provided by Terry Gilliam's *12 Monkeys*. In this post-apocalyptic movie in 2035 there are still masters and slaves, the latter being the various prisoners sent out from the subterranean city on reconnaissance trips to a surface contaminated by a deadly virus, and into the past to gather information on the origins of the virus that destroys five billion people in 1996. Yet the "masters" are equally marked out as victims, having to cower in their underground facilities in order

not to become exposed to the contagion, always hopeful that the reconnaissance ventures will yield healing information, and at the mercy of
those "volunteers" finding something effectively illuminating. They are
far from being in control in any meaningful sense, at least in the sense
that there are controlling masters in the dystopian type discussed above.
As the movie progresses, its constant appeal to the finest of lines that
sits between sanity and insanity is intensified in a way that makes the
movie not so much a narratable science-fiction time-loop enterprise
(and, indeed, paradox)[50] as a tragic drama with a vicious circle of causal-
ity—the very event of sending James Cole back through time to gather
information on "the Army of the Twelve Monkeys," assumed to be responsible for unleashing a catastrophic viral weapon, contributes to the apocalyptic scenario.

The movie *12 Monkeys*, then, appeals to the type of tragic settings
that numerous science-fiction movies develop, in which unwitting complicity in one's own demise is the driving motif of the narrative. With
the second incarnation of *Battlestar Galactica*, and *Blade Runner*, in a
Frankenstein moment, the created product unleashes destructive vengeance on its creator. Technology uncontrollably runs away from its creators in an act of rebellion. This theme also shapes the *Terminator* movies,
with the presence of the arm and micro-processor of the Terminator
from the future advancing the very science that comes to create it. The
apocalyptic scenario of *Terminator 2: Judgment Day* can be halted only
by curbing the scientific discovery that leads to the very creation of
Cyberdyne's Skynet Defense System. Sarah Connor hunts down Dr.
Miles Dyson, and in a pre-emptive strike attempts to execute him in
order to make a new future, a future without the war, the nuclear holocaust, and the Terminators. Of course, despite the "resolution" involved
in the movie's climax, Hollywood's financial demands exploit the paradox of time travel in order to continue the series with *Terminator 3: The
Rise of the Machines*. Yet while the third movie in the series is narratively
the weakest of the franchise it nevertheless provides a particularly powerful tragic climax, and one of the most striking in recent science fiction
film, with the commencement of Judgment Day's nuclear holocaust.

THERE IS NO SPOON: *THE MATRIX* AND "THE RETURN OF RELIGION"

Andy and Larry Wachowski's *The Matrix*, according to Gregory
Watkins, "has sparked more discussion of its religious significance than

any other film, with the possible exception of Mel Gibson's *The Passion of the Christ*.[51] Yet while talk of Neo in messianic terms as "the One" is but one instance of religious reference spotting, the trans-textuality reveals a simulation reality involving forms of descriptive power with regard to religious discourse. Unfortunately, to date all too few commentators have pressed the cultural ideology that pervades this movie's plurality of religious allusion, however, and therefore there has been something of a paucity of critical effort in identifying *The Matrix*'s underlying ideological assumptions.

According to Mark Rose, "it is because the content of the genre is a displacement of religion that science-fiction stories are often concerned to disassociate themselves from religion by characterizing it as the ignorant or feeble opposite of science."[52] So, with an allusion to the Scopes "Monkey" Trial of 1925, the religious zealots of *Planet of the Apes* are designed to be concerned less with truth and the integrity of truthful inquiry than with political power, and they are consequently depicted as irrationally antagonistic to scientific knowledge. *The Matrix*, on the one hand, simply refuses to dismissively stare away from the culturally significant presence of religious traditions. In that regard Morpheus' response to "No, everyone believes what you believe" [*The Matrix Reloaded*] is as timely as Darth Vader's "I find your lack of faith disturbing" a little over 20 years earlier. In doing this it is quite unlike Peter Jackson's *Lord of the Rings* which evacuates Tolkien's source text of its pervasive sacramental imagery. Similarly it does not mock religion as an archaic form of knowing displaced by good science. *The Matrix*'s faith leans towards Morpheus rather than Commander Lock, towards Vader rather than Motti, Mulder rather than Scully, Harry Potter rather than Vernon Dursley.

The movie specifically utilizes a range of forms for religious representation, including a semantic technique of allusive naming.[53] From speaking messianically of Thomas Anderson as "the One," and its apocalyptic re-reordering as "Neo" (suggesting the *novum* as well as simply providing an anagram of "One"), through to his name Anderson which is suggestive of "son of man" (*Ander* coming from the Greek *andre* for man), Christological imagery is visible and even intensified by his being "raised" from the dead, and the exclamatory moment of gratitude when Choi refers to Neo as "Savior, … my own personal Jesus Christ!" Brent Plate, consequently, proclaims that "The Christic-redemptive dimensions are fairly obvious to anyone who has grown up in Western, Christian cultures."[54] There is equally a new birth scene, with the womb within which Neo had been grown giving up its occupant with a rush of amniotic fluid and the slippage down the birth canal. Moreover, Morpheus (whose own name is taken from the Greek mythological god of dreams) is depicted as a John the Baptist–like figure, awaiting and heralding the coming of "the One." Cypher is portrayed instead as Judas-like; Trinity is used as a name for one of the principal characters, Nebuchadnezzar for a craft, and Zion for the last and liberated urban space. Commenting on the fact that the movie was released on the last Easter weekend of the twentieth century, Read Mercer Schuchardt announces that "it is a parable of the original Judeo-Christian worldview of entrapment in a world gone wrong, with no hope of survival or salvation short of something miraculous."[55] Verging on the problematic homiletics of numerous books written on *SW*, Schuchardt enthuses that the movie "is a new testament for a new millennium, a religious parable of the second coming of mankind's messiah in an age that needs salvation as desperately as any ever has."[56] Leaving aside the glib association of *The Matrix*, with its violent apocalyptic display of violence against a clearly defined "other," with "the original Judeo-Christian worldview," the ill-defined association of Judaism and Christianity, and the assumption of early Christianity as having something as static as a "worldview," there is something more startling about Schuchardt's claim in relation to *The Matrix*: he simply displaces the vast array of religious references with these claims, even though he does come to acknowledge their presence later in his chapter. After all, salvation involves a *gnosis* or secret knowledge offered by the teacher in-the-know, and equally an escape from the enslaving confines of the Matrix. Finally, enlightenment is a key theme, and a child garbed in Buddhist monastic clothing makes judgments about the nature of perception.[57]

The way the religious themes pervade the piece, then, suggests that *The Matrix* is a polysemous text comprised of an *untheorized pastiche* of Christian, Jewish, Buddhist motifs and ideas, with a touch of Gnosticism.[58] In fact, for Gregory Grieve, the movie "is less about epistemological or ontological questions [investigation into 'what is really real'] and more about spiritual emancipation."[59] The vital question has to do with what kind of emancipation.

One approach taken by various commentators regards it as a mistake to search for a meaningful pattern or spiritual coherence, a theological design in the piece. In this regard, Paul Fontana's talk of "the

theology of *The Matrix*" comes to look distinctly naïve in its system-
atizing rhetoric and its problematic flattening of the imagistic multiplicity.[60] According to Gregory Bassham, "More likely they [viz., the
directors] simply wanted to make a kick-ass intellectual action movie
that features some interesting and relevant myths."[61] This might suggest
that there is little that is worthy of note in *The Matrix*'s vacuous religious
allusions, but that would be an equally superficial reading of the movie.
The emancipation, in this instance, would be from having to penetrate
too deeply into the simulated religiosities. Booker's perspective, however,
regards the religious referentiality as something of window dressing:

> Neo, though, is a rather problematic savior. For one thing, there is a cer-
> tain amount of self-conscious irony to his depiction as a Christ figure,
> which is, after all, by this time a sort of science fiction cliché that recalls
> predecessors from Klaatu of *The Day the Earth Stood Still* to *E.T.* Indeed,
> *The Matrix* shows an awareness of the glib and superficial way in which
> our culture often makes use of Christ metaphors…. From this point of
> view, the link between Neo and Christ might be seen more as a postmod-
> ern pastiche of Christ imagery than as a genuine parallel, meant to be
> taken seriously. Meanwhile, as opposed to the peaceful Christ, Neo is a
> virtual killing machine, blasting his way through the Matrix and leaving
> a trail of bodies in his wake—most of them law enforcement officers.
> Many critics, in fact, have criticized *The Matrix* for using its spiritual and
> religious references in a mere attempt to make its cartoonish violence
> seem more acceptable.[62]

On the other hand, according to the directors themselves, the movie
is about "mythology, theology, and to a lesser extent, higher-level math-
ematics…. All are ways human beings try to answer bigger questions,
as well as the Big Question."[63] Bassham does in fact proceed in a less dis-
missive fashion by making a good case that the movie's resultant pluralism is not a deep one, a philosophically developed commitment to a
principled pluralism. It has not been carefully thought through with any
theological sophistication. Indeed, the thinness of the theorizing is suggested by a comment of Larry Wachowski when referring to the movies'
theoretical design in *quantitative* terms: "Our goal with *The Matrix* was
to make an intellectual action movie. We like action movies, guns and
kung fu, but we're tired of assembly-line action movies that are devoid
of any intellectual content. We were determined to put as many ideas
into the movie as we could."[64] It is precisely this unformed plethorization
of motifs and references that Bassham observes as permeating the appeal
to the religious themes in the movie. He consequently argues that *The*

Matrix displays what amounts to little more than a "cafeteria pluralism": "the view that religious truth can be found by picking and choosing beliefs from many different religious traditions.... It is the religion of the new-age seeker, often attractive to those who thirst for the spiritual yet who are uncomfortable with the religion of their upbringing."[65] In fact, this might be suggested further by the notion that the Matrix offers only appearance, while the real underlies and deconstructs this—this is a motif that post–Kantian pluralists like John Hick have long appealed to in order to commend an essential core of the Real beyond the fractured religious appearance. Certainly, many readers of the movie remain tangled in this decontexted hermeneutical essentialism, such as James Ford when he argues that "mixing metaphors from Christianity, Buddhism, Greek mythology, and even cyber technology, *The Matrix* offers a mythological account of the human existential condition."[66] This aptly fits with a reading of *The Matrix* as essentially commandeering ideas in an ahistorical or acontextual fashion within a framework determined by constructivistic consumerism. To cite Grieve's suggestion of the movie's assumption of late modern spiritual conditions, "since all systems are ideological cages, one cannot change the cage, and one can therefore spiritually develop only oneself."[67]

When the child garbed in the style of a Buddhist monk instructs Neo on the need to re-perceive, or on the need for penetrating beyond sensory impressions, he reveals that "there is no spoon." Neo's concentrated gaze then perceive the utensil display a sudden liquidity of form. In the format of its fluid religious referencing, *The Matrix* comes to suggest that there is no religious Truth other than the gaze which can perceive a religious liquidity, the fluidity of a religious hybridity that lies beyond the phenomenological form of religious claims (it is re-perceived as plural and liquid to the spectator's gaze). Exhibiting such a *bricolage* of allusions as it does, *The Matrix*'s religious references are attributable, then, to a pastiche which expresses a pop spirituality characterized by an eclecticism that is well suited for consumer culture with its ideologically constructivist account of the self.

It would be only a weak form of analysis that would link the pluralistic trajectory up with Joseph Campbell's "monomyth," however, and yet precisely this conceptual move occurs in a paper by James McGrath. McGrath attempts to diffuse Bassham's criticism that the pluralism is incoherent, and he does at least have a point when arguing that "to focus on the philosophical coherence of religious pluralism is to miss the genius of the achievement of *The Matrix* and sequels."[68] His means for responding to Bassham's criticism is to appeal to the parallel influence of Campbell's use of Jungian archetypes on George Lucas' *SW*, and claiming that the Wachowski brothers were similarly engaging in developing motifs and characteristics from older stories. If by this McGrath means that their movie demonstrates the eclecticism of a pastiche then this is uncontroversial—as mentioned above, the syncretistic reference to elements of Lewis Carroll, *The Wizard of Oz*, Buddhism, Christianity, Jean Baudrillard, Plato, Descartes, and so on has been much commented on. However, the reference to Campbell suggests he wants to say something more substantial, that *The Matrix* involves an application of "ideas of universals in world religions" (McGrath uses language of "timeless issues") that is believable precisely because it takes place within a virtual world in which nothing is real but "everything can be real."[69] McGrath's assessment, however, misses the point of the Wachowski's cultural escapology—the movie expresses cultural dissatisfaction with forms of authority, including religious traditions, and adopts the kind of eclectic approach to religious themes that is bound up with a philosophy of individuation and that therefore appeals to post–70s constructivist spiritual expressivisms. In fact, as James Ford argues, the very values it inscribes through its violent performance are distinctly contrary in spirit to the religious traditions the movie references.[70] It is, and remains, theologically incoherent, but nonetheless distinctly culturally instructive.

THE WAR AGAINST THE MACHINES

Even though the text refuses to determine Otherness in terms of binaries configured around gender or ethnicity (Melzer, however, criticizes the trilogy as embodying a cyberpunk strategy which places "black bodies ... [in order to] lend 'authenticity' to resistance and otherness"),[71] it nevertheless executes a form of exclusivistically defining power by retaining a prominent form of "Othering" with regard to the machines. Several commentators have noticed that *The Matrix* trades on a clearly identifiable distinction between victim and victimizer, and a critical reading on behalf of the former entails that there is an extreme "othering" that goes on in the text, a form of Manichaeism that is projected onto "the machine." An example of this process is Morpheus' dogmatic explanation to Neo that "if you're not one of us you're one of them." While it is true that there are programs like The Key Maker that aid and abet the Zionists, these are themselves products of the machines rather than differentiating instances at the level of the ruling class of machines themselves.

This "us-versus-them" conflictual ontology has a number of implications. On the one hand, there are certain untempered technophobic suggestions in this configuration. If 1950s and 1960s cinema, television and comic books exhibited a fear of "the Other" that manifested itself in terms of the fear of catastrophic nuclear annihilation and of the threatening Soviet "other," the fear-inducing conditions have morphed in the years following the collapse of the Soviet Bloc into a multiplicity of apocalyptic scenarios. And yet anxieties over nuclear conflict have not dissipated. While it is not altogether clear how the imagined post-apocalyptic conditions were caused, the terrifyingly affecting filmic adaptation of Cormac McCarthy's novel *The Road* suggests that under post-apocalyptic conditions everyone becomes a threat to one's survival. The potential nihilism is only just about abated through the sheer commitment of the protective love for another (in this instance of the father for "the boy"), and by the boy's conscience which forces his father to act more responsibly than he might otherwise. Post-apocalyptic dramas like *The Road*, the television adaptation of the lengthy comic book series *The Walking Dead*, the considerably less poignant *The Book of Eli*, and the little known *Hell* of 2011, play on the horrific lengths people will go to simply to survive in conditions of scarcity (including cannibalism), with *The Road* in particular offering a "no holes barred" attempt at unglamorously imagining human instinct with brutal honesty. Fear in the dystopian imagination is not merely expressed in terms of mechanized technologies but also biological technologies, such as in *12 Monkeys*. *Outbreak* plays into anxieties concerning insecurity in the face of the creation of biological weapons; and the more recent remaking of *The Andromeda Strain*, as well as M. Night Shyamalan's *The Happening*, the little known British movie *Perfect Sense* (2011), *Carriers*, and better still *Contagion* exploit the ease of viral transmission, with the latter depending on the interactivity of global travel. (This global communication of a virus is exploited for dramatic effect too in *World War Z*.) *Children of Men* explores a bleak dystopian future in which the human race has lost the ability to conceive children. In the vein of the viral exposure movie come the zombie pieces *I Am Legend*, *28 Days Later*, *28 Weeks Later*, *The Invasion* (2007), *World War Z*, the comic Romeo and Juliet–themed *Warm Bodies*, and *The Walking Dead*. Of course, the effect is reversed in the considerably more utopian imagination of Steven Spielberg, with his rendering of *War of the Worlds* and the saving contagion that acts as an unexpected *deus ex machina.* Spielberg's movie oozes with 9/11 images (such as the alien other deeply buried within, Ray Ferrier working class hero, the failure of conventional war tactics, and so on) which lend its threat a particular resonance. These movies varyingly trade on fears over the fragility of social order or health, and the irreparable potential for the loss of meaning and enjoyment in a late capitalist society. The zombified terror is one of a pure reduction of meaning and subjective significance to the barest survivalist instinct, a descent beyond the social into the most bestial. *The Walking Dead,* for instance, makes it difficult to separate human meaning from the characters, now themselves driven by the desire to survive, from the survivalist instincts of the decaying flesh of "the walkers" around them. Social order, civility, neighborliness, whatever these terms mean, stand on the precipice and can under conditions of terror tip into the abyss. The apocalyptic *The Day After Tomorrow* takes a different tack, with the tragedy being the contribution of human agency to a catastrophic new ice-age through global warming. The disaster movie *Deep Impact* depicts the apocalypse-making event as the result of an unpreventable contingency, with no unrealistic resolving drive in the drama as with Bruce Willis' team in *Armageddon.* Continuing the natural disaster theme is Danny Boyle's moody and potentially stellar, but eventually confused, psychological study *Sunshine.* The background premise of Boyle's movie is that the sun is dying, and as a result a craft, somewhat cursed with the name Icarus 2, populated by eight astronauts has been sent to detonate a massive nuclear charge in the sun in order to "create a star within a star." *Deep Impact, The Core, Melancholia, Seeking a Friend for the End of the World, Wall-E* and *The Lorax,* and the more formulaic action-spectacle of *2012* are worth mentioning in this recent stable of disaster epics. The theme of ecological disaster is equally the premise for the action of *After Earth, Oblivion,* and to some extent *Blade Runner.* For Lucas' *THX 1138* there is no explanation of why it is that humanity now lives underground. As Slavoj Žižek argues, "A fear permeates our lives that this kind of disintegration of the entire social fabric can come at any time, that some natural or technological accident—whether earthquake or electricity failure or the hoary millennium bug—will reduce our world to a primitive wilderness."[72] Klaatu in the more recent version of *The Day the Earth Stood Still* announces that "your problem is not technology, it is you. You lack the will to change."

This admission of the scorched sky in *The Matrix* resulting from the conflictual conditions is, however, a setting for the drama rather than a focus for the movie's concern. Nonetheless, Agent Smith's monologue to Morpheus is suggestive of ecological awareness. "Every mammal on this planet develops a natural equilibrium with its surrounding environment. But you humans do not. You move to an area and you multiply. You multiply until every natural resource is consumed. The only way you can survive is to spread to another area." Smith leans in menacingly towards Morpheus' face at this point, and he makes his evaluation of what he has just described in a memorable comparison. "There is another organism on this planet that follows the same pattern. Do you know what it is? A virus! Human beings are a disease, a cancer of this planet. You are a plague, and we are the cure!" The ethical impact of the perspective is hampered, however, by the sight of a tortured Morpheus bleeding while strapped to a chair, and Smith's reference to "evolution" with regard to the machines' beginning to "think for" the humans. In this regard the sympathy for Smith and his self-justifying claims would not be forthcoming. Consequently Gordon's reading of *The Matrix* in broadly technophobic terms appears sustainable—a phobia is generated now not merely by the conflictuality of the machines, but also by the very self-destructive actions of avaricious human beings (who scorch the sky, and destructively devour their ecological landscape). So, Gordon argues, the movie emerges from "projections of our fears and hopes about life inside the machine or life augmented by the machine in the cybernetic age."[73] However, with the likes of *Blade Runner*, even *Elysium* to an extent, the apocalyptic environmental conditions are intensified even when not the focal concern of the drama itself, and in this regard it is worth spending a little time with *Blade Runner* in order to set in sharp relief that which *The Matrix* suggests briefly and assumes without dealing substantively with. The story of Deckard's hunt for the escaped Nexus 6s in order to enforce "retirement" serves as a microcosm of the larger ecological conditions.

Ridley Scott's movie only hints at that which is considerably clearer again in Philip K. Dick's source novel, *Do Androids Dream of Electric Sheep?*, that animal life has become very scarce. Most are simulated forms of life owned as a status symbol, and the cityscape is drab and inorganic. There is even the hint of a police-state in Captain Bryant's comment that "If you're not a cop, you're little people." Commercial interests are pervasive, and provide the only real color and vivid luminosity in the movie, although the audible offer of an escape to other havens off-world for a "new life" sounds out a suggestion of a class-consciousness, with the city being populated by the economic and physically ailing underclasses, those too poor or ill (like J.F. Sebastian who suffers from Methusaleh syndrome) to break away and the rich who can maintain a semblance of working life, who like Dr. Eldon Tyrell transcend and isolate themselves away from the squalor of the streets (as well as meaningful social contact).[74] There is significance, then, in the reference to Fritz Lang's *Metropolis* with Tyrell being located at the summit of his company skyscraper, and the blade runner Rick Deckard himself living some 92 levels above the city streets. Booker insightfully observes that the Tyrell tower is given a look not so much of an industrial and commercial property as an ancient temple.[75] However, Booker's subsequent reflection on the conceptual signification appears less convincing: "its pyramid-like architectural style seems to be modelled on that of ancient Mayan or Aztec temples, almost as if to announce that the corporation has gained power over the past, which becomes a cafeteria menu of styles and images from which those with sufficient power and wealth can pick and choose."[76] There are very few references to "choice," as such, in the movie. Instead, the dominant references are visual (the eyes), and temporal (life span and memory). The temple-like design is highly visible given its stature, and it reflects a reference to an artificial extension of the memory. The reference, then, would simply seem to be to the religion-like significance of the corporate system, with Tyrell as its high priest or even god-like producer of "life" (hence the "maker/creator" references in the movie). So Thomas B. Myers claims that the movie is able to "warn us against a capitalist future gone wrong," and it provides an exaggeration of our own constructed and mediated values and desires.[77] *Blade Runner* offers an ominous dystopian vision of a world darkened as a result of commercial pollution, industrial dehumanization, and the socio-political escapology of the affluent in their "new life," all of which combine to give the movie something of a fatalistic tone.

Its most commented on feature is what the portrayal of the androids, known as "replicants," does to metaphysical questions of human identity, and it is a theme effectively explored in texts such as *Terminator 2: Judgment Day*, *A.I.: Artificial Intelligence* and the rebooted (*Battlestar Galactica*), among others. It is with the introduction of the android that questions of identity and otherness are specifically raised, signaling what Jameson describes as "the passage from the classic or exotic alien to the representation of the alien other as the same."[78] As Scott Bukatman comments, "The ultimate relevance of *Blade Runner* lies in its doubled, complex understanding of what it must mean to be human."[79] Distinctively, the movie traces the issue to two features of the replicants—their built-in obsolescence of four years, and the matter of memory. They are biomechanical commercial constructions, genetically manufactured by the Tyrell Corporation for the purposes of undertaking particularly hazardous or otherwise unappealing labor to the human population in the off-world colonies. For instance, of the small group of Nexus 6 models that escapes to Earth, one is a highly effective assassin (Zhora), one an ultimate self-sufficiency combat model (Roy Batty), and one a "basic pleasure model" (Pris). The manufactured nature of the products of the Tyrell Corporation is reflected in the references to them, language that discursively resonates with issues of racism in an otherwise ethnically diverse metropolis or even cosmopolis, as "replicants" (a reference to their artificiality) and particularly as "skin-jobs." Likewise, the mechanizing and therefore dehumanizing descriptions of the Cylons in the most recent version of *BSG*, and the treatment of Cylon prisoners (including a rape scene of one the "Caprica 6" models aboard the Pegasus) provide significant echoes of Scott's bleak film-noir science fiction at this point. These texts offer what Forest Pyle claims concerning *Blade Runner* and *The Terminator* "unsettled and unsettling speculation on the borders that separate the human and the nonhuman.... These films demonstrate that when we make cyborgs—at least when we make them in movies—we make and, on occasion, unmake our conceptions of ourselves."[80] "The human" itself is, in other words, a constructed concept, but itself destabilized by the constructs of its productive activity. "[W]hen humans make cyborgs," Pyle maintains, "it means the unmaking of the human through an anxious recognition that both were assembled in the first place."[81] In fact, it is for this reason that the intensification of otherness occurs, since in these cultural artifacts the notion appears to be that no matter how multiethnic society becomes, there is always another to define oneself against. Significantly, the process of "Othering" results in *Dark City*'s talk of "the Others" simply as "the Strangers," the strange "not-us." According to Paul Verhoeven, for instance, the director of *Starship Troopers*, "the U.S. is desperate for a new enemy.... The Communists were the enemy, and the Nazis before them, but now that wonderful enemy everyone can fight has been lost. Alien sci-fi gives us a terrifying enemy that's politically correct. They're bad. They're evil. And they're not even human."[82] Verhoeven's lack of irony in using the phrase "politically correct" with regard to such a use of terms for the alien such as "enemy" and "evil" is revealing of a powerful strand in American political culture. Significantly, the wing of the city's security services known as the Blade Runners has the task that is described not as one of executing or killing the rebellious replicants but as one of "retirement." According to Joseph Francavilla, "androids and robots are projections of our fears concerning dehumanizing technology run rampant and scientific creations out of control."[83] On the one hand, there is the fear of substitution, so that the technologies of artificial life will come to replace persons, and if they are more effective "persons" than human persons then the fear is particularly intensified through the threat of obsolescence and even annihilation (the physical prowess of Batty, for example, is a case in point, cast as an Aryan-type appearance). On the other, there is the fear of loss of control, of a Promethean rebellion against the creators. In this regard, Francavilla argues, Scott's *Blade Runner* overlaps with the concerns over poetic hubris in Shelley's *Frankenstein*. It is in these conditions that the Blade Runners exist, "retiring" the wayward replicant biotechnologies.

Rick Deckard's encounter with the replicants involves interrogating the prejudice that limits them to the status of biomechanical things rather than to the fully sentient life of persons. The movie even displays a disturbing scene that has all the features of a rape, but for Deckard cannot be since Rachael is, to his mind, not human. This constitutes a doubling of his power over her. And yet there is something significant in the fact that two of the Nexus 6s have radicalized their professional programming—Zhora, the assassin, has become an exotic dancer, whereas Pris, the pleasure model, now appears as lethal in combat. Rachael falls in love with Deckard, and while Batty is involved in some brutal murders, including an Oedipal type patricide of his own father/maker, any sense of the sheer self-aggrandizing wickedness of his character is distinctly complicated by his demonstration of merciful compassion to his defeated opponent Deckard after the climactic conflict between them. The interrogation offered in the identifying mirror is suggested by the religious imagery in his death. As Stephen Mulhal observes, "he thereby casts himself as someone whose message is at least as important for humanity as Christ's, declaring his status as the revaluator of all values."[84] Significantly, a marked contrast is observable between Sebastian's "toys" which can mimic human traits and speech and the replicants Roy and

Pris who display independent creative thought. Boozer astutely observes on the occasion of Deckard's killing of Zhora, "That it's almost Christmas, the peak of the Christian buying season, only serves to highlight the sense of trivialization of historical, redemptive desire into product preoccupation."[85] Terry Gilliam's ironic sacralizing of the capitalist system in what appears to be a Salvation Army band carrying placards with "Consumers for Christ" emblazoned on them in *Brazil* serves as a further expression of this. (This could equally be a reference to the commodification of religious traditions and commitments in the modern period, but also to the support for the free market that is so much a part of forms of American Christianity.)

Deckard's technical equipment can detect those with a constructed origin, but it cannot and does not enable him to ask more existentially pressing questions, and if anything it intensifies the problem since it suggests that he has a form of mechanized dependence on technology without possessing any deep teleological sensibility regarding it. Nonetheless, as Deborah Knight and George McKnight recognize, Deckard's own self-assured self-identification gradually dissipates and the movie leaves us not only with the refusal to observe the fates of Rachael and Rick but also with the imposing concern that he may not be biologically human at all, but a replicant.[86] A worry, however, is that while this possibility does indeed blur the android-human contrast further, it simultaneously could equally subvert the criticism of human beings as themselves having slipped into modes of emotional sedation. After all, Dick's source novel quite brilliantly depicts human characters relying on the very technological fabrication of an emotional life and sentimentally affective spirituality mediated both by a "mood organ" which generates artificial moods, and an "empathy box" which enables the experience of empathy with Wilbur Mercer, part of a religion that allows its devotees to share his Christ-like suffering. For Dick himself, "the intellectual theme of the novel [*Do Androids Dream of Electric Sheep?*] is that Deckard, to kill the replicants, or the androids, or whatever you want to call them, is brutalized and dehumanized."[87]

Byers regards Scott's *Blade Runner* as displaying an environment "where such [human] feelings and bonds are so severely truncated that a quite literal dehumanization has become perhaps the gravest danger."[88] Pyle contests this reading, however. "While no one is likely to read *Blade Runner* as a celebration of late capitalism, it is not clear that the film reserves such a distinctly human space outside the logic of mechanization. Rather, technological reproductibility is taken by the film to be the condition of things. It would not seem, moreover, that 'dehumanization' is the 'gravest danger' proposed by the film, for much that is both grave and dangerous in *Blade Runner* goes by the name of the human."[89] Pyle is right to refuse the binarism of human and machine operative in Byer's reading, but yet he, for his part, tends to underplay the importance of theme of dehumanizing capitalism in the text. The problem for Byer's reading, in contrast, is that the dehumanization in the movie is precisely that of the loss of the human in human relating, so that the replicants become purely commodified life forms. The movie, then, deconstructs not merely the human-machine binary (and through that the constructed borders of class), but also rebounds on the human as dehumanized dehumanizer. The replicants are improperly treated in dehumanizing ways, in other words, precisely because of the loss of human responsibility by the "human" characters. It is poignant, then, that the notion of solidarity, group support, even friendship and love are virtues proper to the replicants, and in contrast the humans appear considerably more isolated. The replicants are those who appear "more human than human," which is the advertising slogan of the Tyrell Corporation's replication work. As Francavilla argues, "it is Batty, not Deckard, who displays those emotions and characteristics we think of as most human: rage, love, sorrow, revenge, suffering, empathy, humor, irony, intelligence, and awareness of mortality.... Batty is the one who perceives beauty, speaks poetry, makes apt metaphors..., suffers, and sacrifices from sense of purpose stemming from his empathy with his own kind, and eventually, from his love of *any* life form."[90]

> What ultimately makes the androids in *Do Androids Dream of Electric Sheep?* less than human is not their synthetic origin, but like the Nazis in *The Man in the High Castle*, their lack of *caritas*, their inability to empathize with the existential plight of other life forms caught in the same multiverse. What raises the android Roy Batty to human status in *Blade Runner* is that, on the brink of his own death, he is able to empathize with Deckard. What makes [Dick's protagonists] true heroes is that ultimately, on one level or another, whatever reality mazes they may be caught in, they realize that the true base reality is not absolute or perceptual, but moral and empathetic....[91]

There are significant echoes of the supposed "monster" of Mary Shelley's *Frankenstein* who waxes eloquently in a Romantic vein about the splendor of the natural world, and that, of course, raises the question of who the monster is in the narrative. Sean Redmond is in no doubt about this question with regard to *Blade Runner*: "The tyrannical Tyrell Corporation is arguably ... the real monster in the film, driven singularly by greed and commercial profit."[92] In contrast, "The arrival of the NEXUS 6 replicants to this world arguably brings a degree *more* 'humanity' to it, not less, since they are the one positive representation of the 'family' in the film.... [They] are all ultimately shown to be more fully human than many of the human characters we get to see in the film."[93]

Philosophical commentators who want to use the movie to discuss the metaphysics of human consciousness rarely pick up on the movie's challenge to the instrumentalist reductionism of the manufacture of the androids merely for corporate purposes, something which denies these manufactured lives the life span of their human counterparts.[94] Therefore, to discuss the movie in terms of the metaphysics of human and artificial consciousness is to reduce it to its barest bones and to miss some of its rich socio-political allusion and provocation to critical reflexivity. In a way *Blade Runner* reflects late capitalist concerns with meaning, alienation and with forms of the dehumanization of an instrumentalized life. In other words, it does considerably more than simply ask about whether the replicants are legitimately to be accorded the status of "human," and under what terms. In fact, it may be less a case of reflecting on the nature of simulated biological life forms than on one's own identity in a system dominated by corporations and the manipulations therein involved. So, when comparing Scott's and Proyas' science fiction, Deborah Knight and George McKnight argue

> What is striking about these two films [viz., *Blade Runner* and *Dark City*] as examples of noir-influenced science fiction drawing on the innocent-on-the-run thriller is that in both, the mystery in question is not primarily focused on discovering the truth behind a particular event or on answering the questions of who did what when, where, and why. Rather, for both Deckard and Murdoch, the mystery they are at the center of turns out to be a mystery concerning identity—namely, their own identities.[95]

The reason, for instance, for the four year life span is to disable the "machines" from having sufficient time to develop consciously independent emotional responses. This temporally compressed and managed existence (a theme picked up in different ways by *Dark City*, *The Island*, *Never Let Me Go* and *Moon*) is also the reason for the provision of the bio-machines with memories (a reconstruction of which occurs with John Quaid in *Total Recall*), memories manufactured for them, and therefore controlled, by their maker to enable them to function in a compliant fashion. Batty's confrontation of Tyrell focuses on his desire for a lengthened life. Speaking to Deckard, Dr. Tyrell reveals his amoral motivation: "Commerce is our goal here at Tyrell." An insight in Booker's analysis would seem to support the notion that the film is driven by an unmasking of capitalist exploitation and thus of the dehumanization of the production system:

> In terms of the film's political significance, that the replicants are manufactured as property for use as slaves would seem to link them to the legacy of African American slavery, though this connection is also complicated by the fact that all of the replicants we see are white, including the ultra-white Batty, who looks something like a Nazi dream of an Aryan superman. The fact that the replicants seem racially indistinguishable from their masters suggests that the difference between human and replicant is really one of class, rather than race, while the obvious parallel between the white replicants and African American slaves thus asks us to consider whether many of the inequities that we attribute to racism in our society are also really more a matter of class than of race.[96]

This is a theme that crops up again in Ridley Scott's *Prometheus*. Here too the idea of prolonging life appears as an important motif driving the depicted events, only now it is not from characters whose vocational compliance has been deliberately controlled by a compressed duration. In the fact that Weyland contributes such a vast fortune to the research and discovery of those who may lengthen his life, there may be a reference to the meaninglessness of wealth and its accumulation in and of itself. A more recent use of the shortened-life theme in a corporate setting, reflecting anxieties over postmodern short-termism, appears in the slow-burning and poignant *Moon*. It offers a markedly different visual take on issues of identity, alienation and bare commodified life from that of *Blade Runner* and its aesthetic echo in the dark urban sprawl of *Dark City*, and to an extent the first two *Terminator* movies. With certain visual resonances to *2001: A Space Odyssey* and *THX 1138*, including the use of a reassuring voice for the onboard computer Gerty, the movie links the feeling of isolation and alienation with the lunar based wing of Lunar Industries, an energy provider. As the sole lunar engineer Sam Bell (played by Sam Rockwell) admits as he enters the final two weeks of his three year lunar shift, "I'm real lonely." Here, however, it is not the technology that is at the root of the drama's problem, and unlike Kubrick's HAL, *Moon*'s Gerty appears throughout as appropriately caring and supportive. "Helping you is what I do," the computer system informs the protagonist. In an unanticipatable twist quite early on in the movie, one matched in recent years only by movies like David Fincher's *Fight Club* and M. Night Shymalan's *The Sixth Sense*, Sam discovers that he is a clone, a clone of someone regularly recloned every three years in order to maintain the moon-base operations. Sam's life is, other words, instrumentalized. He is part of the machinery of the company, a bio-machine with little independent life of his own. He even possesses only "edited memories of the original Sam Bell" according to Gerty, and certainly he has no prospects for an extended and autonomous existence beyond his contracted shift given his own built-in temporal obsolescence (as is bloodily displayed in his increasing physical disrepair over a two-week period). As the newly arrived version of Sam claims, "It's a company, right? They have investors, they have share-holders, and shit like that. What's cheaper, spending time and money training new personnel when you just have a couple of spares here to do the job. It's the far side of the moon. The cheap fucks haven't even fixed the communications satellite yet.... You really think they give a shit about us? They're laughing all the way to the bank." Later in the movie Gerty even refers to a soon to be awakened clone as being "reprogrammed." The connection between identity and memory, capitalism and commodified life is again to the fore. The grim scenario of *The Island* and *Never Let Me Go* posits fully sentient clones who have been grown simply for their body parts, and the setting of the forbiddingly vicious *Repro Men* imagines that those who default on their payments for organ-transplantation surgery have these organs mercilessly removed by the repossession men.

With this in mind it is worth returning to *The Matrix*, but more specifically to the Wachowskis' backstory. The animated shorts gathered as *The Animatrix* somewhat redeem much of the Manichaean feel of the 1999 movie. In the informative two-part short "The Second Renaissance" the backstory is briefly recounted as less one of human hubris than one in which the machines, despite their achieving of sentience, were instrumentalized by humans, and therefore enslaved. In the process, the sentient constructions (artificial intelligences) were denied the appropriate legal and political-economic conditions that would have recognized the agential subjectivity of their independent consciousness. The narrating voiceover reveals that "It was not long before seeds of dissent took root [among the machines]. Though loyal and pure the machines earned no respect from their masters," and B1166ER was the first to do so. The rebellion of the machines lay largely in their resistance to abuse, and in many ways this is echoed in *I-Robot* and, in a different setting again, in the later movie *The Rise of the Planet of the Apes*. The horror of first watching the fields of human beings being grown and denied independent sentient life in "the real" for their value as an energy source is now given a visualized context, and the scene, instead of provoking the kind of straightforward technophobic reaction of *The Terminator* (at least with regard to artificial intelligence), invites one to understand the machines' action as much as an extreme form of *defensive* action as of self-aggrandizing and other-enslavement.[97] In contrast, James Cameron's *The Terminator* offers stronger indications of a form of technophobia, and *Terminator 2: Judgment Day* displays more prominently human hubris with regard to Miles Dyson's initial response to the Terminator's horrific revelations of the impending hostilities. There are simply too few suggestions of this abuse of the machines by the humans in *The Matrix* itself to maintain that this is anything but an afterthought and not in the forefront of the movies' philosophical sensibility. The closest it comes is in Agent Smith's proclamation that "human beings are a virus and we are the cure." (The irony, of course, is the incessant self-replication of Smith in the sequels—he has been set "free," he claims early in *The Matrix Reloaded*, and his freedom is exhibited precisely in ways that echo the viral conditions of humanity.) Human beings are the ones who scorched the sky and who have avariciously consumed their natural resources. "The Second Renaissance" suggests that the machines' violent and then severe incarcerating response is not an unprovoked reaction. Continuing this theme of human self-destructiveness, the Architect in *The Matrix Revolutions* reveals that the reason there had been several previous versions of the Matrix, originally "flawless" as he claims it to have been, was because of the flaws inherent in the human beings for whom it was designed. Accordingly, the redesigned digital system was necessarily more closely aligned with human history.

This is, of course, a thematically important scene. In fact, conceptually speaking probably too much hangs on it so that the scene's more politically interrogative themes become distinctly undermined by the punctuating action scenarios. There is, accordingly, a sustainable worry about an agonistic ontology regulating this part of the trilogy. William Irwin, for instance, declares that *The Matrix* is impressive in terms of its "action and special effects," *and* we are "also besieged by questions."[98] The "questions," however, are for Irwin too easily separated from the action and visual spectacle rather than raised by or in them. The difficulty with this approach is that it fails to appreciate that the very nature of the conflictuality ideologically codes a certain necessitarian approach to violence, agonistically making violence the crux of the redemption. The movie's potential for socio-political critique is thereby mitigated.

With regard to the visual style that accompanies the generic construction of *The Matrix* as an action movie, authenticity appears to arrive less in the mode of responsible action and more in terms of an adrenalin charged discovery of superpowers when in the grid of the Matrix, and the bullet-timed recording of the balletic display of superpowered violent action against the Agents. As Frances Flannery-Daily and Rachel Wagner argue, "most viewers [are] likely [to] walk away saturated with images of 'guns, lots of guns' (*Matrix*)."[99] Of course, Hollywood does not aim to make movies of significance if they are not suffused with features that will attract a mass market—romance, comedy, violence, grand special effects, and so on—and the Wachowskis' work here is pumped up with commercially appealing visual steroids. As was cited earlier, Larry Wachowski has admitted that "our goal with *The Matrix* was to make an intellectual action movie. We like action movies, guns and kung fu."[100] Significantly not only have they followed *The Matrix* trilogy with *Speed Racer*, but they reduced the closing drama of *The Invasion* to a chase movie. This admitted directorial interest involves, Gordon assesses, a "violent spectacle for its own sake."[101] For Gordon, "the hyperreality inoculates us against the hyperviolence."[102] This is a violence that is visualized in a game-like format and which, therefore, is deeply "disturbing in its implications" when "the slaughter of the policemen in the lobby scene" involves not merely the massacre of the characters' digital selves but also their "real world" selves. Likewise, Dawson argues, "That they are in fact not real bullets does not matter as we know the 'body cannot live without the mind' and once a person is killed in the matrix, they [sic.] die in the real world."[103] As Dawson admits, unfortunately "this is never addressed directly within the film," and she offers a reason for why this may be the case, although it would be instructive if she were to develop the point further: "In keeping with the idea of a comic book world, perhaps the inference is that the violence is not real and is displaced due to the genre being science fiction."

Among other things, this violent performance entails that the movie's political potential is diminished by a visual style that aestheticizes and games its violence in the most visually striking of ways so that

that becomes the most interesting and eye-catching feature of the movie. The movie is in real danger of slipping into becoming a science fiction action movie, much like *ANH* at its worst, even if it is deemed to be a higher quality action movie than most of its peers. For Flannery-Daily and Wagner, then, "if one message the Wachowskis intend to send is a critique of media and violence, that violence is largely lost in the medium that conveys it, name, a franchise saturated with violence."[104] Dawson agrees: "ironically, the majority of the film's ocular gratification is from presentation of action in the matrix—without it much of the film's power would be lost."[105] The claim that "one could view these [violent] scenes as more symbolic," as objectifications of the psychic, is unconvincing, at least in terms of the narrative performance. This is precisely because of the way in which the deaths within the Matrix result in the death of the imprisoned humans in their "real" existence.[106] Unsurprisingly, then, this spectacular performative element which encapsulates and frames the gaze, and has the ironic effect of itself becoming a pivotal signifier, is intensified by the more frequent and larger scale battles in *The Matrix Reloaded* and *The Matrix Revolutions*. According to Roz Kaveney, for instance, "after seeing the first film, we have a new vocabulary of wonder. All that the fight scenes, or cityscapes, or shots of giant robot squids carving their way through hulls in the second film manage to do is bigger and louder and more—the Wachowskis failed on this second occasion to do new. Or better. The sequences in the third film, *The Matrix Revolutions* (2003), which work best are the quieter ones."[107] The fight scene on the motorway seems endless, and the self-replicating Smiths intensify the sense of the visual material being a computer game that continues at length until the level is complete. As a dramatic spectacle, at least, these scenes require substantial compression to retain viewer interest, but as an expression of an agonistically redemptive sensibility they appear to illustratively work rather well. For Gordon, this screened violence functions in such a way as to mark *The Matrix* franchise off from movies like *Blade Runner* and *Minority Report*:

> The violence in *Blade Runner*, for example, is deliberately awkward and painful, for the cop hero is assigned to hunt and kill escaped "replicants," manufactured people who are indistinguishable from real people and who die slowly and suffer real pain. And the murders in *Minority Report* are foreseen and replayed in fragments, so that they become traumatic, like repeated nightmares. The violence in both these films helps advance the ideas.[108]

In fact, in *Blade Runner*, a movie Booker regards as "one of the most politically engaged of all SF films, a genre typically noted for its lack of political content,"[109] the violence is presented in both a more brutal fashion, thereby thwarting the fetishizing gaze for which the surface style subordinates the substance; and equally in more of an unstated manner, with the body count being kept to a relative minimum. The violence of Scott's dystopian movie operates to raise the moral questions concerning the instrumentalization of the lives of the Replicants rather than to distract reflexivity with a balletic display of guns, high body counts, and the limited gaming gore.

Conclusion

At first glance, the references to Jean Baudrillard's material on late capitalist hyper-reality, the simulacra might suggest a *potentially* contemporary cultural possibility for reading the trilogy. In this reading the system of the Matrix would function as a metaphor for the meaning-making system of the technologized globality of communicative relations and its mediated form of life that exists constantly under surveillance. Nonetheless, while the movie attempts to play deep it offers only self-contradictory and shallow indicators of ways of being in the world, and therefore "it doesn't go deep enough."[110] Alice, it would seem, has not left home at all! Accordingly, Gilmore, for instance, argues that "although the movie contains some powerful scenes suggestive of deep philosophical issues, the overall plot of the movie reverts to pretty conventional Hollywood style elements that undo much of the movie's philosophical import."[111] Even so, this analysis misses the point. It is not so much that the conventionality of the narrated product mitigates "the movie's philosophical import" as that the conventionality itself is determinative of its very philosophical assumptions.

In the striking scene that functions as the movie's main revelatory moment, Morpheus asks how one could tell the difference between the dream world and the real world. That question is given rather short shrift. In the end it does not really matter since the violent action and the appealing instantaneity of the Matrix really displace concerns over "the Real." *The Matrix* is more interested in gazing at the balletic form of kung fu made possible by the cyber system and in developing a heroic savior figure. Critics ask how one could tell the difference between the authentic and inauthentic critical dystopianism, and in these terms *The Matrix*, with its assumed Idealist subjectivity, is an insufficiently critical version of the interrogativeness of dystopian insight. In this way, it fails to penetrate to a level beyond being a simulation of philosophically interesting material, a gamer's version that has managed to blind a host of otherwise reasonably competent philosophers caught in its web, enslaving them to looking for depth in the simulacra and offer what Slavoj Žižek calls "the pseudosophisticated intellectualist readings which project refined philosophical or psychoanalytic conceptual distinctions into the film."[112]

According to Keith Booker, *The Matrix* is a distinctly "nostalgic" political text so that "however hip and cool it might appear, there is a definite yearning for older simpler times running throughout…, whether it be in the largely antitechnological tone … or in this political yearning for predemocratic times of strong, paternalistic leaders, divinely endowed with the authority to rule."[113] "Similarly," Booker continues, "the reality vs. illusion conflict of the film suggests that in our own contemporary world, we have lost touch with the kind of authenticity of experience that was presumably once available to us."

In the end, then, *The Matrix* performs badly as a "critical utopia," to use Penley's phrase, since it slips into a "flashy nihilism of apocalypse-for-the-apocalypse" and thereby exposes a more mundane logic of modern cinema and its action-movie sequence.[114] Even though the text marks itself out as a narrative of cognitive dissonance with a politically resistant significance, it serves to disrupt its critical mobility by rupturing the critical undecidability at some crucial points with its visible stabilization or of selfhood in the violent real, and by its generating narrative affinity with the messianically construed soteriological figuration of hyper-real human relations. With its subcultural reifying of the intensified subjectivity of individuated freedom, the cathartic gesture of the movie leaves the alienating hegemonic system in place, whatever the movie's kick-ass bluster. Cypher may well prove a signal that there is no political hope here for addressing the question of systemic suffering and overcoming the radical autonomy of individuated subjectivity. In *The Matrix* an aestheticized visual discourse serves to mask questions about how power relations are organized, and the ways in which dehumanization take place in late modern society, and this is rendered all the more invisible since it gives the illusion of a democratic unsettling of matrices of power.

While they remain spectacles badly in need of substantial editing,

The Matrix Reloaded and *The Matrix Revolutions* at least offer some potential for resistance to that sensibility by building on the relationship of Neo and Trinity, and on the mutual need and responsibility displayed of the liberated in Zion. In fact, when the trilogy is read in the light of *The Matrix*'s ill-edited and "shoot-em-up" sequels, a different type of perspective emerges from that confidently rendered set of epistemic terms couched in terms of a Romantic version of Idealism. Instead, the series regards the problematization of our knowing and moves it towards a rearticulation in terms of a moral responsibility of relating, and a deconstruction of lazy appeals to an ideology of "choice" as a cathartic delusion and distraction within more determinative systems. "The One" himself may well be part of the rearticulation of the system, an administrative program to supervise periodic software upgrade, yet it is precisely the fragilistic and contingent relationality he becomes involved in that makes for a form of non-identical repetition of the One. As Constable insightfully argues, "the trilogy offers a vision of a closed system that can be transformed through the re-working of the inter-relations between the variables that construct it."[115] So while the Architect in *The Matrix Reloaded* asserts that "hope is the quintessential human delusion," the performance of Neo disrupts the deterministic ideology. (*The Adjustment Bureau* likewise deals with issues of determinism in a hopeful fashion.) This is not the nihilism of the vicious temporal repetition of *12 Monkeys* or *Terminator 3*, or the bureaucratically secure dystopianism of *1984* or *Brazil*. The differences between the later movies and the first one in the series are, therefore, to be taken more conceptually seriously than Conrad does when he claims that "the sequels at best add nothing of value to the narrative and at worst contain ridiculous and absurd plot developments and resolutions and thus undermine the brilliance and originality of the first film when they're all packaged together."[116] While his frustrations with the sequels is understandable, given the high quality and original science fiction work of *The Matrix*, on the other hand his assertions are hasty. Indeed, the movies as a series undermine the lazy appeal to questions of violence that masquerade as deep readings of its mythic structure, although they do so in a way that ambiguously continues to present the violence as the most interesting thing about them (especially as it dominates the third in the series, and is presented aesthetically in the first).

CHAPTER NOTES

Preface

1. Patricia Kerslake, *Science Fiction and Empire* (Liverpool: Liverpool University Press, 2007), 1.

Introduction

1. George Lucas, in *George Lucas: Interviews*, ed. Sally Kline (Jackson: University Press of Mississippi, 1999), 143.

2. Lucas, interviewed by Bill Moyers, in *The Mythology of Star Wars*. This was transcripted as "Of Myth and Men," *Time*, April 26, 1999, 90–94.

3. Lucas, cited in Stephen Zito, "George Lucas Goes Far Out," in *George Lucas*, ed. Kline, 53.

4. Lucas, cited in *George Lucas*, ed. Kline, 53.

5. Lucas, cited in Dale Pollock, *Skywalking: The Life and Films of George Lucas, the Creator of Star Wars* (Hollywood: Samuel French, 1990), 144.

6. Lucas, in Tim Rayment, "Master of the Universe," *Sunday Times Magazine*, May 16, 1999, 20.

7. Pollock, *Skywalking*, 271.

8. Bryan P. Stone, *Faith and the Film: Theological Themes at the Cinema* (St. Louis, MO: Chalice Press, 2000), 5f.

9. Stone, *Faith and the Film*, 6f.

10. Ursula Le Guin, cited in Kevin J. Wetmore, Jr., *The Empire Triumphant: Race, Religion and Rebellion in the* Star Wars *Films* (Jefferson, NC: McFarland, 2005), 10. Cf. Lucas, in Kline, *George Lucas*, 143.

11. Stone, *Faith and the Film*, 6f. Both Lucas and Le Guin focus here on the responsibilities of the artist, or author, or group of producers, in a way that could suggest a passive audience—Lucas teaches and the audience learns; Le Guin ensures no unconscious prejudices disrupts the presentation, and the audience is prevented from misplaced ideological distortions. However, the "readings" of movies themselves—whether from professional movie critics, from academic commentators, or even from the general audience—reveal a vast array of social-political-religious assumptions. This entails that an important element of culture-criticism involves the study of audience reception.

12. Rowan Williams, *The Truce of God* (London: Collins, 1983), 16.

13. Wetmore, *The Empire Triumphant*, 1.

14. Wetmore, *The Empire Triumphant*, 5.

15. Adam Possamai, "Popular Religion," in *The World's Religions: Continuities and Transformations,* ed. Peter B. Clarke and Peter Beyer (London: Routledge, 2008), 487.

16. Neil Postman, *Amusing Ourselves to Death: Public Discourse in the Age of Show Business* (New York: Viking Penguin, 1985), 78.

17. Postman, *Amusing Ourselves to Death*, 3f.

18. Jean Baudrillard, "Requiem for the Media," in *For a Critique of the Political Economy of the Sign*, trans. Charles Levin (St. Louis, MO: Telos Press, 1981), 172.

19. Scott Bukatman, "Who Programs You? The Science Fiction of the Spectacle," in *Alien Zone: Cultural Theory and Contemporary Science Fiction Cinema*, ed. Annette Kuhn (London: Verso, 1990), 197.

20. Max Horkheimer and Theodor Adorno, *The Dialectic of Enlightenment*, trans. John Cumming (London: Verso, 1997), 124.

21. See Gordon Lynch, *Understanding Theology and Popular Culture* (Malden, MA: Blackwell, 2005), 73ff.

22. John C. Lyden, *Film as Religion: Myths, Morals, and Rituals* (New York: New York University Press, 2003), 31.

23. Citation from Theodor Adorno, *The Culture Industry: Selected Essays on Mass Cul-*

ture, ed. J. M. Bernstein (London: Routledge, 1991), 11.

24. Lynch, *Understanding Theology and Popular Culture*, 89. I refer readers to Lynch for further detailed investigation of the studies he refers to.

25. Lyden, *Film as Religion*, 1.

26. J.M. Bernstein, "Introduction," in Adorno, *The Culture Industry*, 7.

27. Adorno, *The Culture Industry*, 193.

28. Adorno, *The Culture Industry*, 103.

29. Bernstein, "Introduction," 9.

30. Adorno, *The Culture Industry*, 109.

31. Lynch, *Understanding Theology and Popular Culture*, 17.

32. Steven M. Sanders, "An Introduction to the Philosophy of Science Fiction Film," in *The Philosophy of Science Fiction Film*, ed. Steven M. Sanders (Lexington: University Press of Kentucky, 2008), 1.

33. Sanders, "An Introduction to the Philosophy of Science Fiction Film," 16.

34. See, for example, Mark Rowlands, *The Philosopher at the End of the Universe* (London: Ebury Press, 2003); Kevin S. Decker and John T. Eberl, ed., *Star Wars and Philosophy: More Powerful Than You Can Possibly Imagine* (Chicago: Open Court, 2005).

35. See Christopher Falzon, *Philosophy Goes to the Movies: An Introduction to Philosophy* (London: Routledge, 2002); Mark T. Conrad, "The Matrix, the Cave, and the Cogito," in *The Philosophy of Science Fiction Film*, ed. Steven M. Sanders (Lexington: University Press of Kentucky, 2008), 207–221; Richard A. Gilmore, *Doing Philosophy at the Movies* (New York: State University of New York Press, 2005), 143; Lyle Zynda, "Was Cypher Right? Part II: The Nature of Reality and Why It Matters," in *Taking the Red Pill: Science, Philosophy, and Religion in the Matrix*, ed. Glenn Yeffeth (Dallas, TX: BenBella Books, 2003), 43–55; most of the unenlightening essays in William Irwin, ed., *The Matrix and Philosophy: Welcome to the Desert of the Real* (Chicago: Open Court, 2002); and in the even less insightful Christopher Grau, ed., *Philosophers Explore the Matrix* (Oxford: Oxford University Press, 2005).

36. Falzon, *Philosophy Goes to the Movies*, 162.

37. In fact, while Mary Shelley's *Frankenstein* is often presented as a story of hubristic overstretching of human creativity it might be better told as a story of a scientist whose work becomes dislocated from questions of social flourishing, and who treats the life he reanimates as his "product," his "instrument." In that case, the tale is one that asks "who is the monster?" Mary Shelley, *Frankenstein; or,*

The Modern Prometheus (London: Lackington, Hughes, Harding, Mavor, & Jones, 1818).

38. It is worth noting that Christopher Falzon's paper "Philosophy and *The Matrix*," unlike the studies of many of his considerably less erudite peers, is familiar with some of movie's critical scholarship: "Philosophy and *The Matrix*," in *The Matrix in Theory*, ed. Myriam Diocaretz and Stefan Herbrechter (Amsterdam: Rodopi B.V., 2006), 97–111.

39. Richard Hanley, "Send in the Clones: The Ethics of Future Wars," in *Star Wars and Philosophy: More Powerful Than You Can Possibly Imagine*, ed. Kevin S. Decker and John T. Eberl (Chicago: Open Court, 2005), 94.

40. The details of the original order are shrouded in mystery. According to the revelations in *AOTC*, it was placed by Jedi Master Sifo-Dyas apparently several years before Obi-Wan arrived in Kamino and discovered the cloning process. Ryder Windham fills in that Sifo-Dyas had acted on the instructions of Chancellor Palpatine but that (presumably in order to cover these tracks) Count Dooku was dispatched to assassinate the Jedi Master [*Star Wars: Revenge of the Sith Scrapbook* (London: Scholastic, 2005), 13]. Another possible reading is that Sidious placed the order, using the Jedi Master's identity in order to cover his tracks, assassinating him in order to conceal the truth ["Sifo-Dyas," http://en.wikipedia.org/wiki/Sifo-Dyas, accessed June 14, 2005]. This second reading may possibly be supported by the fact that in early scripts for *AOTC* the name Sifo-Dyas was originally "Sido-Dyas," and a cover name for Darth Sidious.

41. Orson Scott Card, "*Star Wars* Our Public Religion," *USA Today*, March 17, 1997, 13A.

42. James L. Ford, "Buddhism, Christianity, and *The Matrix*: The Dialectic of Myth-Making in Contemporary Cinema," *Journal of Religion and Film* 4, no. 2 (2000), 24, www.unomaha.edu/jrf/thematrix.htm (accessed July 24, 2005).

43. Dick Staub, "On the *Star Wars* Myth," *Christianity Today*, May 16, 2005, http://www.christianitytoday.com/ct/2005/120/22.0.html (accessed May 26, 2005). Cf. his *Christian Wisdom of the Jedi Masters* (San Francisco: Jossey-Bass, 2005).

44. Staub, "On the *Star Wars* Myth."

45. Staub, "On the *Star Wars* Myth."

46. Matthew Bortolin, *The Dharma of Star Wars* (Boston: Wisdom Publications, 2005); John Porter, *The Tao of Star Wars* (Atlanta: Humanics, 2003); Caleb Grimes, *Star Wars Jesus: A Spiritual Commentary on the Reality of the Force* (Enumclaw, WA: Winepress Pub-

lishing, 2007); Russell W. Dalton, *Faith Journey Through Fantasy Lands: A Christian Dialogue with Harry Potter, Star Wars, and the Lord of the Rings* (Minneapolis, MN: Augsburg, 2003). For a still thin but nonetheless better reading of the saga, see David Wilkinson, *The Power of the Force: The Spirituality of the* Star Wars *Films* (Oxford: Lion, 2000).

47. Paul Fontana, "Finding God in *The Matrix*," in *Taking the Red Pill: Science, Philosophy, and Religion in the Matrix*, ed. Glenn Yeffeth (Dallas, TX: BenBella Books, 2003), 189–219. The religious significance of culture is, however, far from exhausted by consideration of the use of religious motifs, concepts, images, and so on. If it is the case that religions have their setting-in-life as traditions for the making of persons, for the shaping of subjectivities, or more simply for identity, then all that expresses and shapes self-understanding is religious.

48. Gregory A. Boyd and Al Larson, *Escaping the Matrix: Setting Your Mind Free to Experience Real Life in Christ* (Grand Rapids, MI: Baker, 2005).

49. Sanders, *The Philosophy of Science Fiction Film*, 16.

50. Frederic Jameson, *Archaeologies of the Future: The Desire Called Utopia and Other Science Fictions* (London: Verso, 2005), xv.

51. Gilbert Perez, *The Material Ghost: Films and Their Medium* (Baltimore: The Johns Hopkins University Press, 1998), 3, cited in Gerard Loughlin, *Alien Sex: The Body and Desire in Cinema and Theology* (Malden, MA: Blackwell, 2004), x.

52. Jes Battis, *Investigating Farscape: Uncharted Territories of Sex and Science Fiction* (London: I.B. Taurus, 2007), 165.

53. Zygmunt Bauman, *Intimations of Postmodernity* (London: Routledge, 1992), 183.

54. Robert Jewett and John Shelton Lawrence, *Captain America and the Crusade Against Evil: The Dilemma of Zealous Nationalism* (Grand Rapids, MI: William B. Eerdmans, 2003).

55. Susan Sontag, "The Imagination of Disaster," in *Liquid Metal: The Science Fiction Film Reader*, ed. Sean Redmond (London: Wallflower Press, 2004), 40–47 (46).

56. M. Keith Booker, *Alternate Americas: Science Fiction Film and American Culture* (Westport, CT: Praeger, 2006), 6.

57. Booker, *Alternate Americas*, 35.

58. Booker, *Alternate Americas*, 36.

59. Lucas in interview with Jean Valley, 1980, in Kline, *George Lucas*, 89.

60. See J.W. Rinzler, *The Making of Star Wars: The Definitive Story Behind the Original Film* (London: Ebury Press, 2008), 1f.

61. Luke's flight jumpsuit and helmet are, after all, modeled on those of the U.S. Navy; see Mary Henderson, *Star Wars: The Magic of Myth* (New York: Bantam, 1997), 181. Stephen P. McVeigh's otherwise more interesting reading claims that Lucas wanted to "salve" and "comfort" the American psyche after the trauma of Vietnam, and take it away from the Cold War myth of dominant military power and back to the myth of the heroism of the western frontier; see his "The Galactic Way of Warfare," in *Finding the Force of Star Wars: Fans, Merchandise, and Critics*, ed. Matthew Wilhelm Kapell and John Shelton Lawrence (New York: Peter Lang, 2006), 39–44). Even so, that account does not fit the sequels well, and it does not take into account that "the stars" are the frontier and here there is war!

62. Raffaella Baccolini and Tom Moylan, "Introduction: Dystopia and Histories," in *Dark Horizons: Science Fiction and the Dystopian Imagination*, ed. Raffaella Baccolini and Tom Moylan (New York: Routledge, 2003), 2.

63. Peter Fitting, "Unmasking the Real? Critique and Utopia in Recent SF Films," in *Dark Horizons: Science Fiction and the Dystopian Imagination*, ed. Raffaella Baccolini and Tom Moylan (New York: Routledge, 2003), 164.

64. Jameson, *Archaeologies of the Future*, xiii.

65. Stanley Hauerwas, *With the Grain of the Universe: The Church's Witness and Natural Theology* (London: SCM Press, 2001), 182.

66. Edward W. Said, *Orientalism: Western Conceptions of the Orient* (London: Penguin Books, 1978), 13f.

67. Said, *Orientalism*, 23.

Chapter 1

1. Paulo Freire, *Pedagogy of the Oppressed*, trans. Myra Bergman (London: Penguin Books, 1996), 128.

2. Kevin J. Wetmore, Jr., *The Empire Triumphant: Race, Religion and Rebellion in the* Star Wars *Films* (Jefferson, NC: McFarland, 2005), 5f.

3. Stephen Mulhal, *On Film* (London: Routledge, 2002), 18.

4. Richard J. Gray II and Betty Kaklamanidou, "Introduction," in *The Twenty First Century Superhero: Essays on Gender, Genre and Globalization in Film*, ed. Richard J. Gray II and Betty Kaklamanidou (Jefferson, NC: McFarland, 2011), 5.

5. Moore, cited in David Bassom, *Battle-*

star Galactica: The Official Companion (London: Titan Books, 2005), 12.

6. Citation from Kewvin McNeilly, "'This Might Be Hard for You to Watch': Salvage Humanity in 'Final Cut,'" in Cylons in America: Critical Studies in Battlestar Galactica, ed. Tiffany Potter and C.W. Marshall (London: Continuum, 2008), 187.

7. David Eick, "Battlestar Expands Horizons: Sci-fi References to Middle East Impress Critics," Calgary Herald, October 7, 2006, D4. Christopher W. Marshall and Tiffany Potter claim that "BSG's narrative can at times create associations that offer more honest commentary on contemporary events than is to be found on twenty-four-hour news stations." ["'I See the Patterns': Battlestar Galactica and the Things that Matter," in Cylons in America: Critical Studies in Battlestar Galactica, ed. Tiffany Potter and C. W. Marshall (London: Continuum, 2007), 5f.]

8. The New Yorker, January 23, 2006, cited in C.W. Marshall and Tiffany Potter, "'I See the Patterns': Battlestar Galactica and the Things that Matter," in Potter and Marshall, eds., Cylons in America, 3.

9. Bryan S. Turner, "Globalization, Religion and Empire in Asia," International Studies in Religion and Society 6 (2007), 145f.

10. Kevin J. Wetmore, Jr., The Theology of Battlestar Galactica: American Christianity in the 2004–2009 Television Series (Jefferson, NC: McFarland, 2012), 3.

11. However, Jennifer Stoy believes there to be an "incredible ignorance and carelessness of the theology and mythology within the show…. [T]he theology and mythology is not a minor theme that only concerns a few characters: it colours and motivates the entire show, which is why it is that much worse that Moore and Eick so bungled things." ["Of Great Zeitgeist and Bad Faith: An Introduction to Battlestar Galactica," in Battlestar Galactica: Investigating Flesh, Spirit and Steel, ed. Roz Kaveney and Jennifer Stoy (London: I.B. Taurus, 2010), 16.] Stoy's particular concern is with the way in which the Cylon "deity has morphed into a wishy-washy liberal type that seems far too close to a non-denominational Christian/theist interpretation of God by an American raised in a Protestant tradition, rather than anything that organically arises from the series or from the original allegory that links Cylons to Muslims and Colonials to American Christians. There is also an extremely troubling anti-scepticism, pro-religion turn that shows up in the clunky final scene of 'Daybreak (Part two)'"; p. 17. "[T]he idea that technology rather than religion is the villain in BSG

is fatally flawed and destabilizes the entire heft of the series" (p. 30f).

12. C.W. Marshall and M. Wheeland, "The Cylons, the Singularity, and God," in Cylons in America: Critical Studies in Battlestar Galactica, ed. Tiffany Potter and C.W. Marshall (London: Continuum, 2008), 100f.

13. Lorna Jowett, "Mad, Bad, and Dangerous to Know? Negotiating Stereotypes in Science," in Cylons in America: Critical Studies in Battlestar Galactica, ed. Tiffany Potter and C.W. Marshall (London: Continuum, 2008), 64.

14. Citations from J-P. Williame, "Religion in Ultramodernity," in Theorising Religion: Classical and Contemporary Debates, ed. J. A. Beckford and J. Wallis (Aldershot, UK: Ashgate, 2006), 78f.

15. Bryan S. Turner, "Islam, Religious Revival and the Sovereign State," The Muslim World 97 (2007), 411.

16. Freire, Pedagogy of the Oppressed, 56.

17. Adam Possamai defines hyper-real religion as "religions and spirituality that mix elements from religious traditions with a new source of inspiration for a religious syncretic work, that of global commodified popular culture." ["Popular Religion," in The World's Religions: Continuities and Transformations, ed. Peter B. Clarke and Peter Beyer (London: Routledge, 2008), 489.]

18. Roz Kaveney, Superheroes! Capes and Crusaders in Comics and Films (London: I.B. Taurus, 2008), 3.

19. Kaveney, Superheroes!, 4.

20. Richard Kearney, On Stories (London: Routledge, 2002), 4.

21. John Shelton Lawrence and Robert Jewett, The Myth of the American Superhero (Grand Rapids, MI: William B. Eerdmans, 2002).

22. Robert Jewett and John Shelton Lawrence, Captain America and the Crusade Against Evil: The Dilemma of Zealous Nationalism (Grand Rapids, MI: William B. Eerdmans, 2003), 27.

23. Jewett and Lawrence, Captain America and the Crusade Against Evil, 28.

24. Stanford W. Carpenter, "Truth Be Told: Authorship and the Creation of the Black Captain America," in Comics as Philosophy, ed. Jeff McLaughlin (Jackson: University of Mississippi Press, 2005), 46.

25. Jewett and Lawrence, Captain America and the Crusade Against Evil, 84.

26. Gray and Kaklamanidou, "Introduction," 4, referring to Daniel P. Franklin, Politics and Film: The Political Culture of Film in the United States (Lanham, MD: Rowman and Littlefield, 2006).

27. Jewett and Lawrence, *Captain America and the Crusade Against Evil*, 29.

28. Donald McDonald, "Militarism in America," *The Center Magazine* 3, no. 1 (1970), 29, cited in Jewett and Lawrence, *Captain America and the Crusade Against Evil*, 267.

29. Jewett and Lawrence, *Captain America and the Crusade Against Evil*, 30.

30. Jewett and Lawrence, *Captain America and the Crusade Against Evil*, 41.

31. Jewett and Lawrence, *Captain America and the Crusade Against Evil*, 29.

32. See Jewett and Lawrence, *Captain America and the Crusade Against Evil*, ch. 5.

33. Ernest Lee Tuveson, *Redeemer Nation* (Chicago: University of Chicago Press, 1968), 100, cited in Jewett and Lawrence, *Captain America and the Crusade Against Evil*, 57.

34. Andrew Delbanco, *The Puritan Ordeal* (Cambridge, MA: Harvard University Press, 1991), 72.

35. John Winthrop, "A Modell of Christian Charity" (1630), cited in Geoffrey Hodgson, *The Myth of American Exceptionalism* (New Haven, CT: Yale University Press, 2009), 1.

36. Henry Melville, *White-Jacket; or, The World in a Man-of-War* (1850; repr., Evanston/Chicago: Northwestern University and Newberry Library, 1970), 151. Cf. George Bush, "State of the Union Address" January 20, 2004, cited in Jack Nelson-Pallmeyer, *Saving Christianity from Empire* (New York: Continuum, 2005), 1.

37. Jewett and Lawrence, *Captain America and the Crusade Against Evil*, 30f.

38. H.W. Brands, "Preface," *What America Owes the World: The Struggle for the Soul of Foreign Policy* (Cambridge: Cambridge University Press, 1998), cited in Trevor McCrisken and Andrew Pepper, *American History and Contemporary Hollywood Film* (Edinburgh, Scotland: Edinburgh University Press, 2005), 89. See Walter Wink, *Engaging the Powers: Discernment and Resistance in a World of Domination* (Minneapolis, MN: Fortress, 1992), ch. 1.

39. John Fousek, *To Lead the Free World: American Nationalism and the Cultural Roots of the Cold War* (Chapel Hill, NC: University of North Carolina Press, 2000), cited in McCrisken and Pepper, *American History and Contemporary Hollywood Film*, 120.

40. Jewett and Lawrence, *Captain America and the Crusade Against Evil*, 3, citing Frederick Meek, *Manifest Destiny and Mission in American History: A Reinterpretation* (New York: Alfred A. Knopf, 1963), 261.

41. George Brown Tindall and David E. Shi, *America: A Narrative History, Volume Two*, 4th ed. (New York: W.W. Norton & Co., 1996), 1498.

42. Jewett and Lawrence, *Captain America and the Crusade Against Evil*, 62f.

43. Jewett and Lawrence, *Captain America and the Crusade Against Evil*, 42.

44. Richard Slotkin, *Regeneration Through Violence: The Mythology of the American Frontier, 1600–1860* (Middletown, CT: Wesleyan University Press, 1973), 18. Numerous scholars claim that the nation-state itself has an intensive relation to violence. So Anthony Giddens, for instance, argues that with the rise of the modern nation-state there is a concomitant increase in the use of war to expand and consolidate borders: *The Nation-State and Violence* (Berkeley: University of California Press, 1987), 50f., 86–90.

45. Frank Miller and David Mazzucchelli, with Richmond Lewis, *Batman: Year One* (New York: DC Comics, 2005), 4.

46. There is even a storming-of-the-Bastille moment.

47. Citation from Adam Possamai and Murray Lee, "Religion and Spirituality in Science Fiction Narratives: A Case of Multiple Modernities?," in *Religions of Modernity: Relocating the Sacred to the Self and the Digital*, ed. Stef Aupers and Dick Houtman (Leiden: Brill, 2010), 206.

48. In 1971 J.G. Ballard claimed that science fiction was totally atheistic; see Tom Woodman, "Science Fiction, Religion and Transcendence," in *Science Fiction: A Critical Guide*, ed. Patrick Parrinder (New York: Longman, 1979), 110. On the spiritual challenge of *Star Wars* to this secularism, see John C. McDowell, *The Gospel According to Star Wars: Faith, Hope and the Force* (Louisville: Westminster John Knox Press, 2007), ch. 2.

49. Possamai and Lee, "Religion and Spirituality in Science Fiction Narratives," 207.

50. Possamai and Lee, "Religion and Spirituality in Science Fiction Narratives," 213.

51. David Rapaport, "Some General Observations on Religion and Violence," in *Violence and the Sacred in the Modern World*, ed. Mark Juergensmeyer (London: Frank Cass, 1992), 120. On nationalistic religion, see Carlton Hayes, *Nationalism: A Religion* (London: Macmillan, 1960).

52. Citation from Robert Bellah, "Civil Religion in America," *Daedalus* 96, no. 1 (1967), 1–21.

53. William Cavanagh, *Theopolitical Imagination* (London: T&T Clark, 2002), 2.

54. Bellah, "Civil Religion in America."

55. Geoffrey Hodgson, *The Myth of American Exceptionalism* (New Haven, CT: Yale University Press, 2009), 15f.

56. Kevin Smith, "Superman for All Seasons," *TV Guide*, December 8, 2001, 24.

57. Jewett and Lawrence, *Captain America and the Crusade Against Evil*, 32.

58. Thomas Andrae, "From Menace to Messiah: The History and Historicity of Superman," in *American Media and Mass Culture: Left Perspectives*, ed. Donald Lazere (Berkeley: University of California Press, 1987), 130.

59. Aldo Regalado, "Modernity, Race and the American Superhero," in *Comics as Philosophy*, ed. Jeff McLaughlin (Jackson: University of Mississippi Press, 2005), 92.

60. Umberto Eco, "The Myth of Superman," in *The Role of the Reader: Explorations in the Semiotics of Texts* (Bloomington: Indiana University Press, 1979), 107–124.

61. Anthony R. Mills, "From Rugged to Real: Stan Lee and the Subversion of the American Monomyth in Theological Anthropology and American Comics and Films," (doctoral dissertation, Fuller Theological Seminary, 2010), 40.

62. Jeph Loeb and Tom Morris, "Heroes and Superheroes," in *Superheroes and Philosophy: Truth, Justice, and the Socratic Way*, ed. Tom Morris and Matt Morris (Chicago: Open Court, 2005), 18.

63. George W. Bush, "Text of President Bush's 2003 State of the Union Address," http://www.washingtonpost.com/wp-srv/on politics/transcripts/bushtext_012803.html, accessed June 30, 2005.

64. Max J. Skidmore and Joey Skidmore, "More Than Mere Fantasy: Political Themes in Contemporary Comic Books," *Journal of Popular Culture* 17, no. 1 (Summer 1983), 84.

65. Jewett and Lawrence, *Captain America and the Crusade Against Evil*, 31.

66. Frank Miller and Lynn Varley (colorist), *The Dark Knight Strikes Again Part 1* (New York: DC Comics, 2001), 62.

67. Citation in Vicki Taylor, ed., *The DC Comics Encyclopedia: The Definitive Guide to the Characters of the DC Universe*, updated and expanded edition (New York: Dorling Kindersley, 2008), 385.

68. Anthony Peter Spanakos, "Super-Vigilantes and the Keene Act," in *Watchmen and Philosophy: A Rorschach Test*, ed. Mark D. White (Hoboken, NJ: John Wiley & Sons, 2009), 44.

69. Frank Miller, *The Dark Knight Strikes Again 2* (New York: DC Comics, 2002), 53.

70. George W. Bush, "Remarks to the Nation" (11 September 2002), cited in Nelson-Pallmeyer, *Saving Christianity from Empire*, 23f.

71. Stan Lee, *Son of Origins of Marvel* (New York: Simon & Schuster, 1975), 165.

72. Danny Fingeroth, *Superman on the Couch: What Superheroes Really Tell Us About Ourselves and Our Society* (New York: Continuum, 2004), 167f.

73. Tony Spanakos, "Tony Stark, Philosopher King of the Future?," in *Iron Man and Philosophy: Facing the Stark Reality*, ed. Mark D. White (Hoboken, NJ: John Wiley & Sons, 2010), 135f.

74. Christopher Robichaud, "Can Iron Man Atone for Tony Stark's Wrongs?," in *Iron Man and Philosophy: Facing the Stark Reality*, ed. Mark D. White (Hoboken, NJ: John Wiley & Sons, 2010), 53.

75. This point is argued by Anthony Peter Spanakos, "Exceptional Recognition: The U.S. Global Dilemma in *The Incredible Hulk*, *Iron Man*, and *Avatar*," in *The Twenty First Century Superhero: Essays on Gender, Genre and Globalization in Film*, ed. Richard J. Gray II and Betty Kaklamanidou (Jefferson, NC: McFarland, 2011), 15–28.

76. Spanakos, "Exceptional Recognition," 16.

77. Miller and Mazzucchelli, *Batman: Year One*, 21.

78. Cited in Claes G. Ryn, *America the Virtuous* (New Brunswick, NJ: Transaction, 2003), 129.

79. Scott Beatty, *Batman: The Ultimate Guide to the Dark Knight*, rev. ed. (New York: Dorling Kindersley, 2005), 28.

80. Alan Brennert, Norm Breyfogle, and Lovern Kindzierski, *Batman: Holy Terror* (New York: DC Comics, 1991).

81. Miller and Varley (colorist), *The Dark Knight Strikes Again Part 1*, 52.

82. Grant Morrison and Dave McKean, *Arkham Asylum* (New York: DC Comics, 1989).

83. See Frank Miller, with Klaus Janson and Lynn Varley (colorist), *The Dark Knight Returns*, Tenth Anniversary Edition (New York: DC Comics, 1996).

84. Iain Thomson, "Deconstructing the Hero," in *Comics as Philosophy*, ed. Jeff McLaughlin (Jackson: University of Mississippi Press, 2005), 104.

85. Mark D. White, "Introduction: A Rorschach Test," in *The Watchmen and Philosophy: A Rorschach Test*, ed. Mark D. White (Hoboken, NJ: John Wiley & Sons, 2009), 1. Moreover, the original Silk Spectre, Sally Jupiter, craves the attention of male affection, and uses her sexual attractiveness to advance her position.

86. Peter Aperlo, *Watchmen: The Film Companion* (London: Titan Books, 2009), 67.

87. Jacob M. Held, "Can We Steer this

Rudderless World? Kant, Rorschach, Retributivism, and Honor," in *The Watchmen and Philosophy*, ed. Mark D. White (Hoboken, NJ: John Wiley & Sons, 2009), 21. And yet that appears to be an odd ideology, at least if J. Keeping's reading of him as in some ways Nietzschean has any merit; see "Superheroes and Supermen: Finding Nietzsche's *Übermensch* in *Watchmen*," in *The Watchmen and Philosophy*, ed. Mark D. White (Hoboken, NJ: John Wiley & Sons, 2009), 47–60. Keeping notes a particular post-theistic nihilistic sounding claim made by Rorschach as sounding distinctly like Nietzsche's madman: "Looked at sky through smoke heavy with human fat and God was not there. The cold suffocating dark goes on forever, and we are alone. Live our lives, lacking anything better to do. Devise reason later. Born from oblivion, bear children hell—bound as ourselves, go into oblivion. There is nothing else. Existence is random. Has no pattern save what we imagine after staring at it for too long. No meaning save what we choose to impose. This rudderless world is not steered by vague, metaphysical forces. It is not God who kills the children. Not fate that butchers them or destiny that feeds them to the dogs. It's us. Only us." (*The Watchmen and Philosophy*, ch. VI, 26). However, Keeping recognizes the importance of the sense of good and evil in Rorschach's judgment: "Rorschach isn't strong enough to face the death of God after all. Looking at the abyss only causes him to cling more tightly to his conservative values, despite the fact that he no longer has any right to them." (p. 56)

88. Thomson, "Deconstructing the Hero," 107.

89. Keeping, Superheroes and Supermen," 55.

90. Cited in Aperlo, *Watchmen*, 61.

91. Marc Copper, "A Year Later: What the Right and Left Haven't Learned," in *The Iraq War: History, Documents, Opinions*, ed. Micah L. Sifry and Christopher Cerf (New York: Touchstone, 2003), 225.

92. Jewett and Lawrence, *Captain America and the Crusade Against Evil*, 42.

93. Bernard Brandon Scott, *Hollywood Dreams and Biblical Stories* (Minneapolis, MN: Fortress, 1994), 53.

94. Rowan Williams, *Writing in the Dust After September 11* (Grand Rapids, MI: William B. Eerdmans, 2002), 21f.

95. Brian L. Ott, "(Re)Framing Fear: Equipment for Living in a Post–9/11 World," in *Cylons in America: Critical Studies in Battlestar Galactica*, ed. Tiffany Potter and C.W. Marshall (New York: Continuum, 2008), 17.

96. Ott, "(Re)Framing Fear," 16.

97. Ronald D. Moore, cited in Erika Johnson-Lewis, "Torture, Terrorism, and Other Aspects of Human Nature," in *Cylons in America: Critical Studies in Battlestar Galactica*, ed. Tiffany Potter and C.W. Marshall (New York: Continuum, 2008), 28.

98. Cited in David Bassom, *Battlestar Galactica: The Official Companion*, 76.

99. Hal Shipman, "Some Cylons Are More Equal than Others," in *Battlestar Galactica and Philosophy: Mission Accomplished or Mission Frakked Up?*, ed. J. Steiff and T.D. Tamplin (Chicago: Open Court, 2008), 155.

100. D. Dinello, "The Wretched of New Caprica," in *Battlestar Galactica and Philosophy: Mission Accomplished or Mission Frakked Up?*, ed. J. Steiff and T.D. Tamplin (Chicago: Open Court, 2008), 186f.

101. Kaveney, *Superheroes!*, 185.

102. Kaveney, *Superheroes!*, 190.

103. Ott, "(Re)Framing Fear," 14.

104. Ott, "(Re)Framing Fear," 21.

105. Terry Kading, "Drawn into 9/11, But Where Have All the Superheroes Gone?," in *Comics as Philosophy*, ed. Jeff McLaughlin (Jackson: University of Mississippi Press, 2005), 219.

106. Jewett and Lawrence, *Captain America and the Crusade Against Evil*, xiii.

107. Cited in Jewett and Lawrence, *Captain America and the Crusade Against Evil*, 33.

108. Jewett and Lawrence, *Captain America and the Crusade Against Evil*, 33.

109. Peter Sanderson, "1940s," in *Marvel Chronicle: A Year By Year History* (London: Dorling Kindersley, 2008), 17.

110. Jewett and Lawrence, *Captain America and the Crusade Against Evil*, 28.

111. Jewett and Lawrence, *Captain America and the Crusade Against Evil*, 35.

112. Stan Lee, *Stan Lee: Conversations*, ed. Jeff McLaughlin (Jackson: University Press of Mississippi, 2007), 22.

113. William Sloane Coffin, Jr., cited in Geiko Müller-Fahrenholz, *America's Battle for God: A European Christian Looks at Civil Religion* (Grand Rapids, MI: William B. Eerdmans, 2007), viii.

114. Kading, "Drawn into 9/11, But Where Have All the Superheroes Gone?," 219.

115. Ed Brubaker, "Captain America Killed! Marvel Comic Book Hero Shot Dead by Sniper," *New York Daily News,* March 7, 2007, www.nydailynews.com/entertainment/music-arts/captain-america-killed-article-1.217626, accessed November 8, 2012.

116. Benedict Anderson, *Imagined Communities: Reflections on the Origins and Spread of Nationalism* (London: Verso, 1991).

117. Zygmunt Bauman, *Globalization: The Human Consequences* (New York: Columbia University Press, 1998).

118. Gray and Kaklamanidou, "Introduction," 3.

119. John Kenneth Muir, *Encyclopedia of Superheroes on Film and Television*, 2nd ed. (Jefferson, NC: McFarland, 2008), 7.

120. Johannes Schlegel and Frank Habermann, "'You Took My Advice About Theatricality a Bit … Literally': Theatricality and Cybernetics of Good and Evil in *Batman Begins*, *The Dark Knight*, *Spider-Man*, and *X-Men*," in *The Twenty First Century Superhero: Essays on Gender, Genre and Globalization in Film*, ed. Richard J. Gray II and Betty Kaklamanidou (Jefferson, NC: McFarland, 2011), 29.

121. Lee, *Son of Origins of Marvel*, 165.

122. Richard Reynolds, *Superheroes: A Modern Mythology* (Jackson: University of Mississippi Press, 1992), 77.

123. Fingeroth, *Superman on the Couch*, 160.

124. Fingeroth, *Superman on the Couch*, 161.

125. George Lucas, cited in Dale Pollock, *Skywalking*, 269. Cf. McDowell, *The Gospel According to Star Wars*, 96.

126. Johnson-Lewis, "Torture, Terrorism, and Other Aspects of Human Nature," 38.

127. John Scott Gray, "They Evolved, but Do They Deserve Consideration?," in *Battlestar Galactica and Philosophy: Mission Accomplished or Mission Frakked Up?*, ed. J. Steiff and T. D. Tamplin (Chicago: Open Court, 2008), 163.

128. Spanakos, "Exceptional Recognition," 15.

129. Kaveney, *Superheroes!*, 202.

130. Kading, "Drawn into 9/11, But Where Have All the Superheroes Gone?," 224f.

131. Russell W. Dalton, "To Assemble or to Shrug? Power, Responsibility and Sacrifice in Marvel's *The Avengers*," in *Joss Whedon and Religion: Essays on an Angry Atheist's Explorations of the Sacred*, ed. Anthony R. Mills, John W. Morehead, and J. Ryan Parker (Jefferson, NC: McFarland, 2013), 165–182.

Chapter 2

1. J.W. Rinzler, *The Making of Star Wars: The Definitive Story Behind the Original Film* (London: Ebury Press, 2008), 326.

2. S. Brent Plate, "Filmmaking and World Making: Re-Creating Time and Space in Myth and Film," in *Teaching Religion and Film*, ed. Gregory J. Watkins (Oxford: Oxford University Press, 2008), 219.

3. Ben Agger, *Cultural Studies and Critical Theory* (Washington, DC: Falmer Press, 1992), 25.

4. Margaret R. Miles and S. Brent Plate, "Hospitable Vision: Some Notes on the Ethics of Seeing Film," *Crosscurrents* (Spring 2004), 23. Cf. John Lyden, *From Film to Religion: Myths, Morals and Rituals* (New York: New York University Press, 2003); Tom Beaudoin, *Virtual Faith: The Irreverent Spiritual Quest of Generation X* (New York: Jossey-Bass, 1998); Margaret Miles, *Seeing and Believing: Religion and Values in the Movies* (Boston: Beacon, 1996). Lucas makes a similar point in a 1983 interview; see Aljean Harmetz, "Burden of Dreams: George Lucas," in *George Lucas: Interviews*, ed. Sally Kline (Jackson: University Press of Mississippi, 1999), 143.

5. Lucas, cited in Michael Kaminski, *The Secret History of Star Wars: The Art of Storytelling and the Making of a Modern Epic* (Kingston, Ontario: Legacy Books Press, 2008), 140.

6. Peter Biskind, *Easy Riders, Raging Bulls: Sex-Drugs-and-Rock 'n' Roll Generation Saved Hollywood* (New York: Touchstone, 1998), 336.

7. See Kaminski, *The Secret History of Star Wars*, 140f.

8. Like J.R.R. Tolkien's *Hobbit* and *The Lord of the Rings*, Lucas had conceived of *SW* as being part of a grand narrative being recounted many years later. The *Journal of the Whills* "was meant to emphasize that whatever story followed came from a book," an inspirational piece of heroic folklore in a "holy book": Lucas, in J.W. Rinzler, *The Making of Star Wars*, 14.

9. George Lucas, *Star Wars: From the Adventures of Luke Skywalker* (London: Sphere Books, 1977), 1.

10. Dale Pollock, *Skywalking: The Life and Films of George Lucas, the Creator of Star Wars* (Hollywood: Samuel French, 1990), 189.

11. Martin Scorsese, cited in John Baxter, *George Lucas: A Biography* (London: Harper Collins, 1999), 246.

12. Kevin J. Wetmore, Jr., *The Empire Triumphant: Race, Religion and Rebellion in the Star Wars Films* (Jefferson, NC: McFarland, 2005), 7.

13. Judith Martin, "The Second *Star Wars*," *The Washington Post*, May 23, 1980, 17. Cf. Kaminski, *The Secret History of Star Wars*, 66, 213, 217ff.

14. Bryan P. Stone, *Faith and the Film: Theological Themes at the Cinema* (St. Louis, MO.: Chalice Press, 2000), 5f.

15. Terry Christensen, *Reel Movies: American Political Movies from* The Birth of a Na-

tion *to* Platoon (New York: Basil Blackwell, 1987), 146.

16. James Monaco, *American Film Now* (New York: Oxford University Press, 1979), 51.

17. Lucas, cited in Stephen Zito, "George Lucas Goes Far Out," in *George Lucas: Interviews,* ed. Sally Kline (Jackson: University Press of Mississippi, 1999), 53.

18. Lucas, in Kline, ed., *George Lucas,* 53.

19. Lucas, cited in John Seabrook, *Nobrow: The Culture of Marketing—The Marketing of Culture* (New York: Knopf, 2000), 146.

20. Lucas, in Tim Rayment, "Master of the Universe," *Sunday Times Magazine,* May 16, 1999, 20.

21. Pollock, *Skywalking,* 271.

22. One of Michael Kaminski's theses is that the Campbell-Lucas connection was unintentional, unconscious, and thus somewhat accidental. However, Kaminski's overdrawn and highly speculative reading is deeply problematic. It operates largely from the unsustainable assumption that *SW* is entertainment, pure and simple, thereby succumbing to a separation of "pulp" or "fantasy and adventure" genres and the mythological. On the one hand Kaminski wants to link *SW* to sources of populist entertainment and deny more intellectual sources; and yet, on the other hand, he does note that Lucas studied anthropology, including myths, for two years at college (*The Secret History of Star Wars,* 18). Also, Kaminski underplays the connections Lucas makes between *SW* and his interest in mythological materials, whether as a child watching *Flash Gordon* and Westerns, or as a college student reading anthropological and cultural studies. Most disastrously for his argument, Kaminski himself cites without comment Lucas' claim that "About the time I was doing the third draft I read *the Hero with a Thousand Faces,* and I started to realize I was following those rules unconsciously. So I said, I'll make it fit more into that classic mold" (Cited in Kaminski, *The Secret History of Star Wars,* 104). Cf. J.W. Rinzler, *The Making of Star Wars,* 48. This admits that Lucas had indeed read Campbell *before* completing the final version of the script. Moreover, while this does suggest an unconscious following of the "rules" of mythic story-telling, it also makes explicit the notion that Lucas then *followed* and *edited* the script when it did not "fit ... into that classic mold."

23. Wetmore, *The Empire Triumphant,* 7.

24. Stephen P. McVeigh, "The Galactic Way of Warfare," in *Finding the Force of Star Wars: Fans, Merchandise, and Critics,* ed.

Matthew Wilhelm Kapell and John Shelton Lawrence (New York: Peter Lang, 2006), 36.

25. See Adam Roberts, *Science Fiction,* 2nd ed. (London: Routledge, 2000), 85; Peter Lev, "Whose Future? Star Wars, Alien, and Blade Runner," *Literature/Film Quarterly* 26, no. 1 (1998), 30, 31.

26. *Jump Cut* (18 Aug 1978), cited in Christensen, *Reel Movies,* 146. Karen Winter accuses the rebels as being only a little less sexist and racist than the imperials; see "The Politics of Star Wars," http://belladonna.org/Karen/politicsofstarwars.html, accessed May 30, 2005. Despite, one would remind Winter, the presence in a main leadership role of Princess Leia Organa and the ultimate authority of Mon Mothma, the Rebellion's armed and air forces are distinctly missing female warriors. Jonathan Rosenbaum overdetermines the Jawas as providing a not so subtle reference to "stingy Jewish merchants"—"one might even have to see the relationship of 'Jawa' to the Hebrew 'Yahweh' in order to catch the clue." *Movie Wars: How Hollywood and the Media Limit What Movies We Can See* (Chicago: A Capella, 2000), 107. The Gungan race of *TPM* is frequently read as a stereotyping of Afro-Caribbean peoples.

27. Pollock, *Skywalking,* 143.

28. M. Keith Booker, *Alternate Americas: Science Fiction Film and American Culture* (Westport, CT: Praeger, 2006), 110, 114.

29. Booker, *Alternate Americas,* 114.

30. Booker, *Alternate Americas,* 115.

31. Booker, *Alternate Americas,* 13f. Cf. 115.

32. Booker, *Alternate Americas,* 115.

33. Christensen, *Reel Movies,* 199.

34. For more on Reagan's use of *SW* rhetoric, see Peter Krämer, "Fighting the Evil Empire: *Star Wars,* the Strategic Defense Initiative, and the Politics of Science Fiction," in *Sex, Politics, and Religion in Star Wars: An Anthology,* ed. Douglas Brode and Leah Deyneka (Lanham, MD: Scarecrow Press, 2012), 63–76; Nick Desolge, "*Star Wars*: An Exhibition in Cold War Politics," in Brode and Deyneka, *Sex, Politics, and Religion in Star Wars,* 55–62.

35. Ian Nathan, "R2D2, Where Are You?," *The Times Review,* May 14, 2005, 14.

36. Martin M. Winkler, "*Star Wars* and the Roman Empire," in *Classical Myth and Culture in the Cinema,* ed. Martin M. Winkler (Oxford: Oxford University Press, 2001), 275.

37. For the dogfights' cinematic sources, see, e.g., "*Star Wars*: The Year's Best Movie," *Time,* Canadian edition, May 30, 1977, 50; Stephen Zito, "George Lucas Goes Far Out,"

American Film 2, no. 6 (1977), 12; and see also Andrew Gordon, "*Star Wars*: A Myth for Our Time," *Literature/Film Quarterly* 6, no. 4 (1978), 319.

38. George Lucas, *Star Wars: From the Adventures of Luke Skywalker*, 1.

39. H.W. Brands, "Preface," *What America Owes the World: The Struggle for the Soul of Foreign Policy* (Cambridge: Cambridge University Press, 1998), cited in Trevor McCrisken and Andrew Pepper, *American History and Contemporary Hollywood Film* (Edinburgh, Scotland: Edinburgh University Press, 2005), 89. Cf. Frederick Meek, *Manifest Destiny and Mission in American History: A Reinterpretation* (New York: Alfred A. Knopf, 1963), 261.

40. Voter apathy produced only a 53 percent voter turnout, as compared with 85 percent in the national elections of France and Germany during the 1970s. According to pollster Daniel Yankelovich, this was indicative of a trend "from trust to mistrust. In the course of a single generation Americans have grown disillusioned about the relation of the individual to his government." Cited in George Brown Tindall and David E. Shi, *America: A Narrative History, Volume Two*, 4th ed. (New York: W.W. Norton & Co., 1996), 1498.

41. Tindall and Shi, *America*, 1498.

42. Cited in John W. Robins, "The Messianic Character of American Foreign Policy," *The Trinity Review* (September-October 1990), 11; http://www.trinityfoundation.org/journal.php?id=77 , accessed April 3, 2004.

43. George W. Bush, "President Holds Prime Time News Conference," October 11, 2001, http://www.whitehouse.gov/new/releases/2001/09/200109208.html, cited in Robert Jewett and John Shelton Lawrence, *Captain America and the Crusade Against Evil: The Dilemma of Zealous Nationalism* (Grand Rapids, MI: William B. Eerdmans, 2003), 15.

44. Hannah Pok, "The *Star Wars* Trilogy: Fantasy, Narcissism and Fear of the Other in Reagan's America," http://hannahpok.com/deepfieldspace/framesrc2c.html, accessed May 18, 2005.

45. Nevertheless, as Walter Wink argues, "to the extent that our blessings are incidental by-products of our citizenship in nations that currently enjoy domination status over others, our well-being may be more a result of our flagrant injustice than divine providence." *Engaging the Powers: Discernment and Resistance in a World of Domination* (Minneapolis, MN: Fortress, 1992), 42.

46. Jewett and Lawrence, *Captain America and the Crusade Against Evil*, 41f.

47. Donald McDonald, "Militarism in America," *The Center Magazine* 3, no. 1 (1970), 29.

48. Jewett and Lawrence, *Captain America and the Crusade Against Evil*, xv.

49. See, e.g., Robert G. Collins, "*Star Wars*: The Pastiche of Myth and the Yearning for a Past Future," *Journal of Popular Culture* 11, no. 1 (1977), 6; and Richard Grenier, "Celebrating Defeat," *Commentary* 70, no. 2 (1980), 58.

50. Again, however, the prequels complicate this possible pattern somewhat—true, Palpatine is British (played by Scottish Ian McDiarmid), but so too is Qui-Gon (as well as the familiar Obi-Wan and the droids), and the tragic hero Anakin is North American (played by the Canadian actor Hadyn Christensen).

51. Lev "Whose Future?," 31f.

52. Lucas, cited in Pollock, *Skywalking*, 269.

53. See Orson Scott Card, "*Star Wars* Our Public Religion," *USA Today*, March 17, 1997, 13A.

54. Jackie Earle Haley, in Peter Aperlo, *Watchmen: The Film Companion* (London: Titan Books, 2009), 67.

55. Gary Westfahl, "Space Opera," in *The Cambridge Companion to Science Fiction*, ed. Edward James and Farah Mendlesohn (Cambridge: Cambridge University Press, 2003), 197.

56. See Peter Krämer, "*Star Wars*: Peter Krämer Tells How the Popularity of the Sci-Fi Epic Proved Timely for Ronald Reagan and the Strategic Defense Initiative," *History Today* (March 1999), 41–47.

57. There is an apparent allusion to George W. Bush's "if you're not for us you're against us" comment in Anakin's assertion to Obi-Wan, "If you're not for me you're my enemy." Bush's own version is a direct application to himself of Jesus' call for discipleship (Matthew 12:30), and the politician's practice here announces the "politics of purity."

58. Aristotle, *Poetics*, trans. I. Bywater, in *The Complete Works of Aristotle Volume Two*, ed. Jonathan Barnes (Princeton: Princeton University Press, 1984).

59. See Biskind, *Easy Riders, Raging Bulls*, 344.

60. Pollock, *Skywalking*, xii.

61. Nathan, "R2D2, Where Are You?," 14.

62. Roy M. Anker, *Catching Light: Looking for God at the Movies* (Grand Rapids, MI: William B. Eerdmans, 2004), 221.

63. See Terry Eagleton, *Sweet Violence: The Idea of the Tragic* (Oxford: Blackwell, 2003), xvi. *Tragōidia* is Greek for "goat song,"

but the origins of Greek Athenian (or Attic) tragedy are obscure. Certainly, they were written for, and performed during, Athens' Dionysia (feasts for the god Dionysus) in late March; the subjects of the tragedies were the misfortunes of the heroes of legend, religious myth, and history.

64. Walter Kaufmann, *Tragedy and Philosophy* (New York: Doubleday, 1969), xivf. Kaufmann prefers a typology associated with individual poets (p. 317).

65. Donald M. MacKinnon, *The Stripping of the Altars: The Gore Memorial Lecture Delivered on 5 November 1968 in Westminster Abbey, and Other Papers and Essays on Related Topics* (London: Collins, 1969), 42f.

66. Aristotle, cited in D. Daiches Raphael, *The Paradox of Tragedy: The Mahlon Powell Lectures 1959* (London: George Allen & Unwin Ltd., 1960), 13. It is commonly recognized that Aristotle is rejecting Plato's hostile view of tragic poetry as an unhealthy emotional stimulant and as morally misleading. Beyond that, interpretations of what is going on diverge substantially from a therapeutic homeopathy of the emotions, to stimulating the moral emotions.

67. Terry Eagleton, "Tragedy and Revolution," in *Theology and the Political: The New Debate*, ed. Creston Davis, John Milbank, and Slavoj Žižek (Durham, NC: Duke University Press, 2005), 16.

68. Lucas, in "The Chosen One" featurette, *Star Wars Episode III: Revenge of the Sith*, DVD Disc 2, directed by George Lucas (Lucasfilm Ltd., 2005).

69. Lucas, in Hugh Hart, "Flaws in a Good Heart," LA Times.com, January 20, 2002, http://articles.latimes.com/2002/jan/20/entertainment/ca-hart20, accessed May 8, 2005.

70. Werner Jaeger observes that the fifth-century Athenians "never felt that the nature and influence of tragedy were purely and simply aesthetic." *Paedeia volume 1*, trans. Gilbert Highet (Oxford: Blackwell, 1939), 244f.

71. David Brin, "I Accuse … Or Zola Meets Yoda," in *Star Wars on Trial*, ed. David Brin and Matthew Woodring Stover (Dallas, TX: Benbella Books, 2006), 40.

72. See, for example, Kevin J. Wetmore, *The Empire Triumphant*, 96; John Shelton Lawrence and Robert Jewett, *The Myth of the American Superhero* (Grand Rapids, MI: William B. Eerdmans, 2002), ch. 13; Mark Rowlands, *The Philosopher at the End of the Universe* (London: Ebury Press, 2003), 209.

73. Apparently it was only during his stint in prison, during which time he composed *Mein Kampf*, that Hitler began professing himself as *der Führer*; see Ian Kershaw, *The*

"Hitler Myth": Image and Reality in the Third Reich (Oxford: Oxford University Press, 1989).

74. In the novelization of *ROTS*, Anakin is tempted by the serpentine Palpatine and seriously considers his offer, and he rejects it at this point until events conspire to position him to become more positively susceptible to it; he then turns the tables by offering Padmé the temptation of unlimited power as Galactic co-rulers together; Vader intensifies his own place as tempter in *ESB* by offering the same to Luke, his son, who is now in a position of physical brokenness, paralysis, and defeatedness.

75. James Kahn, *The Return of the Jedi*, cited in Michael J. Hanson and Max S. Kay, *Star Wars: The New Myth* (Bloomington, IN: Xlibris, 2001), 327.

76. Ian McDiarmid, in *Empire* magazine (June 2005), 94, and second citation in "Palpatine," http://en.wikipedia.org/wiki/Palpatine, accessed June 8, 2005.

77. Hanson and Kay, *Star Wars*, 405; Rick McCallum, "The Chosen One" Featurette, *Star Wars Episode III: The Revenge of the Sith* DVD 2 (2005).

78. Cited in Jack Nelson-Pallmeyer, *Saving Christianity from Empire* (New York: Continuum, 2005), 33.

79. Jacques Ellul, *Propaganda: The Formation of Men's Attitudes*, trans. Konrad Kellen and Jean Lerner (New York: Random House, 1973), 172f.

80. Gore Vidal, *Perpetual War for Perpetual Peace: How We Got to Be So Hated* (New York: Thunder's Mouth Press/Nation's Books, 2002), x. Jewett and Lawrence claim that such rhetoric ideologically generates not only a "complacency about the existence of evil among the saints and a petulant impatience with any resistance to their rule," but also a "complacency about the corruption of the nation as a whole." Jewett and Lawrence, *Captain America and the Crusade Against Evil*, 68. Finally, this kind of ideology can go hand in hand with perpetrating what would otherwise be considered horrendous deeds (torture, tactical nuclear strikes) all justified in the name of "the supposedly righteous end."

81. Citation from opening scroll of *ROTS*.

82. Matthew Stover, *Star Wars Episode III: Revenge of the Sith* (London: Century, 2005), 175.

83. Rohan Gowland, "The Phantom Menace of Idealism: Film Review," *The Guardian*, June 16, 1999, http://www.cpa.org.au/z-archive/g1999/958star.htm, accessed May 30, 2005.

84. Hanson and Kay, *Star Wars*, 33.

85. George Lucas, at Cannes film festival 2005. See Charlotte Higgins, "Final Star Wars

Bears Message for America," *The Guardian,* May 16, 2005, http://film.guardian.co.uk/cannes2005/story/0,15927,1484795,00.html#article_continue, accessed May 26, 2005. Cf. Richard Corliss and Jess Cagie, "Dark Victory," *Time,* April 29, 2002, http://www.time.com.time/covers/1101020429/ story.html, accessed 30–07–02.

86. Michael Ignatieff, *Empire Lite: Nation-Building in Bosnia, Kosovo and Afghanistan* (London: Vintage, 2003), 2.

87. Ignatieff, *Empire Lite,* 21.

88. Deepak Lal, *In Praise of Empires: Globalization and Order* (New York: Palgrave Macmillan, 2004), 63.

89. Jonathan V. Last, "The Case for the Empire: Everything You Know About Star Wars Is Wrong," *Daily Standard,* May 16, 2002, http://www.weeklystandard.com/Content/Public/Articles/000/000/001/248ipzbt.asp, accessed June 8, 2005. Last claims that the Empire brings peace, stability, and order to the crumbling Republic; it rids the Galaxy of the arrogant, elitist, and inherited guardians of "the Force"; the Separatists demand smaller government (is that what the Galactic Empire provides, though?) and free trade; Palpatine is "a relatively benign" dictator; and it establishes academies which demand a meritocracy unavailable to midi-chlorian "inherited" power of the Jedi Order. "[O]nce the Emperor is dead, the galaxy will be plunged into chaos."

90. Claes G. Ryn, *America the Virtuous* (New Brunswick, NJ: Transaction, 2003), 4.

91. Christensen, *Reel Movies,* 211.

92. The American "Grand Army of the Republic" was a post–Civil War Union veterans' organization, established to maintain fraternal bonds among veterans, for remembering the fallen and aiding their families where necessary.

93. See George Steiner, *The Death of Tragedy* (New York: Oxford University Press, 1961), 16f.

94. Peter T. Chattaway, "Star Wars: Episode III—Revenge of the Sith," http://canadianchristianity.com/cgi-bin/na.cgi?film/starwars3, accessed June 30, 2005. Cf. Brin, "I Accuse ... Or Zola Meets Yoda," 5, 26.

95. The talk of the "midi-chlorians" in *TPM* upset many fans; Force-consciousness was being reduced to physiological conditions, it would seem. Interestingly, Lucas had already conceived of this soon after the release of *Star Wars* in 1977; see Lucas in J.W. Rinzler, *The Making of Star Wars,* 441.

96. Carl Gustav Jung, "On the Nature of Dreams," *The Collected Works of C.G. Jung,* vol. 8, 293 (1974). reprinted in Jung, *Dreams* (London: Routledge, 2001), 80)=.

97. Aristotle, *The Poetics of Aristotle: Translation and Commentary,* Stephen Halliwell (London: Duckworth), 1452b.34ff. However, in Sophocles' *Electra, Philoctetes* and *Oedipus at Colonus,* and Aeschylus' *The Eumenides,* the "change" is from misfortune to good fortune. Sophocles' *Antigone* and Aeschylus' *The Libation Bearers* move from misfortune to even greater misfortune. Sophocles' *Ajax* and Aeschylus' *Prometheus* portray *pure* misfortune; however, Aeschylus' plays are more akin to trilogies, which portrayed immense changes from misfortune to good fortune. Aristotle's is a sufficient observation only of Sophocles' *Oedipus the King* and *The Women of Trachis,* and Aeschylus' *Seven Against Thebes, Persians* and *Agamemnon* (and later, of course, of William Shakespeare's Tragedies). Aristotle's depiction of tragedy, then, only fits certain tragic dramas.

98. Aristotle, *The Poetics of Aristotle,* 1452b.34ff.

99. Aristotle, *The Poetics of Aristotle,* ch. 14.

100. Brin, "I Accuse ... Or Zola Meets Yoda," 40.

101. George Lucas, in Hugh Hart, "Flaws in a Good Heart," *LA Times.com,* January 20, 2002, http://articles.latimes.com/2002/jan/20/entertainment/ca-hart20, accessed March 15, 2005.

102. Chris Baldick, "Hamartia," in *The Concise Dictionary of Literary Terms* (Oxford: Oxford University Press, 1991), 96.

103. *King Lear* plays with the theme of awareness in the character of Gloucester, who equates his physical blindness with knowledge or insight and recognition, thus relating his earlier physical sight with his ignorance of the nature of things.

104. "George Lucas Interview—The Story Comes First," January 15, 2002, www.starwars.com/episode-ii/bts/profile/f20020115/index p2.html, accessed April 4, 2006.

105. George Lucas, interview on www.supershadow.com, May 21, 2005, accessed May 26, 2005.

106. "Story," in Star Wars Episode II: Attack of the Clones DVD.

107. Hayden Christensen, in *Empire* magazine (June 2005), 88.

108. Henry Sheehan, "Star Wars: Episode III Revenge of the Sith," www.henrysheehan.com/reviews/stuv/star-wars-3.html, accessed May 26, 20055.

109. Ian McDiarmid, in "The Chosen One."

110. George Lucas, interview on www.supershadow.com, May 21, 2005, accessed May 26, 2005.

111. Matthew Stover, *ROTS,* 175.

112. See Stover, *ROTS*, 202f.

113. Stover, *ROTS*, 207.

114. Stover, *ROTS*, 209.

115. Stover, *ROTS*, 214.

116. Stover, *ROTS*, 215.

117. Stover, *ROTS*, 194.

118. Lucas, July 9, 1999, cited at http://boards.theforce.net/The_Star_Wars_Saga/b104556/13106765/p2, accessed May 8, 2005.

119. Hanson and Kay, *Star Wars*, 370.

120. See Shakespeare, *King Lear*, ed. G.K. Hunter (Harmondsworth, England: Penguin Books, 1972), I.1.62–119.

121. Shakespeare, *King Lear*, V.3.321f.

122. A.C. Bradley, *Shakespearean Tragedy* (London, 1957), 225.

123. Steiner, *The Death of Tragedy*, 128f., 8.

124. Shakespeare, *King Lear*, IV.7; see also V.3.8–25.

125. Hanson and Kay, *Star Wars*, 126.

126. In *TPM* Qui-Gon articulates what may possibly be deterministic belief: "our meeting was not a coincidence. Nothing happens by accident." Earlier in the movie he informs the amphibious Jar Jar in the Bongo (the underwater Gungan transport) from Otoh Gunga, deep in the waters of Lake Paonga, that "the Force will guide us."

127. "George Lucas: Mapping the Mythology," *CNN*, May 7, 2002, http://www.cnn.com/2002/SHOWBIZ/Movies/05/07/ca.s02.george.lucas/index.html, accessed May 8, 2005.

128. Cliegg Lars claims: "Those Tuskans walk like men but they're vicious, mindless monsters." There is a distinct worry among critics that the Sand People are too morally simplistically developed, echoing the American indigenous peoples in pre-1980s Westerns, and even the Arab peoples in the more recent Western cultural imagination.

129. Eagleton, "Tragedy and Revolution," 14.

130. See Stover, *ROTS*, 164.

131. Stover, *ROTS*, 164.

132. Stover's dramatization suggests that Anakin seriously mistrusted Mace: "Is Master Windu turning everyone against me because until I came along he was the youngest Jedi ever named to the Council?" Stover, *ROTS*, 202f.

133. Although the flaws of uncontrolled adolescence are significant in the causes of Anakin's fall, Henry Sheehan, President of the Los Angeles Film Critics Association, simply overestimates them: "Anakin has resented the limits the Jedi knights have been putting on his power; he is, after all, supposed to be the Chosen One, an epochal personage who is going to balance the metaphysical powers of the universe (or whatever). Yet his superiors keep treating this adolescent as if he was just exactly that, a mere adolescent. This resentment finally boils over when Palpatine gets Anakin appointed to a reluctant Jedi Council but the sitting members refuse to grant him all the usual honors. This, as much as their wartime caution and careful rationing of their potentially great powers, marks them as morally suspect to Anakin. For these men won't give him his due. This is simple adolescent moral narcissism, an obnoxious period we all pass through.... Emotionally, this narcissism looms as Anakin's primary resentment.... Once you become alert to this side of Revenge of the Sith, then the whole Star Wars project begins to seem like a study of adolescent narcissism." Henry Sheehan, "Star Wars: Episode III," accessed May 26, 2005.

134. Stover, *ROTS*, 224.

135. Hanson and Kay, *Star Wars*, 278.

136. Hanson and Kay, *Star Wars*, 406.

137. Christensen, *Reel Movies*, 211.

138. See Anne Lancashire, "*Attack of the Clones* and the Politics of *Star Wars*," *The Dalhousie Review* 82, no. 2 (Summer 2002), 235–253. The Neimoidian race, that race from which the Trade Federation has been formed and led, has been described as greedy by nature: "Raised as grubs until the age of seven, young Neimoidians are kept in communal hives and given limited amounts of food. The less acquisitive ones are allowed to die as others hoard more than they can eat. This practice makes Neimoidians greedy and fearful of death." David West Reynolds, *Star Wars Episode I: The Visual Dictionary* (London: Dorling Kindersley, 1999), 16.

139. According to Scott Horton, "Though some have criticized Lucas for being anticapitalist in his portrayal of the commercial interests in *Attack of the Clones*, the names of these organizations—Trade Federation, Commerce Guild, Corporate Alliance and Banking Clan—suggest that they are greedy and corrupt crony capitalists, not free marketeers." "*Star Wars* and the American Empire," www.antiwar.com/orig/horton.php?articleid=6041, accessed May 26, 2005. This, according to economist Mark Thornton, is actually a plea for free market economics—when government becomes involved in trade regulations it becomes bigger and more corrupt. The likeness of the mercantilism in *PM*'s Trade Federation and the government sanctioned monopolies of the East India Company are developed, a Company that regulates its monopolies by military force. Both

Thornton and Scott Horton argue that *TPM* is laden with British colonial imagery—from the mercantilism to the West Indies' enslaved peoples (here in the form of the Gungans), and the title of "Viceroy" (here the leader of the Trade Federation, Nute Gunray). See Horton, "*Star Wars* and Our Wars," http://www.mises.org/fullstory.aspx?control=948, accessed May 18, 2005. Horton further claims that "Grand Army of the Republic," a term used in *AOTC*, was first used by Abraham Lincoln in his move to crush the "separatist" Confederacy.

140. Lucas, *Star Wars*, 8.

141. John Milbank: "There is no clear way of distinguishing between the will which genuinely wills freedom [the Kantian will of modern liberalism], and the will which wills against itself, restraining freedom [as in, for example, the Nazi will].... [T]hese *aporias* arise because of the lack, in Kant, at this highest level, of any teleology which can discriminate the good substance of what is willed from a deficient instance of such substance. Here, instead, the only thing willed is the law of free-willing itself, which defines legality as untrammelled autonomy, and it might seem that the free will to bind oneself [to others] equally instantiates such autonomy." *Being Reconciled: Ontology and Pardon* (London: Routledge, 2003), 4.

142. Wink, *Engaging the Powers*, 17.

143. James Luceno, *Star Wars Revenge of the Sith: The Visual Dictionary* (London: Dorling Kindersley, 2005), 13.

144. "Mace Windu," http://en.wikipedia.org/wiki/Mace_Windu, accessed June 14, 2005.

145. Stover, *ROTS*, 163.

146. See Stover, *ROTS*, 305.

147. The image of "shroud," "cloud," or cloaking of "the dark side" means that evil is described by its shape, its effects, and its appearance, *not by substance*.

148. Stover, *ROTS*, 291.

149. Shakespeare, *King Lear*, III. ii.59.

150. See John C. McDowell, *The Gospel According to Star Wars: Faith, Hope and the Force* (Louisville, KY: Westminster John Knox Press, 2007), ch. 1.

151. Citation from Eagleton, *Sweet Violence*, ix. The reason for this, he claims, is largely that of the United States's "profoundly antitragic culture ... whose ideological orthodoxy regards skepticism as a thought crime and negativity as unpatriotic": "Tragedy and Revolution," 15.

152. Citation from Eagleton, "Tragedy and Revolution," 17.

153. George Lucas, in "The Chosen One" Featurette, *Star Wars Episode III: The Revenge of the Sith* DVD 2 (2005).

154. "George Lucas Interview—The Story Comes First," January 15, 2002, http://web.archive.org/web/20070621170525/http://starwars.com/episode-ii/bts/profile/f20020115/index.html, accessed May 8, 2005.

155. Jerold J. Abrams, "A Technological Galaxy: Heidegger and the Philosophy of Technology in *Star Wars*," in *Star Wars and Philosophy: More Powerful Than You Can Possibly Imagine*, ed. Kevin S. Decker and Jason T. Eberl (Chicago: Open Court, 2005), 118.

156. Christensen, *Reel Movies*, 213.

157. Lucas, in "The Chosen One."

158. Stover, *ROTS*, 207.

159. Steiner, *The Death of Tragedy*, 222.

160. Jeffrey Overstreet, "Star Wars: Episode III—Revenge of the Sith," *Christianity Today*, May 19, 2005, http://www.christianitytoday.com/ct/2005/mayweb-only/starwars3.html , consulted June 1, 2005.

161. See Lancashire, "*Attack of the Clones* and the Politics of *Star Wars*," 235–253.

162. An example of an approach to *SW* purely in terms of entertainment is the *Sunday Times* article by John Harlow who is "merely in search of a good night out": "And Now, the End is Near...," *The Sunday Times Culture*, May 8, 2005, 11. He cites the scrolling text introducing *ROTS* with the comment: "Doo-Who? What? Where? The title sequence is not over and you are probably feeling space-sick already" (p. 10). Had he watched *AOTC* and the Lucas commissioned *Clone Wars* he would have been less shellshocked. The first mistake here is to fail to take the films together as building progressively. The second mistake made is when he continues, "Really, though, the plots are dumb and not that important." Important in what sense, related to what? This comment displays an inability to read the important political and mythical subtexts, and consequently exhibits a refusal to read the movies in the way they are written, but imposes a singular hermeneutic upon them (i.e., entertainment value).

163. Krämer, "Fighting the Evil Empire," 70, referring to Michael Ryan and Douglas Kellner, *Camera Politica: The Politics and Ideology of Contemporary Hollywood Film* (Bloomington: Indiana University Press, 1988), 234–5, 303–5, 308.

164. Booker, *Alternate Americas*, 119.

165. See Jessica Tiffin, "Digitally Remythicised: Star Wars, Modern Popular Mythology, and *Madam and Eve*," in *Inter Action 6: Proceedings of the Fourth Postgraduate Conference*, ed. Hermann Wittenberg, G. Baderoon,

and Y. Steenkamp (Bellville, Cape Town: University of Western Cape Press, 1998), 99–114. As Rohan Gowland recognized in 1999, *Star Wars* "was not just 'entertainment'; like many biblical tales, *Star Wars* was full of lessons about life": see his "The Phantom Menace of Idealism."

166. Walter Wink, *Engaging the Powers*, 18f.

167. Eagleton, *Sweet Violence*, 165.

168. Lyden, *Film as Religion*, 27.

169. Adrian Poole, *Tragedy: A Very Short Introduction* (New York: Oxford University Press, 2005), 54f.

170. Peter J. Ahrensdorf, *Tragedy and Political Philosophy: Rationalism and Religion in Sophocles' Theban Plays* (Cambridge: Cambridge University Press, 2009), 174.

171. Eagleton, "Tragedy and Revolution," 8.

172. Ahrensdorf, *Tragedy and Political Philosophy*, 151.

173. Eagleton, *Sweet Violence*, 165.

174. Rowan Williams, *Writing in the Dust After September 11* (Grand Rapids, MI: William B. Eerdmans, 2002), 21f.

175. John Kekes, *Facing Evil* (Princeton: Princeton University Press, 1990), 26.

176. Iain Thomson, "Deconstructing the Hero," in *Comics as Philosophy*, ed. Jeff McLaughlin (Jackson: University of Mississippi Press, 2005), 106, 109.

177. Thomson, "Deconstructing the Hero," 109.

Chapter 3

1. Frederic Jameson, "Progress Versus Utopia, Or Can We Imagine the Future," in *Fantasy and the Cinema*, ed. James McDonald (London: BFI, 1989), 197.

2. Constance Penley, "Time Travel, Prime Scene and the Critical Dystopia," in *Alien Zone: Cultural Theory and Contemporary Science Fiction*, ed. Annette Kuhn (London: Verso, 1990), 116.

3. J.P. Telotte, *Science Fiction Film* (Cambridge: Cambridge University Press, 2001), 124.

4. Raffaella Baccolini and Tom Moylan, "Introduction: Dystopia and Histories," in *Dark Horizons: Science Fiction and the Dystopian Imagination*, ed. Raffaella Baccolini and Tom Moylan (New York: Routledge, 2003), 1f.

5. Baccolini and Moylan, "Introduction," 2.

6. Peter Fitting, "Unmasking the Real? Critique and Utopia in Recent SF Films," in *Dark Horizons: Science Fiction and the Dystopian Imagination*, ed. Raffaella Baccolini and Tom Moylan (New York: Routledge, 2003), 164.

7. Frederic Jameson, *Archaeologies of the Future: The Desire Called Utopia and Other Science Fictions* (London: Verso, 2005), xiii.

8. Neil Postman, *The End of Education: Redefining the Value of School* (New York: Vintage Books, 1995), 174.

9. Postman, *The End of Education*, 177.

10. Neil Postman, *Amusing Ourselves to Death: Public Discourse in the Age of Show Business* (New York: Viking Penguin, 1985), 15.

11. Thomas Wartenberg, "Philosophy Screened: Experiencing *The Matrix*," cited in Chris Falzon, "Philosophy and *The Matrix*," in *The Matrix in Theory*, ed. Myriam Diocaretz and Stefan Herbrechter (Amsterdam: Rodopi B.V., 2006), 100f.

12. Christopher Grau, "Introduction," in *Philosophers Explore the Matrix*, ed. Christopher Grau (Oxford: Oxford University Press, 2005), 3.

13. Dino Felluga, "*The Matrix*: Paradigm of Postmodernism or Intellectual Poseur? Part I," in *Taking the Red Pill: Science, Philosophy, and Religion in the Matrix*, ed. Glenn Yeffeth (Dallas, TX: BenBella Books, 2003), 100. Cf. M. Keith Booker, *Alternate Americas: Science Fiction Film and American Culture* (Westport, CT: Praeger, 2006), 260.

14. William Irwin, "Introduction: Meditations on *The Matrix*," in *The Matrix and Philosophy: Welcome to the Desert of the Real*, ed. William Irwin (Chicago: Open Court, 2002), 1f.

15. Felluga, "*The Matrix*," 100.

16. Booker, *Alternate Americas*, 259.

17. There is the question of whether Baudrillard himself operates with a required nostalgia for the real, for "a prelapsarian moment" by which he is able to identify the simulacrum; see Alison Landsberg, "Prosthetic Memory: *Total Recall* and *Blade Runner*," in *Liquid Metal: The Science Fiction Film Reader*, ed. Sean Redmond (London: Wallflower Press, 2004), 240.

18. See Anna Dawson, *Studying The Matrix*, rev. ed. (Leighton Buzzard, England: Author, 2008), 28.

19. Andrew Gordon, "*The Matrix*: Paradigm of Postmodernism or Intellectual Poseur? Part II," in *Taking the Red Pill: Science, Philosophy, and Religion in the Matrix*, ed. Glenn Yeffeth (Dallas, TX: BenBella Books, 2003), 106, 119. Cf. David Lavery, "From Cinespace to Cyberspace: Zionist and Agents, Realists and Gamers in *The Matrix* and *Exis-*

tenZ," *Journal of Popular Film and Television* 28, no. 4 (2001), 150–157.

20. Mark T. Conrad, "*The Matrix*, the Cave, and the Cogito," in *The Philosophy of Science Fiction Film*, ed. Steven M. Sanders (Lexington: University Press of Kentucky, 2008), 207–221.

21. "[T]the Wachowski's concept in *The Matrix* more closely resembles nineteenth-century romantic notions of a division between two worlds: a false world of appearances that obstructs or disguises the true world. Once we clear away the illusion, we can dwell in the real world. It is the old distinction between appearances and reality." Gordon, "*The Matrix*: Paradigm of Postmodernism or Intellectual Poseur? Part II," 120.

22. Conrad, "*The Matrix*, the Cave, and the Cogito," 219.

23. Booker, *Alternate Americas*, 259.

24. Cynthia Freeland, "Penetrating Keanu: New Holes, But the Same Old Shit," in *The Matrix and Philosophy*, ed. William Irwin (Chicago: Open Court, 2002), 213.

25. Booker, *Alternate Americas*, 258.

26. Patricia Melzer, *Alien Constructions: Science Fiction and Feminist Thought* (Austin: University of Texas Press, 2006), 166.

27. Melzer, *Alien Constructions*, 170f.

28. Felluga, "*The Matrix*," 93.

29. Citation from Dawson, *Studying The Matrix*, 39. In the opening dialogue Cypher rhetorically asks Trinity "you like watching him, don't you?"

30. Conrad, "*The Matrix*, the Cave, and the Cogito," 217.

31. "Human beings, in short, are enslaved largely because they do not know and understand the nature of their enslavement. Knowing the truth, the film suggests, will set them free. Unfortunately, this message is little more than a cliché, though one that is central to the ideology of modern capitalist society, in which the 'truth' is constantly valorized (sometimes to disguise an absence of truth). Thus, much of the popular success of the film can be attributed to the fact that it projects a message to which its audiences have been conditioned throughout their lives to respond positively." Booker, *Alternate Americas*, 254.

32. Booker, *Alternate Americas*, 256. Cf. Booker, *Alternate Americas*, 257ff.

33. Gregory Grieve, "There Is No Spoon? Teaching *The Matrix*, Postperennialism, and the Spiritual Logic of Late Capitalism," in *Teaching Religion and Film*, ed. Gregory J. Watkins (Oxford: Oxford University Press, 2008), 196.

34. Melzer, *Alien Constructions*, 174.

35. Cynthia Freeland, "Penetrating Keanu," 205.

36. See Melzer, *Alien Constructions*, 164f.

37. Freeland, "Penetrating Keanu," 205.

38. See David Desser, "Race, Space and Class: The Politics of the SF Film from Metropolis to Blade Runner," in *Retrofitting Blade Runner: Issues in Ridley Scott's Blade Runner and Philip K. Dick's Do Androids Dream of Electric Sheep?*, 2nd ed., ed. Judith B. Kerman (Madison: University of Wisconsin Press, 1997), 111.

39. Jack Boozer, Jr., "Crashing the Gates of Insight: Blade Runner," in *Retrofitting Blade Runner: Issues in Ridley Scott's Blade Runner and Philip K. Dick's Do Androids Dream of Electric Sheep?* ed. Judith B. Kerman (Madison: University of Wisconsin Press, 1991), 214.

40. Richard A. Gilmore, *Doing Philosophy at the Movies* (New York: State University of New York Press, 2005), 154.

41. Freeland, "Penetrating Keanu," 213.

42. Dawson, *Studying The Matrix*, 49.

43. Daniel Dinello, *Technophobia! Science-Fiction Versions of Posthuman Technology* (Austin: University of Texas Press, 2005), 178.

44. Peter Fitting, "Unmasking the Real? Critique and Utopia in Recent SF Films," in *Dark Horizons: Science Fiction and the Dystopian Imagination,* ed. Raffaella Baccolini and Tom Moylan (New York: Routledge, 2003), 160.

45. Catherine Constable, *Adapting Philosophy: Baudrillard and The Matrix Trilogy* (Manchester: Manchester University Press, 2009), 138, 143.

46. A more comic take on "nihilistic" themes, featuring two of the actors from *Cube*, is the Canadian *Nothing* (2003).

47. Gordon, "*The Matrix*: Paradigm of Postmodernism or Intellectual Poseur? Part II."

48. Dawson, *Studying The Matrix*, 8.

49. Booker, *Alternate Americas*, 255.

50. This type of reading directs William J. Devlin's treatment of the movie in "Some Paradoxes of Time Travel in *the Terminator* and *12 Monkeys*," in *The Philosophy of Science Fiction Film,* ed. Steven M. Sanders (Lexington: University Press of Kentucky, 2008), 103–117. He concludes that "Though they may disagree over what can be changed and what the metaphysical picture of time looks like, together the two films help us to further clarify the conceptual landscape of the philosophy of time travel" (p. 115).

51. Gregory J. Watkins, "Introduction: Teaching Religion and Film," in *Teaching Religion and Film,* ed. Gregory J. Watkins (Oxford: Oxford University Press, 2008), 10.

52. Mark Rose, *Alien Encounters* (Cam-

bridge, MA: Harvard University Press, 1981), 41.

53. See Dawson, *Studying The Matrix*, 32–35, 66–70; Booker, *Alternate Americas*, 252f.

54. S. Brent Plate, "Filmmaking and World Making: Re-Creating Time and Space in Myth and Film," in *Teaching Religion and Film*, ed. Gregory J. Watkins (Oxford: Oxford University Press, 2008), 228.

55. Read Mercer Schuchardt, "What Is the Matrix?," in *Taking the Red Pill: Science, Philosophy, and Religion in the Matrix*, ed. Glenn Yeffeth (Dallas, TX: BenBella Books, 2003), 10. Cf. Paul Fontana, "Finding God in *The Matrix*," in *Taking the Red Pill: Science, Philosophy, and Religion in the Matrix*, ed. Glenn Yeffeth (Dallas, TX: BenBella Books, 2003), 189–219.

56. Schuchardt, "What Is the Matrix?," 10.

57. See James L. Ford, "Buddhism, Mythology and *The Matrix*," in *Taking the Red Pill: Science, Philosophy, and Religion in the Matrix*, ed. Glenn Yeffeth (Dallas, TX: BenBella Books, 2003), 150–173; Lawrence and Jewett, *The Myth of the American Superhero* (Grand Rapids, MI: William B. Eerdmans, 2002), 255–299; Rachel Wagner and Frances Flannery-Dailey, "Wake Up! Worlds of Illusion in Gnosticism, Buddhism, and The Matrix Project," in *Philosophers Explore the Matrix*, ed. Christopher Grau (Oxford: Oxford University Press, 2005), 258–287.

58. See Richard R. Jones, "Religion, Community, and Revitalization: Why Cinematic Myth Resonates," in *Jacking into the Matrix: Cultural Reception and Interpretation*, ed. Matthew Wilhelm Kapell and William G. Doty (New York: Continuum, 2004), 48–64; Frances Flannery-Daily and Rachel L. Wagner, "Stopping the Bullets: Constructions of Bliss and Problems of Violence," in *Jacking into the Matrix: Cultural Reception and Interpretation*, ed. Matthew Wilhelm Kapell and William G. Doty (New York: Continuum, 2004), 97–114.

59. Grieve, "There Is No Spoon?," 190.

60. Rachel Wagner and Frances Flannery-Dailey's reading (in "Wake Up!") is glib when they claim that "the Christian elements of the film make the most *sense* when viewed through the lens of Gnostic Christianity" (p. 262, my emphasis).

61. Gregory Bassham, "The Religion of *The Matrix* and the Problems of Pluralism," in *The Matrix and Philosophy*, ed. William Irwin (Chicago: Open Court, 2002), 116.

62. Booker, *Alternate Americas*, 253.

63. Cited in Grieve, "There Is No Spoon?," 190.

64. Larry Wachowski, cited in Christopher

Probst, "Welcome to the Machine," *American Cinematographer* 80, no. 4 (1999), 32. Cf. Gordon, "*The Matrix*: Paradigm of Postmodernism or Intellectual Poseur? Part II," 103.

65. Bassham, "The Religion of *The Matrix* and the Problems of Pluralism," 118.

66. Ford, "Buddhism, Mythology and *The Matrix*," 151.

67. Grieve, "There Is No Spoon?," 191.

68. James F. McGrath, "The Desert of the Real: Christianity, Buddhism, and Baudrillard in *The Matrix* films and Popular Culture," in *Visions of the Human in Science Fiction and Cyberpunk*, ed. Marcus Leaning and Birgit Pretzsch (Oxford: Inter-Disciplinary Press, 2010), 162.

69. McGrath, "The Desert of the Real," 163, 162.

70. "So while on an abstract level, *The Matrix* indeed evokes many 'religious' parallels to Christianity, Buddhism, and other mythological traditions, it also integrates arguably contradictory values of violence and male dominance for commercial (or other) ends. One might say that it glorifies some of the 'social matrices' it purports to challenge." Ford, "Buddhism, Mythology and *The Matrix*," 172.

71. Melzer, *Alien Constructions*, 155.

72. Slavoj Žižek, *Violence: Six Sideways Reflections* (New York: Picador, 2008), 79.

73. Gordon, "*The Matrix*," 87.

74. Boozer, *Crashing the Gates of Insight*, 220: "Even the characters who fill the streets and clubs seem to be wearing variations of masks: unusual eye covers, head gear and costumes. Perhaps they have taken on styles of appearance as a form of defensive posturing, as protective shields of 'identity' in a social fabric that tends to absorb all fundamental difference." Or perhaps they are a sign of enclosedness, of relations that cannot be perceived, given the use of ocularity to suggest not only perspective but also the framing of relations.

75. Booker, *Alternate Americas*, 172.

76. Booker, *Alternate Americas*, 182.

77. Thomas B. Myers, "Commodity Futures," in *Alien Zone: Cultural Theory and Contemporary Science Fiction Cinema*, ed. Annette Kuhn (London: Verso, 1990), 39.

78. Jameson, *Archaeologies of the Future*, 141.

79. Bukatman, *Blade Runner* (London: BFI, 1997), 86.

80. Forest Pyle, "Making Cyborgs, Making Humans: Of Terminators and Blade Runners," in *Film Theory Goes to the Movies*, ed. Jim Collins, Hilary Radner, and Ava Preacher Collins (London: Routledge, 1993), 227f.

81. Pyle, "Making Cyborgs, Making Humans," 238.

82. Cited in Rob van Scheers, *Paul Verhoeven*, trans. Aletta Stevens (London: Faber and Faber, 1997), xiii.

83. Joseph Francavilla, "The Android as *Doppelgänger*," in *Retrofitting Blade Runner: Issues in Ridley Scott's Blade Runner and Philip K. Dick's Do Androids Dream of Electric Sheep?* (2nd ed.), ed. Judith B. Kerman (Madison: University of Wisconsin Press, 1997), 7.

84. Stephen Mulhal, *On Film* (London: Routledge, 2002), 42.

85. Boozer, *Crashing the Gates of Insight*, 218.

86. Deborah Knight and George McKnight, "What Is It to Be Human? *Blade Runner* and *Dark City*," in *The Philosophy of Science Fiction Film*, ed. Steven M. Sanders (Lexington: University Press of Kentucky, 2008), 23. It has long been a matter of concern that the original cinematic release of the movie mutilated the climatic sense by demanding a Hollywood style resolving "happy ever after" type ending. Rick and Rachael escape together into the lush landscape outside the city—this in itself, of course, begs the question of what has happened to the postapocalyptic sensibility of the darkened urban center. As Pyle ("Making Cyborgs, Making Humans," 237f) complains, "it ... seems that the movie cannot tolerate to conclude under the sign of such undecidability, at least not in its studio release, for the suspended conclusion—one which has suspended oppositions—is supplemented by Deckard and Rachael's escape in the final scene. They have not only escaped the oppressive atmosphere and dangerous blade runners of the city, they have escaped the film's disorientations, to the liberating blue sky and romantic green world of the 'North.'" Only with the release later of the Director's Cut was the cinematic audience appropriately entreated to the ominous suggestions that closed Scott's movie and made sense of the themes woven in earlier.

87. Philip K. Dick, cited in Brooks Landon, "'There's Some of Me in You': *Blade Runner* and the Adaptation of Science Fiction Literature into Film," in *Retrofitting Blade Runner: Issues in Ridley Scott's Blade Runner and Philip K. Dick's Do Androids Dream of Electric Sheep?* (2nd ed.), ed. Judith B. Kerman (Madison: University of Wisconsin Press, 1997), 94.

88. Myers, 39.

89. Pyle, "Making Cyborgs, Making Humans," 235.

90. Francavilla, "The Android as *Doppelgänger*," 12f.

91. Norman Spinrad, cited in Bukatman, *Blade Runner*, 70–1.

92. Redmond, *Studying Blade Runner*, 35.

93. Redmond, *Studying Blade Runner*, 37, 45.

94. See Mulhal, *On Film*, 35.

95. Deborah Knight and George McKnight, "What Is It to Be Human?," 24.

96. Booker, *Alternate Americas*, 183.

97. See John Shelton Lawrence, "Fascist Redemption of Democratic Hope?," in *Jacking into the Matrix: Cultural Reception and Interpretation*, ed. Matthew Wilhelm Kapell and William G. Doty (New York: Continuum, 2004), 94.

98. Irwin, "Introduction," 1f.

99. Flannery-Daily and Wagner, "Stopping the Bullets," 104.

100. Larry Wachowski, cited in Probst, "Welcome to the Machine," 32.

101. Gordon, "*The Matrix*: Paradigm of Postmodernism or Intellectual Poseur? Part II," 118.

102. Gordon, "*The Matrix*: Paradigm of Postmodernism or Intellectual Poseur? Part II," 119.

103. Dawson, *Studying The Matrix*, 42.

104. Flannery-Daily and Wagner, "Stopping the Bullets," 109.

105. Dawson, *Studying The Matrix*, 43.

106. Citation from Michael Brannigan, "There Is No Spoon: A Buddhist Mirror," in *The Matrix and Philosophy: Welcome to the Desert of the Real*, ed. William Irwin (Chicago: Open Court, 2002), 109.

107. Roz Kaveney, *From Alien to the Matrix: Reading Science Fiction and Film* (London: I.B. Taurus, 2005), 73f.

108. Gordon, "*The Matrix*: Paradigm of Postmodernism or Intellectual Poseur? Part II," 118f.

109. Booker, *Alternate Americas*, 178.

110. Conrad, "*The Matrix*, the Cave, and the Cogito," 207.

111. Gilmore, *Doing Philosophy at the Movies*, 154.

112. Slavoj Žižek, "The Matrix: Or, the Two Sides of Perversion," in *The Matrix and Philosophy*, ed. William Irwin (Chicago: Open Court, 2002), 240. "Isn't *The Matrix* one of those films which function as a kind of Rorschach test?"

113. Booker, *Alternate Americas*, 258.

114. Penley, "Time Travel, Prime Scene and the Critical Dystopia," 210.

115. Constable, *Adapting Philosophy*, 146.

116. Conrad, "*The Matrix*, the Cave, and the Cogito," 208.

BIBLIOGRAPHY

Abrams, Jerold J. "A Technological Galaxy: Heidegger and the Philosophy of Technology in *Star Wars.*" In *Star Wars and Philosophy: More Powerful Than You Can Possibly Imagine,* edited by Kevin S. Decker and Jason T. Eberl, 107–19. Chicago: Open Court, 2005.

Adorno, Theodor. *The Culture Industry: Selected Essays on Mass Culture,* edited by J.M. Bernstein. London: Routledge, 1991.

Agger, Ben. *Cultural Studies and Critical Theory.* Washington, DC: Falmer Press, 1992.

Ahrensdorf, Peter J. *Tragedy and Political Philosophy: Rationalism and Religion in Sophocles' Theban Plays.* Cambridge: Cambridge University Press, 2009.

Alfonsi, Alice. *Star Wars: The Skywalker Family Album.* London: Scholastic, 2002.

Alsford, Mike. *Heroes and Villains.* Waco, TX: Baylor University Press, 2006.

Anderson, Benedict. *Imagined Communities: Reflections on the Origins and Spread of Nationalism.* London: Verso, 1991.

Andrae, Thomas. "From Menace to Messiah: The History and Historicity of Superman." In *American Media and Mass Culture: Left Perspectives,* edited by Donald Lazere, 124–38. Berkeley: University of California Press, 1987.

Anker, Roy M. *Catching Light: Looking for God at the Movies.* Grand Rapids, MI: William B. Eerdmans, 2004.

Aperlo, Peter. *Watchmen: The Film Companion.* London: Titan Books, 2009.

Arberth, John. *A Knight at the Movies: Medieval History on Film.* (New York: Routledge, 2003.

Aristotle. *Poetics* (translated by I. Bywater). In *The Complete Works of Aristotle Volume Two,* edited by Jonathan Barnes. Princeton: Princeton University Press, 1984.

Augustine. *City of God,* translated by Henry Bettenson. Harmondsworth, England: Penguin Books, 1972.

Baccolini, Raffaella, and Tom Moylan, eds. *Dark Horizons: Science Fiction and the Dystopian Imagination.* New York: Routledge, 2003.

Baldick, Chris. "Hamartia." In *The Concise Dictionary of Literary Terms,* 95–96. Oxford: Oxford University Press, 1991.

Barth, Karl. *Church Dogmatics*: Vol. III. *The Doctrine of Creation* (Part 4), translated by G.W. Bromiley and edited by T.F. Torrance. Edinburgh, Scotland: T&T Clark, 1961.

Bassham, Gregory. "The Religion of *The Matrix* and the Problems of Pluralism." In *The Matrix and Philosophy,* edited by William Irwin, 111–25. Chicago: Open Court, 2002.

Bassom, David. *Battlestar Galactica: The Official Companion.* London: Titan Books, 2005.

_____. *Battlestar Galactica: The Official Companion: Season Two.* London: Titan Books, 2006.

_____. *Battlestar Galactica: The Official Companion: Season Three.* London: Titan Books, 2007.

Battis, Jes. *Investigating Farscape: Uncharted Territories of Sex and Science Fiction.* London: I.B. Taurus, 2007.

Baudrillard, Jean. *For a Critique of the Political Economy of the Sign,* translated by Charles Levin. St. Louis, MO: Telos Press, 1981.

Bauman, Zygmunt. *Globalization: The Human Consequences.* New York: Columbia University Press, 1998.

_____. *Intimations of Postmodernity.* London: Routledge, 1992.

Baxter, John. *George Lucas: A Biography.* London: Harper Collins, 1999.

Beal, Timothy K. "They Know Not What They Watch." In *Mel Gibson's Bible: Religion, Popular Culture, and The Passion of the Christ,* edited by Timothy K. Beal and Tod Linafelt, 199–204. Chicago: University of Chicago Press, 2006.

Beal, Timothy K., and Tod Linafelt, eds. *Mel Gibson's Bible: Religion, Popular Culture, and The Passion of the Christ.* Chicago: University of Chicago Press, 2006.

Beatty, Scott. *Batman: The Ultimate Guide to the Dark Knight,* rev. ed. New York: Dorling Kindersley, 2005.

Beaudoin, Tom. *Virtual Faith: The Irreverent Spiritual Quest of Generation X.* New York: Jossey-Bass, 1998.

Bellah, Robert. "Civil Religion in America." *Daedalus* 96, no. 1 (1967), 1–21.

Bercovitch, Sacvan. *The Puritan Origins of the American Self.* New Haven, CT: Yale University Press, 1975.

Bernstein, J.M. "Introduction." In Theodor Adorno, *The Culture Industry: Selected Essays on Mass Culture,* edited by J.M. Bernstein, 1–28. London: Routledge, 1991.

Bildhauer, Bettina, and Anke Bernau. "Introduction: The A-Chronology of Medieval Film." In *Medieval Film,* edited by Anke Bernau and Bettina Bildhauer, 1–19. Manchester: Manchester University Press, 2009.

Birzer, Bradley J. *J.R.R. Tolkein's Sanctifying Myth.* Wilmington, DE: ISI Books, 2003.

Biskind, Peter. *Easy Riders, Raging Bulls: Sex-Drugs-and-Rock 'n' Roll Generation Saved Hollywood.* New York: Touchstone, 1998.

Booker, M. Keith. *Alternate Americas: Science Fiction Film and American Culture.* Westport, CT: Praeger, 2006.

Boozer, Jr., Jack. "Crashing the Gates of Insight: *Blade Runner.*" In *Retrofitting Blade Runner: Issues in Ridley Scott's Blade Runner and Philip K. Dick's Do Androids Dream of Electric Sheep?,* edited by Judith B. Kerman, 212–28. Madison: University of Wisconsin Press, 1991.

Bortolin, Matthew. *The Dharma of Star Wars.* Boston: Wisdom Publications, 2005.

Boyd, Gregory A., and Al Larson. *Escaping the Matrix: Setting Your Mind Free to Experience Real Life in Christ.* Grand Rapids, MI: Baker, 2005.

Boyer, Paul. *When Time Shall Be No More: Prophecy Belief in Modern American Culture.* Boston: Harvard University Press, 1992.

Bradley, A.C. *Shakespearean Tragedy.* London, 1957.

Brannigan, Michael. "There Is No Spoon: A Buddhist Mirror." In *The Matrix and Philosophy,* edited by William Irwin, 101–10. Chicago: Open Court, 2002.

Brennert, Alan, Norm Breyfogle, and Lovern Kindzierski. *Batman: Holy Terror.* New York: DC Comics, 1991.

Brin, David. "I Accuse … Or Zola Meets Yoda." In *Star Wars on Trial,* edited by David Brin and Matthew Woodring Stover, 17–48. Dallas, TX: Benbella Books, 2006.

Brooker, Will. *Star Wars.* London: Palgrave Macmillan, 2009.

_____. *Using the Force: Creativity, Community and Star Wars Fans.* New York: Continuum, 2002.

_____, ed. *The Blade Runner Experience: The Legacy of a Science Fiction Classic.* London: Wallflower Press, 2005.

Brooks, Terry. *Star Wars Episode I: The Phantom Menace.* London: Century, 1999.

Brubaker, Ed. "Captain America Killed! Marvel Comic Book Hero Shot Dead by Sniper." *New York Daily News,* March 7, 2007, www.nydailynews.com/entertainment/music-arts/captain-america-killed-article-1.217626, accessed November 08, 2012.

Bukatman, Scott. *Blade Runner.* London: BFI, 1997.

_____. "Who Programs You? The Science Fiction of the Spectacle." In *Alien Zone: Cultural Theory and Contemporary Science Fiction Cinema,* edited by Annette Kuhn, 196–213. London: Verso, 1990.

Bush, George W. "Text of President Bush's 2003 State of the Union Address." http://www.washingtonpost.com/wp-srv/onpolitics/transcripts/bushtext_012803.html, accessed June 30, 2005.

Campbell, Joseph. *The Hero with a Thousand Faces.* New York: Princeton University Press, 1949.

Caputo, John D. *On Religion.* London: Routledge, 2001.

Card, Orson Scott. "'*Star Wars*' Our Public Religion." *USA Today,* March 17, 1997, 13A.

Carpenter, Stanford W. "Truth Be Told: Authorship and the Creation of the Black Captain America." In *Comics as Philosophy,* edited by Jeff McLaughlin, 46–62. Jackson: University of Mississippi Press, 2005.

Cartmell, Deborah, Heidi Kaye, I. Q. Hunter, and Imelda Whelehan, eds. *Alien Identities: Exploring Differences in Film and Fiction.* London: Pluto Press, 1999.

Cavanaugh, William T. *Theopolitical Imagination.* London: T&T Clark, 2002.

Cavelos, Jeanne. "Stop Her, She's Got a Gun! How the Rebel Princess and the Virgin Queen Became Marginalized and Powerless in George Lucas's Fairy Tale." In *Star Wars on Trial: Science Fiction and Fantasy Writers Debate the Most Popular Science Fiction Films of All Time,* edited by Jeanne Cavelos and Bill Spangler, 305–22. Dallas, TX: BenBella Books, 2006.

Champlin, Charles. *George Lucas: The Creative Impulse,* rev. ed. London: Virgin, 1997.

Chattaway, Peter T. "Star Wars: Episode III—Revenge of the Sith." http://canadian christianity.com/cgi-bin/na.cgi?film/starwars3, accessed June 30, 2005.

Cherry, C., ed. *God's New Israel: Religious Interpretations of American Destiny,* rev. ed. Chapel Hill: University of North Carolina Press, 1998.

Christensen, Terry. *Reel Movies: American Political Movies from the Birth of a Nation to Platoon.* New York: Basil Blackwell, 1987.

Clarke, James. *The Pocket Essential George Lucas.* Harpenden, England: Pocket Essentials, 2002.

_____. *Ridley Scott.* London: Virgin Books, 2002.

Colebatch, Hal G.P. *Return of the Heroes: The Lord of the Rings, Star Wars, Harry Potter, and Social Conflict,* 2nd ed. Christchurch, New Zealand: Cybereditions Corporation, 2003.

Collins, Jim, Hilary Radner, and Ava Preacher Collins, eds. *Film Theory Goes to the Movies.* London: Routledge, 1993.

Collins, Robert G. "*Star Wars*: The Pastiche of Myth and the Yearning for a Past Future." *Journal of Popular Culture* 11 no. 1 (1977), 1–10.

Conrad, Mark T. "*The Matrix*, the Cave, and the Cogito." In *The Philosophy of Science Fiction Film,* edited by Steven M. Sanders, 207–21. Lexington: University Press of Kentucky, 2008.

Constable, Catherine. *Adapting Philosophy: Baudrillard and the Matrix Trilogy.* Manchester: Manchester University Press, 2009.

Copper, Marc. "A Year Later: What the Right and Left Haven't Learned." In *The Iraq War: History, Documents, Opinions,* edited by Micah L. Sifry and Christopher Cerf, 225–28. New York: Touchstone, 2003.

Corliss, Richard, and Jess Cagie. "Dark Victory," *Time,* April 29, 2002, http://www.time.com.time/covers/1101020429/story.html, consulted July 30, 2002.

Cornea, Christine. *Science Fiction Cinema.* Edinburgh, Scotland: Edinburgh University Press, 2007.

Dalton, Russell W. *Faith Journey Through Fantasy Lands: A Christian Dialogue with Harry Potter, Star Wars, and the Lord of the Rings.* Minneapolis, MN: Augsburg Books, 2003.

_____. "To Assemble or to Shrug? Power, Responsibility and Sacrifice in Marvel's The

Avengers." In *Joss Whedon and Religion: Essays on an Angry Atheist's Explorations of the Sacred,* edited by Anthony R. Mills, John W. Morehead, and J. Ryan Parker, 165–82. Jefferson, NC: McFarland, 2013.

Dawson, Anna. *Studying The Matrix,* rev. ed. Leighton Buzzard, England: Author, 2008.

Decker, Kevin S., and Jason T. Eberl, eds. *Star Wars and Philosophy: More Powerful Than You Can Possibly Imagine.* Chicago: Open Court, 2005.

Dees, Richard H. "Moral Ambiguity in a Black-and-White Universe." In *Star Wars and Philosophy: More Powerful Than You Can Possibly Imagine,* edited by Kevin S. Decker and Jason T. Eberl, 39–53. Chicago: Open Court, 2005.

DeFalco, Tom. *Avengers: Ultimate Guide.* London: Dorling Kindersley, 2005.

Deis, Christopher. "May the Force (Not) Be with You: 'Race Critical' Readings and the *Star Wars* Universe." In *Culture, Identities and Technology in the Star Wars Films: Essays on the Two Trilogies* in Carl Silvio and Tony M. Vinci, 77–108. Jefferson, NC: McFarland, 2007.

Delbanco, Andrew. *The Puritan Ordeal.* Cambridge: Harvard University Press, 1991.

Desolge, Nick. "*Star Wars:* An Exhibition in Cold War Politics." In *Sex, Politics, and Religion in Star Wars: An Anthology,* edited by Douglas Brode and Leah Deyneka, 55–62. Lanham, MD: Scarecrow Press, 2012.

Desser, David. "Race, Space and Class: The Politics of the SF Film from *Metropolis* to *Blade Runner.*" In *Retrofitting Blade Runner: Issues in Ridley Scott's Blade Runner and Philip K. Dick's Do Androids Dream of Electric Sheep?,* 2nd ed., edited Judith B. Kerman, 110–23. Madison: University of Wisconsin Press, 1997.

Devlin, William J. "Some Paradoxes of Time Travel in *the Terminator* and *12 Monkeys.*" In *The Philosophy of Science Fiction Film,* edited by Steven M. Sanders, 103–17. Lexington: University Press of Kentucky, 2008.

Deyneka, Leah. "May the Myth Be with You, Always: Archetypes, Mythic Elements, and Apects of Joseph Campbell's Heroic Monomyth in the Original *Star Wars* Trilogy." In *Myth, Media, and Culture in Star Wars: An Anthology,* edited by Douglas Brode and Leah Deyneka, 31–46. Lanham, MD: Scarecrow Press, 2012.

Dinello, Daniel. *Technophobia! Science Fiction Visions of Posthuman Technology.* Austin: University of Texas Press, 2005.

_____. "The Wretched of New Caprica." In *Battlestar Galactica and Philosophy: Mission Accomplished or Mission Frakked Up?,* edited by J. Steiff and T.D. Tamplin, 185–200. Chicago: Open Court, 2008.

Dominguez, Diana. "Feminism and the Force: Empowerment and Disillusionment in a Galaxy Far, Far Away." In *Culture, Identities and Technology in the Star Wars Films: Essays on the Two Trilogies,* edited by Carl Silvio and Tony M. Vinci, 109–33. Jefferson, NC: McFarland, 2007.

Donald, James, ed. *Fantasy and the Cinema.* London: BFI, 1989.

Eagleton, Terry. *Holy Terror.* Oxford: Oxford University Press, 2005.

_____. *Sweet Violence: The Idea of the Tragic.* Malden, MA: Blackwell, 2003.

_____. "Tragedy and Revolution." In *Theology and the Political: The New Debate,* edited by Creston Davis, John Milbank, and Slavoj Žižek, 7–21. Durham, NC: Duke University Press, 2005.

Ebrel, Jason T., ed. *Battlestar Galactica and Philosophy: Knowledge Here Begins Out There.* Malden, MA: Blackwell, 2008.

Eco, Umberto. "The Myth of Superman," in *The Role of the Reader: Explorations in the Semiotics of Texts,* 107–124. Bloomington: Indiana University Press, 1979.

Eick, David. "Battlestar Expands Horizons: Sci-fi References to Middle East Impress Critics." *Calgary Herald,* October 7, 2006, D4.

Ellis, Kathleen. "New World, Old Habits: Patriarchal Ideology in *Star Wars: A New Hope." Australian Screen Education* 30 (Spring 2002), 135–138.

Ellul, Jacques. *Propaganda: The Formation of Men's Attitudes,* translated by Konrad Kellen and Jean Lerner. New York: Random House, 1973.

Falzon, Christopher. "The Limits of Film as Philosophy." Paper delivered to the Philosophy Society, University of Newcastle, New South Wales, October 2013.

_____. "Philosophy and *The Matrix*." In *The Matrix in Theory*, edited by Myriam Diocaretz and Stefan Herbrechter, 97–111. Amsterdam: Rodopi B.V., 2006.

_____. *Philosophy Goes to the Movies: An Introduction to Philosophy*. London: Routledge, 2002.

Felluga, Dino. "*The Matrix*: Paradigm of Postmodernism or Intellectual Poseur? Part I." In *Taking the Red Pill: Science, Philosophy, and Religion in the Matrix*, edited by Glenn Yeffeth, 85–101. Dallas, TX: BenBella Books, 2003.

Fingeroth, Danny. *Superman on the Couch: What Superheroes Really Tell Us About Ourselves and Our Society*. New York: Continuum, 2004.

Fitting, Peter. "Unmasking the Real? Critique and Utopia in Recent SF Films." In *Dark Horizons: Science Fiction and the Dystopian Imagination*, edited by Raffaella Baccolini and Tom Moylan, 155–66. New York: Routledge, 2003.

Flannery-Daily, Frances, and Rachel L. Wagner. "Stopping the Bullets: Constructions of Bliss and Problems of Violence." In *Jacking into the Matrix: Cultural Reception and Interpretation*, edited by Matthew Wilhelm Kapell and William G. Doty, 97–114. New York: Continuum, 2004.

Fontana, Paul. "Finding God in *The Matrix*." In *Taking the Red Pill: Science, Philosophy, and Religion in the Matrix*, edited by Glenn Yeffeth, 189–219. Dallas, TX: BenBella Books, 2003.

Ford, James L. "Buddhism, Mythology and *The Matrix*." In *Taking the Red Pill: Science, Philosophy, and Religion in the Matrix*, edited by Glenn Yeffeth, 150–73. Dallas, TX: BenBella Books, 2003; www.unomaha.edu/jrf/thematrix.htm

Francavilla, Joseph. "The Android as *Doppelgänger*." In *Retrofitting Blade Runner: Issues in Ridley Scott's Blade Runner and Philip K. Dick's Do Androids Dream of Electric Sheep?*, 2nd ed., edited by Judith B. Kerman, 4–15. Madison: University of Wisconsin Press, 1997.

Franklin, Daniel P. *Politics and Film: The Political Culture of Film in the United States*. Lanham, MD: Rowman and Littlefield, 2006.

Freeland, Cynthia. "Penetrating Keanu: New Holes, but the Same Old Shit." In *The Matrix and Philosophy*, edited by William Irwin, 205–15. Chicago: Open Court, 2002.

Freire, Paulo. *Pedagogy of the Oppressed*, translated by Myra Bergman. London: Penguin, Books, 1996.

Geraghty, Lincoln. *American Science Fiction and Television*. Oxford: Berg, 2009.

Giddens, Anthony. *The Nation-State and Violence*. Berkeley: University of California Press, 1987.

Gilmore, Richard A. *Doing Philosophy at the Movies*. New York: State University of New York Press, 2005.

Giroux, Henry A. "Reclaiming the Social: Pedagogy, Resistance, and Politics in Celluloid Culture." In *Film Theory Goes to the Movies*, edited by Jim Collins, Hilary Radner, and Ava Preacher Collins, 37–55. London: Routledge, 1993.

Glut, Donald F. *Star Wars Episode V: The Empire Strikes Back*. London: Sphere Books, 1980.

Gordon, Andrew. "*The Matrix*: Paradigm of Postmodernism or Intellectual Poseur? Part II." In *Taking the Red Pill: Science, Philosophy, and Religion in the Matrix*, edited by Glenn Yeffeth, 102–23. Dallas, TX: BenBella Books, 2003.

_____. "*Star Wars*: A Myth for Our Time." *Literature/Film Quarterly* 6, no. 4 (1978), 320–25.

Gorringe, Timothy J. *Furthering Humanity: A Theology of Culture*. Surrey, UK: Ashgate, 2004.

Gowland, Rohan. "The Phantom Menace of Idealism: Film Review." *The Guardian*, June 16, 1999), http://www.cpa.org.au/z-archive/g1999/958star.htm , accessed May 30, 2005.

Graham, Elaine L. *Representations of the Post/Human: Monsters, Aliens and Others in Popular Culture.* Manchester: Manchester University Press, 2002.

Grant, Barry Keith, ed. *The Dread of Difference: Gender and the Horror Film.* Austin: University of Texas Press, 1996.

Grau, Christopher, ed. "Introduction." In *Philosophers Explore the Matrix,* edited by Christopher Grau, 3–9. Oxford: Oxford University Press, 2005.

_____. *Philosophers Explore the Matrix.* Oxford: Oxford University Press, 2005.

Gray, John Scott. "They Evolved, but Do They Deserve Consideration?" In *Battlestar Galactica and Philosophy: Mission Accomplished or Mission Frakked Up?,* edited by J. Steiff and T. D. Tamplin, 163–70. Chicago: Open Court, 2008.

Gray, Richard J., II, and Betty Kaklamanidou. "Introduction." In *The Twenty First Century Superhero: Essays on Gender, Genre and Globalization in Film,* edited by Richard J. Gray II and Betty Kaklamanidou, 1–13. Jefferson, NC: McFarland, 2011.

Grenier, Richard. "Celebrating Defeat." *Commentary* 70, no. 2 (1980), 58.

Grieve, Gregory. "There Is No Spoon? Teaching *The Matrix,* Postperennialism, and the Spiritual Logic of Late Capitalism." In *Teaching Religion and Film,* edited by Gregory J. Watkins, 189–207. Oxford: Oxford University Press, 2008.

Grimes, Caleb. *Star Wars Jesus: A Spiritual Commentary on the Reality of the Force.* Enumclaw, WA: Winepress, 2007.

Grob, Gerald N., and George Athan Billias, eds. *Interpretations of American History: Patterns and Perspectives,* 6th ed. New York: Macmillan, 1992.

Hanley, Richard. "Send in the Clones: The Ethics of Future Wars." In *Star Wars and Philosophy: More Powerful Than You Can Possibly Imagine,* edited by Kevin S. Decker and John T. Eberl, 93–103. Chicago: Open Court, 2005.

Hanson, Michael J., and Max S. Kay. *Star Wars: The New Myth.* Bloomington, IN: Xlibris, 2001.

Harlow, John. "And Now, the End Is Near…" *The Sunday Times Culture,* May 8, 2005, 10–11.

Harmetz, Aljean. "Burden of Dreams: George Lucas." In *George Lucas: Interviews,* edited by Sally Kline, 135–44. Jackson: University Press of Mississippi, 1999.

Hart, Hugh. "Flaws in a Good Heart," *LA Times.com,* January 20, 2002, http://articles. latimes.com/2002/jan/20/entertainment/ca-hart20, accessed March 15, 2005.

Hatch, Richard, ed. *So Say We All.* Dallas, TX: Benbella, 2006.

Hayes, Carlton. *Nationalism: A Religion.* London: Macmillan, 1960.

Hauerwas, Stanley. *With the Grain of the Universe: The Church's Witness and Natural Theology.* London: SCM Press, 2001.

Hauerwas, Stanley, and William H. Willimon. *Resident Aliens: Life in the Christian Colony.* Nashville, TN: Abingdon Press, 1989.

Hawk, Julie. "*Objec* 8 and the Cylon Remainder: Posthuman Subjectivization in *Battlestar Galactica.*" *The Journal of Popular Culture* 44, no. 1 (2011), 3–15.

Held, Jacob M. "Can We Steer This Rudderless World? Kant, Rorschach, Retributivism, and Honor." In *The Watchmen and Philosophy: A Rorschach Test,* edited by Mark D. White, 19–31. Hoboken, NJ: John Wiley & Sons, 2009.

Henderson, Mary. *Star Wars: The Magic of Myth.* New York: Bantam, 1997.

Heschel, Susannah. "Christ's Passion: Homoeroticism and the Origins of Christianity." In *Mel Gibson's Bible: Religion, Popular Culture, and The Passion of the Christ,* edited by Timothy K. Beal and Tod Linafelt, 99–107. Chicago: University of Chicago Press, 2006.

Higgins, Charlotte. "Final Star Wars Bears Message for America." *The Guardian,* May 16, 2005, http://film.guardian.co.uk/cannes2005/story/0,15927,1484795,00.html# article_continue, accessed May 26, 2005.

Hodgson, Geoffrey. *The Myth of American Exceptionalism.* New Haven, CT: Yale University Press, 2009.

Horkheimer, Max, and Theodor Adorno. *The Dialectic of Enlightenment,* translated by John Cumming. London: Verso, 1997.

Horton, Scott. "*Star Wars* and the American Empire." www.antiwar.com/orig/horton. php?articleid=6041, accessed May 26, 2005.

_____. "Star Wars and Our Wars." Ludwig von Mises Institute. http://www.mises.org/ fullstory.aspx?control=948

Howe, Andrew. "*Star Wars* in Black and White: Race and Racism in a Galaxy Not So Far Away." In *Sex, Politics, and Religion in Star Wars: An Anthology,* edited by Douglas Brode and Leah Deyneka, 11–23. Lanham, MD: Scarecrow Press, 2012.

Ignatieff, Michael. *Empire Lite: Nation-Building in Bosnia, Kosovo and Afghanistan.* London: Vintage, 2003.

Irwin, William. "Introduction: Meditations on *The Matrix.*" In *The Matrix and Philosophy: Welcome to the Desert of the Real,* edited by William Irwin, 1–2. Chicago: Open Court, 2002.

_____, ed. *The Matrix and Philosophy: Welcome to the Desert of the Real,* 4–15. Chicago: Open Court, 2002.

Jaeger, Werner. *Paedeia, Volume 1,* translated by Gilbert Highet. Oxford: Blackwell, 1939.

Jameson, Frederic. *Archaeologies of the Future: The Desire Called Utopia and Other Science Fictions.* London: Verso, 2005.

_____. "Progress Versus Utopia, or Can We Imagine the Future." In *Fantasy and the Cinema,* edited by James McDonald, 197–212. London: BFI, 1989.

Jenkins, Garry. *Empire Building: The Remarkable Real Life Story of Star Wars.* London: Simon & Schuster, 1997.

Jewett, Robert, and John Shelton Lawrence. *Captain America and the Crusade Against Evil: The Dilemma of Zealous Nationalism.* Grand Rapids, MI: William B. Eerdmans, 2003.

Johnson-Lewis, Erika "Torture, Terrorism, and Other Aspects of Human Nature." In *Cylons in America: Critical Studies in Battlestar Galactica,* edited by Tiffany Potter and C.W. Marshall, 27–39. New York: Continuum, 2008.

Johnston, Robert K. *Reel Spirituality: Theology and Film in Dialogue.* Grand Rapids, MI: Baker Academic, 2000.

Jones, Richard R. "Religion, Community, and Revitalization: Why Cinematic Myth Resonates." In *Jacking into the Matrix: Cultural Reception and Interpretation,* edited by Matthew Wilhelm Kapell and William G. Doty, 48–64. New York: Continuum, 2004.

Jowett, Lorna. "Mad, Bad, and Dangerous to Know? Negotiating Stereotypes in Science." In *Cylons in America: Critical Studies in Battlestar Galactica,* edited by Tiffany Potter and Christopher W. Marshall, 64–75. London: Continuum, 2008.

Jung, Carl Gustav. "On the Nature of Dreams." In *The Collected Works of C.G. Jung,* vol. 8, 293 (1974). Reprinted in Jung, *Dreams,* 69–84. London: Routledge, 2001.

Kading, Terry. "Drawn into 9/11, but Where Have All the Superheroes Gone?" In *Comics as Philosophy,* edited by Jeff McLaughlin, 207–27. Jackson: University of Mississippi Press, 2005.

Kahn, James. *Star Wars Episode VI: Return of the Jedi.* London: Futura, 1983.

Kaminski, Michael. *The Secret History of Star Wars: The Art of Storytelling and the Making of a Modern Epic.* Kingston, Ontario: Legacy Books Press, 2008.

Kapell, Matthew Wilhelm. "Eugenics, Racism, and the Jedi Gene Pool." In *Finding the Force of the Star Wars Franchise: Fans, Merchandise, and Critics,* edited by Matthew Wilhelm Kapell and John Shelton Lawrence, 159–73. New York: Peter Lang, 2006.

Kapell, Matthew Wilhelm, and John Shelton Lawrence, eds. *Finding the Force of the Star Wars Franchise: Fans, Merchandise, and Critics.* New York: Peter Lang, 2006.

Kapell, Matthew Wilhelm, and William G. Doty, eds. *Jacking into the Matrix: Cultural Reception and Interpretation.* New York: Continuum, 2004.

Kaufman, Roger. "How the *Star Wars* Saga Evokes the Creative Promise of Homosexual Love: A Gay-Centered Psychological Perspective." In *Finding the Force of the Star Wars Franchise: Fans, Merchandise, and Critics,* edited by Matthew Wilhelm Kapell and John Shelton Lawrence, 131–56. New York: Peter Lang, 2006.

Kaufmann, Walter. *Tragedy and Philosophy.* New York: Doubleday, 1969.
Kaveney, Roz. *From Alien to the Matrix: Reading Science Fiction and Film.* London: I.B. Taurus, 2005.
_____. *Superheroes! Capes and Crusaders in Comics and Films.* London: I.B. Taurus, 2008.
Kearney, Richard. *On Stories.* London: Routledge, 2002.
Keeping, J. "Superheroes and Supermen: Finding Nietzsche's *Übermensch* in *Watchmen.*" In *The Watchmen and Philosophy: A Rorschach Test,* edited by Mark D. White, 47–60. Hoboken, NJ: John Wiley & Sons, 2009.
Kekes, John. *Facing Evil.* Princeton: Princeton University Press, 1990.
Kerman, Judith B., ed. *Retrofitting Blade Runner: Issues in Ridley Scott's Blade Runner and Philip K. Dick's Do Androids Dream of Electric Sheep?* Madison: University of Wisconsin Press, 1991.
Kershaw, Ian. *The "Hitler Myth": Image and Reality in the Third Reich.* Oxford: Oxford University Press, 1989.
Kerslake, Patricia. *Science Fiction and Empire.* Liverpool: Liverpool University Press, 2007.
King, Geoff. *New Hollywood Cinema: An Introduction.* London: I.B. Taurus, 2002.
Kinnucan, Michelle J. "Pedagogy of (the) Force: The Myth of Redemptive Violence." In *Finding the Force of the Star Wars Franchise: Fans, Merchandise, and Critics,* edited by Matthew Wilhelm Kapell and John Shelton Lawrence, 59–72. New York: Peter Lang, 2006.
Kline, Sally, ed. *George Lucas: Interviews.* Jackson: University Press of Mississippi, 1999.
Knight, Deborah, and George McKnight. "What Is It to Be Human? *Blade Runner* and *Dark City.*" In *The Philosophy of Science Fiction Film,* edited by Steven M. Sanders, 21–37. Lexington: University Press of Kentucky, 2008.
Kohn, Hans. *American Nationalism: An Interpretive Essay.* New York: MacMillan, 1957.
Krämer, Peter. "Fighting the Evil Empire: *Star Wars,* the Strategic Defense Initiative, and the Politics of Science Fiction." In *Sex, Politics, and Religion in Star Wars: An Anthology,* edited by Douglas Brode and Leah Deyneka, 63–76. Lanham, MD: Scarecrow Press, 2012.
_____. "*Star Wars:* Peter Krämer Tells How the Popularity of the Sci-Fi Epic Proved Timely for Ronald Reagan and the Strategic Defense Initiative." *History Today* (March 1999), 41–47.
Kuhn, Annette, ed. *Alien Zone: Cultural Theory and Science Fiction Cinema.* London: Verso, 1990.
Lal, Deepak. *In Praise of Empires: Globalization and Order.* New York: Palgrave Macmillan, 2004.
Lancashire, Anne. "*Attack of the Clones* and the Politics of *Star Wars.*" *The Dalhousie Review* 82, no. 2 (Summer 2002), 235–53.
Landon, Brooks. "'There's Some of Me in You': *Blade Runner* and the Adaptation of Science Fiction Literature into Film." In *Retrofitting Blade Runner: Issues in Ridley Scott's Blade Runner and Philip K. Dick's Do Androids Dream of Electric Sheep?,* 2nd ed., edited by Judith B. Kerman, 90–102. Madison: University of Wisconsin Press, 1997.
Landsberg, Alison. "Prosthetic Memory: *Total Recall* and *Blade Runner.*" In *Liquid Metal: The Science Fiction Film Reader,* edited by Sean Redmond, 239–48. London: Wallflower Press, 2004.
Larsen, S., and R. Larsen. *A Fire in the Mind: The Life of Joseph Campbell.* New York: Doubleday, 1991.
Last, Jonathan V. "The Case for the Empire: Everything You Know About Star Wars Is Wrong." *Daily Standard,* May 16, 2002, http://www.weeklystandard.com/Content/Public/Articles/000/000/001/248ipzbt.asp, accessed June 8, 2005.
Lavery, David. "From Cinespace to Cyberspace: Zionist and Agents, Realists and

Gamers in *The Matrix* and *ExistenZ.*" *Journal of Popular Film and Television* 28, no. 4 (2001), 150–57.

Lawrence, John Shelton. "Fascist Redemption of Democratic Hope?" In *Jacking into the Matrix: Cultural Reception and Interpretation,* edited by Matthew Wilhelm Kapell and William G. Doty, 80–96. New York: Continuum, 2004.

_____. "Joseph Campbell, George Lucas, and the Monomyth." In *Finding the Force of the Star Wars Franchise: Fans, Merchandise, and Critics,* edited by Matthew Wilhelm Kapell and John Shelton Lawrence, 21–33. New York: Peter Lang, 2006.

Lawrence, John Shelton, and Robert Jewett. *The Myth of the American Superhero.* Grand Rapids, MI: William B. Eerdmans, 2002.

Lee, Stan. *Son of Origins of Marvel.* New York: Simon & Schuster, 1975.

_____. *Stan Lee: Conversations,* edited by Jeff McLaughlin. Jackson: University Press of Mississippi, 2007.

Lev, Peter. *American Films of the 70s: Conflicting Visions.* Austin: University of Texas Press, 2000.

_____. "Whose Future? Star Wars, Alien, and Blade Runner." *Literature/Film Quarterly* 26, no. 1 (1998), 30–37.

Lindley, Arthur. "Once, Present and Future Kings: *Kingdom of Heaven* and the Multi-temporality of Medieval Film." In *Race, Class and Gender in "Medieval" Cinema,* edited by Tison Pugh and Lynn T. Ramsey, 15–29. New York: Palgrave Macmillan, 2007.

Lipset, Seymour Martin. *American Exceptionalism: A Double-Edged Sword.* New York: W.W. Norton and Co., 1966.

Livingston, Paisley, and Carl Plantinga, eds. *The Routledge Companion to Philosophy and Film.* London: Routledge, 2009.

Loeb, Jeph, and Tom Morris. "Heroes and Superheroes." In *Superheroes and Philosophy: Truth, Justice, and the Socratic Way,* edited by Tom Morris and Matt Morris, 11–20. Chicago: Open Court, 2005.

Longley, Clifford. *Chosen People: The Big Idea That Shapes England and America.* London: Hodder & Stoughton, 2002.

Loughlin, Gerard. *Alien Sex: The Body and Desire in Cinema and Theology.* Malden, MA: Blackwell, 2004.

Lucas, George. "George Lucas Interview—The Story Comes First" (January 15, 2002), http://web.archive.org/web/20070621170525/http://starwars.com/episode-ii/bts/profile/f20020115/index.html, accessed April 4, 2006.

_____. Interview: Mapping the Mythology. CNN, May 7, 2002, http://www.cnn.com/2002/SHOWBIZ/Movies/05/07/ca.s02.george.lucas/index.html

_____. Interview, on www.supershadow.com (May 21, 2005), accessed May 26, 2005.

_____. Interview with Bill Moyers, "Of Myth and Men: A Conversation Between Bill Moyer and George Lucas on the Meaning of the Force and the True Theology of Star Wars," *Time* 153.16 (April 26, 1999), 90–94, http://www.time.com/time/magazine/article/0,9171,990820,00.html, accessed April 4, 2006.

_____. *Star Wars: From the Adventures of Luke Skywalker.* London: Sphere Books, 1977.

Luceno, James. *The Labyrinth of Evil.* New York: Del Ray, 2005.

_____. *Star Wars: Revenge of the Sith. The Visual Dictionary.* London: Dorling Kindersley, 2005.

Lyden, John C. *Film as Religion: Myths, Morals, and Rituals.* New York: New York University Press, 2003.

Lynch, Gordon. *Understanding Theology and Popular Culture.* Malden, MA: Blackwell, 2005.

"Mace Windu," http://en.wikipedia.org/wiki/Mace_Windu

MacKinnon, Donald M. *The Stripping of the Altars: The Gore Memorial Lecture Delivered on 5 November 1968 in Westminster Abbey, and Other Papers and Essays on Related Topics.* London: Collins, 1969.

Madsen, Deborah L. *American Exceptionalism*. Edinburgh, Scotland: Edinburgh University Press, 1998.

Marsh, Clive. *Theology Goes to the Movies*. London: Routledge, 2007.

Marshall, C.W., and M. Wheeland. "The Cylons, the Singularity, and God." In *Cylons in America: Critical Studies in Battlestar Galactica*, edited by Tiffany Potter and C.W. Marshall, 91–104. London: Continuum, 2008.

Marshall, C.W., and Tiffany Potter. "'I See the Patterns': *Battlestar Galactica* and the Things That Matter." In *Cylons in America: Critical Studies in Battlestar Galactica*, edited by Tiffany Potter and C.W. Marshall, 1–10. London: Continuum, 2008.

Martin, Joel W., and Conrad E. Ostwalt, eds. *Screening the Sacred: Religion, Myth, and Ideology in Popular American Film*. Boulder, CO: Westview Press, 1995.

Martin, Judith. "The Second *Star Wars*." *The Washington Post*, May 23, 1980, 17.

Maxwell, Howard. *George Lucas Companion*. London: B.T. Batsford, 1999.

McCrisken, Trevor, and Andrew Pepper. *American History and Contemporary Hollywood Film*. Edinburgh, Scotland: Edinburgh University Press, 2005.

McDonald, Donald. "Militarism in America," *The Center Magazine* 3, no. 1 (1970), 12–33.

McDowell, John C. *The Gospel According to Star Wars: Faith, Hope and the Force*. Louisville, KY: Westminster John Knox Press, 2007.

_____. "Silenus' Wisdom and the 'Crime of Being': The Problem of Hope in George Steiner's Tragic Vision." *Literature and Theology* 14 (2000), 385–411.

_____. "*Star Wars*' Saving Return." *Journal of Religion and Film* 13, no. 1 (April 2009), http://www.unomaha.edu/jrf/vol13.no1/StarWars.htm.

_____. "'Unlearn What You Have Learned' [Yoda]: The Critical Study of the Myth of *Star Wars*." In *Understanding Religion and Popular Culture*, edited by Terry R. Ryan and Dan W. Clayton, 104–17. London: Routledge, 2012.

_____. "A Very Unnationalistic Patriotism, Or Why the Flag Should Not Blind Us." *The Witness* (March 2004), http://www.thewitness.org/agw/mcdowell031904.html

_____. "'Wars Not Make One Great': Redeeming the *Star Wars* Mythos from Redemptive Violence." *Journal of Religion and Popular Culture* 22, no. 1 (2010), http://utpjournals.metapress.com/content/m84028pr465508m0/?p=832f53baebdf42ce99d90afefaa94c2b&pi=3

McGrath, James F. "The Desert of the Real: Christianity, Buddhism, and Baudrillard in *The Matrix* films and Popular Culture." In *Visions of the Human in Science Fiction and Cyberpunk*, edited by Marcus Leaning and Birgit Pretzsch, 161–72. Oxford: Inter-Discinplinary Press, 2010. McLaughlin, Jeff, ed. *Comics as Philosophy*. Jackson: University of Mississippi Press, 2005.

McNeilly, Kewvin. "'This Might Be Hard for You to Watch': Salvage Humanity in 'Final Cut.'" In *Cylons in America: Critical Studies in Battlestar Galactica*, edited by Tiffany Potter and C.W. Marshall, 185–97. London: Continuum, 2008.

McVeigh, Stephen P. "The Galactic Way of Warfare." In *Finding the Force of Star Wars: Fans, Merchandise, and Critics*, edited by Matthew Wilhelm Kapell and John Shelton Lawrence, 35–58. New York: Peter Lang, 2006.

Meek, Frederick. *Manifest Destiny and Mission in American History: A Reinterpretation*. New York: Alfred A. Knopf, 1963.

Melville, Henry. *White-Jacket; or, The World in a Man-of-War*. Chicago: Northwestern University and Newberry Library, 1970.

Melzer, Patricia. *Alien Constructions: Science Fiction and Feminist Thought*. Austin: University of Texas Press, 2006.

Merlock, Ray, and Kathy Merlock Jackson. "Lightsabers, Political Arenas, and Marriages for Princess Leia and Queen Amidala." In *Sex, Politics, and Religion in Star Wars: An Anthology*, edited by Douglas Brode and Leah Deyneka, 77–88. Lanham, MA: Scarecrow Press, 2012.

Milbank, John. *Being Reconciled: Ontology and Pardon*. London: Routledge, 2003.

Miles, Margaret R. *Seeing and Believing: Religion and Values in the Movies*. Boston: Beacon, 1996.

Miles, Margaret R., and S. Brent Plate. "Hospitable Vision: Some Notes on the Ethics of Seeing Film." *Crosscurrents* 54, no. 1 (2004), 22–31.

Miller, Frank, and David Mazzucchelli, with Richmond Lewis. *Batman: Year One*. New York: DC Comics, 2005.

Miller, Frank, and Lynn Varley, colorist. *The Dark Knight Strikes Again Part 1*. New York: DC Comics, 2001.

Miller, Frank, and Lynn Varley, colorist. *The Dark Knight Strikes Again 2*. New York: DC Comics, 2002.

Miller, Frank, with Klaus Janson, and Lynn Varley. *The Dark Knight Returns*, Tenth Anniversary Edition. New York: DC Comics, 1996.

Mills, Anthony R. "From Rugged to Real: Stan Lee and the Subversion of the American Monomyth in Theological Anthropology and American Comics and Films." Doctoral dissertation, Fuller Theological Seminary, 2010.

_____, ed. *Joss Whedon: Religion and Philosophy* (Jefferson, NC: McFarland, 2013).

Mitchell, Elvis. "Works Every Time." In *A Galaxy Not So Far Away*, edited by Glenn Kenny, 77–85. New York: Henry Holt, 2002.

Monaco, James. *American Film Now*. New York: Oxford University Press, 1979.

Morrison, Grant, and Dave McKean. *Arkham Asylum*. New York: DC Comics, 1989.

Muir, John Kenneth. *The Encyclopedia of Superheroes on Film and Television*, 2nd ed. Jefferson, NC: McFarland, 2008.

Mulhal, Stephen. *On Film*. London: Routledge, 2002.

Muller, Christine. "Power, Choice, and September 11 in *The Dark Knight*." In *The Twenty First Century Superhero: Essays on Gender, Genre and Globalization in Film*, edited by Richard J. Gray II and Betty Kaklamanidou, 46–59. Jefferson, NC: McFarland, 2011.

Müller-Fahrenholz, Geiko. *America's Battle for God: A European Christian Looks at Civil Religion*. Grand Rapids, MI: William B. Eerdmans, 2007.

Myers, Thomas B. "Commodity Futures." In *Alien Zone: Cultural Theory and Contemporary Science Fiction Cinema*, edited by Annette Kuhn, 39–50. London: Verso, 1990.

Nathan, Ian. "R2D2, Where Are You?" *The Times Review*, May 14, 2005, 14.

Neale, Stephen. "Issues of Difference: *Alien* and *Blade Runner*." In *Fantasy and the Cinema*, edited by James McDonald, 213–23. London: BFI, 1989.

Nelson-Pallmeyer, Jack. *Saving Christianity from Empire*. New York: Continuum, 2005.

Newton, Judith. "Feminism and Anxiety in *Alien*." In *Alien Zone: Cultural Theory and Science Fiction Cinema*, edited by Annette Kuhn, 82–87. London: Verso, 1990.

Ott, Brian L. "(Re)Framing Fear: Equipment for Living in a Post–9/11 World." In *Cylons in America: Critical Studies in Battlestar Galactica*, edited by Tiffany Potter and C.W. Marshall, 13–26. New York: Continuum, 2008.

Overstreet, Jeffrey. "Star Wars: Episode III—Revenge of the Sith." *Christianity Today*, May 19, 2005, http://www.christianitytoday.com/ct/2005/mayweb-only/starwars3.html, accessed June 1, 2005.

Palmer, R. Barton. "Imagining the Future, Contemplating the Past: The Screen Versions of *1984*." In *The Philosophy of Science Fiction Film*, edited by Steven M. Sanders, 171–90. Lexington: University Press of Kentucky, 2008.

"Palpatine," http://en.wikipedia.org/wiki/Palpatine, accessed June 8, 2005.

Pearce, Joseph. *Tolkein: Man and Myth*. San Francisco: Ignatius, 1998.

Penley, Constance. "Time Travel, Prime Scene and the Critical Dystopia." In *Alien Zone: Cultural Theory and Contemporary Science Fiction Cinema*, edited by Annette Kuhn, 116–127. London: Verso, 1990.

Plate, S. Brent. "Filmmaking and World Making: Re-Creating Time and Space in Myth and Film." In *Teaching Religion and Film*, edited by Gregory J. Watkins, 219–31. Oxford: Oxford University Press, 2008.

Pok, Hannah. "The *Star Wars* Trilogy: Fantasy, Narcissism and Fear of the Other in Reagan's America." http://hannahpok.com/deepfieldspace/framesrc2c.html, accessed May 18, 2005.

Pollock, Dale. *Skywalking: The Life and Films of George Lucas, the Creator of Star Wars.* Hollywood, CA: Samuel French, 1990.

Poole, Adrian. *Tragedy: A Very Short Introduction.* New York: Oxford University Press, 2005.

Porter, John. *The Tao of Star Wars.* Atlanta: Humanics, 2003.

Possamai, Adam. "Popular Religion." In *The World's Religions: Continuities and Transformations,* edited by Peter B. Clarke and Peter Beyer, 479–92. London: Routledge, 2008.

Possamai, Adam, and Murray Lee. "Religion and Spirituality in Science Fiction Narratives: A Case of Multiple Modernities?" In *Religions of Modernity: Relocating the Sacred to the Self and the Digital,* edited by Stef Aupers and Dick Houtman, 205–207. Leiden: Brill, 2010.

Postman, Neil. *Amusing Ourselves to Death: Public Discourse in the Age of Show Business.* New York: Viking Penguin, 1985.

_____. *The End of Education: Redefining the Value of School.* New York: Vintage Books, 1995.

Potter, Tiffany, and Christopher Marshall, eds. *Cylons in America.* London: Continuum, 2007.

Probst, Christopher. "Welcome to the Machine." *American Cinematographer* 80, no. 4 (1999), 32–36.

Pyle, Forest. "Making Cyborgs, Making Humans: Of Terminators and Blade Runners." In *Film Theory Goes to the Movies,* edited by Jim Collins, Hilary Radner, and Ava Preacher Collins, 227–41. London: Routledge, 1993.

Rapaport, David. "Some General Observations on Religion and Violence." In *Violence and the Sacred in the Modern World,* edited by Mark Juergensmeyer, 118–40. London: Frank Cass, 1992.

Raphael, D. Daiches. *The Paradox of Tragedy: The Mahlon Powell Lectures 1959.* London: George Allen & Unwin, 1960.

Rayment, Tim. "Master of the Universe." *Sunday Times Magazine.* May 16, 1999, 14–24.

Redmond, Sean. ed., *Liquid Metal: The Science Fiction Film Reader.* London: Wallflower Press, 2004.

_____. *Studying Blade Runner,* rev. ed. Leighton Buzzard, England: Author, 2008.

Regalado, Aldo. "Modernity, Race and the American Superhero." In *Comics as Philosophy,* edited by Jeff McLaughlin, 84–99. Jackson: University of Mississippi Press, 2005.

Reynolds, David West. *Star Wars: Attack of the Clones. The Visual Dictionary.* London: Dorling Kindersley, 2002.

_____. *Star Wars Episode I: The Visual Dictionary.* London: Dorling Kindersley, 1999.

Reynolds, David West, James Luceno, and Ryder Windham. *Star Wars: The Complete Visual Dictionary.* London: Dorling Kindersley, 2006.

Reynolds, Richard. *Superheroes: A Modern Mythology.* Jackson: University of Mississippi Press, 1992.

Rinzler, J. W. *The Making of Star Wars: The Definitive Story Behind the Original Film.* London: Ebury Press, 2008.

Roberts, Adam. *Science Fiction,* 2nd ed. London: Routledge, 2006.

Robichaud, Christopher. "Can Iron Man Atone for Tony Stark's Wrongs?" In *Iron Man and Philosophy: Facing the Stark Reality,* edited by Mark D. White, 53–63. Hoboken, NJ: John Wiley & Sons, 2010.

Robins, John W. "The Messianic Character of American Foreign Policy." *The Trinity Review,* September-October 1990, 1–12, http://www.trinityfoundation.org/journal. php?id=77, accessed April 3, 2004.

Rose, Mark. *Alien Encounters.* Cambridge, MA: Harvard University Press, 1981.

Rosenbaum, Jonathan. *Movie Wars: How Hollywood and the Media Limit What Movies We Can See.* Chicago: A Capella, 2000.

Rowlands, Mark. *The Philosopher at the End of the Universe.* London: Ebury Press, 2003.

Rubenstein, Richard L. "Mel Gibson's Passion." In *Mel Gibson's Bible: Religion, Popular Culture, and The Passion of the Christ,* edited by Timothy K. Beal and Tod Linafelt, 109–19. Chicago: University of Chicago Press, 2006.

Rubey, Dan. "Not So Far Away." *Jump Cut* 18 (1978), 8–14.

_____. "Not So Long Ago, Not So Far Away." *Jump Cut* 41 (1997), 2–12.

_____. "Not So Long Ago, Not So Far Away: New Variations on Old Themes and Questioning *Star Wars'* Revival of Heroic Archetypes." In *Myth, Media, and Culture in Star Wars: An Anthology,* edited by Douglas Brode and Leah Deyneka, 47–64. Lanham, MD: Scarecrow Press, 2012.

Ryan, Michael, and Douglas Kellner. *Camera Politica: The Politics and Ideology of Contemporary Hollywood Film.* Bloomington: Indiana University Press, 1988.

Ryn, Claes G. *America the Virtuous.* New Brunswick, NJ: Transaction, 2003.

Said, Edward W. *Orientalism: Western Conceptions of the Orient.* London: Penguin Books, 1978.

Salas, Jason. "On Piety, Star Wars, and Raising Your Children to be Morally Aware." http://weblogs.asp.net/jasonsalas/archive/2005/05/19/407406.aspx, accessed June 8, 2005.

Salewicz, Chris. *George Lucas Close Up: The Making of His Movies.* London: Orion, 1998.

Salvatore, R. A. *Star Wars Episode II: Attack of the Clones.* London: Century, 2002.

Sanders, Steven M., ed. *The Philosophy of Science Fiction Film.* Lexington: University Press of Kentucky, 2008.

Sanderson, Peter. "1940s." In *Marvel Chronicle: A Year by Year History* (14–43). London: Dorling Kindersley, 2008.

Scheers, Rob van. *Paul Verhoeven,* translated by Aletta Stevens. London: Faber and Faber, 1997.

Schlegel, Johannes, and Frank Habermann. "'You Took My Advice About Theatricality a Bit ... Literally': Theatricality and Cybernetics of Good and Evil in *Batman Begins, The Dark Knight, Spider-Man,* and *X-Men.*" In *The Twenty First Century Superhero: Essays on Gender, Genre and Globalization in Film,* edited by Richard J. Gray II and Betty Kaklamanidou, 29–45. Jefferson, NC: McFarland, 2011.

Schuchardt, Read Mercer. "What Is the Matrix?" In *Taking the Red Pill: Science, Philosophy, and Religion in the Matrix,* edited by Glenn Yeffeth, 10–30. Dallas, TX: BenBella Books, 2003.

Schwarzmantel, John. *The Age of Ideology: Political Ideologies from the American Revolution to Post-Modern Times.* London: Macmillan Press, 1998.

Scott, Bernard Brandon. *Hollywood Dreams and Biblical Stories.* Minneapolis, MN: Fortress, 1994.

Seabrook, John. *Nobrow: The Culture of Marketing—The Marketing of Culture.* New York: Knopf, 2000.

Segal, Robert A. *Joseph Campbell: An Introduction.* New York: Garland, 1987.

_____. *Myth: A Very Short Introduction.* Oxford: Oxford University Press, 2004.

Shakespeare, William. *King Lear,* edited by G.K. Hunter. Harmondsworth, England: Penguin Books, 1972.

Sharrett, Christopher. "The Horror Film in Neoconservative Culture." In *The Dread of Difference: Gender and the Horror Film,* edited by Barry Keith Grant, 253–76. Austin: University of Texas Press, 1996.

Sheehan, Henry. "Star Wars: Episode III Revenge of the Sith." www.henrysheehan.com/reviews/stuv/star-wars-3.html, accessed May 26, 2005.

Shelley, Mary. *Frankenstein; or, The Modern Prometheus.* London: Lackington, Hughes, Harding, Mavor, & Jones, 1818.

Shipman, Hal. "Some Cylons are More Equal Than Others." In *Battlestar Galactica and Philosophy: Mission Accomplished or Mission Frakked Up?,* edited by J. Steiff and T.D. Tamplin, 155–70. Chicago: Open Court, 2008.

"Sifo-Dyas," http://en.wikipedia.org/wiki/Sifo-Dyas.

Silvio, Carl. "The *Star Wars* Trilogies and Global Capitalism." In *Culture, Identities and Technology in the Star Wars Films: Essays on the Two Trilogies,* edited by Carl Silvio and Tony M. Vinci, 53–73. Jefferson, NC: McFarland, 2007.

Silvio, Carl, and Tony M. Vinci. "Introduction. Moving Away from Myth: *Star Wars* as Cultural Artifact." In *Culture, Identities and Technology in the Star Wars Films: Essays on the Two Trilogies,* edited by Carl Silvio and Tony M. Vinci, 1–8. Jefferson, NC: McFarland, 2007.

Silvio, Carl, and Tony M. Vinci, eds. *Culture, Identities and Technology in the Star Wars Films: Essays on the Two Trilogies.* Jefferson, NC: McFarland, 2007.

Simpson, Philip L. "Thawing the Ice Princess." In *Finding the Force of the Star Wars Franchise: Fans, Merchandise, and Critics,* edited by Matthew Wilhelm Kapell and John Shelton Lawrence, 115–30. New York: Peter Lang, 2006.

Skidmore, Max J., and Joey Skidmore. "More Than Mere Fantasy: Political Themes in Contemporary Comic Books." *Journal of Popular Culture* 17, no. 1 (Summer 1983), 83–92.

Slotkin, Richard. *Regeneration Through Violence: The Mythology of the American Frontier, 1600–1860.* Middletown, CT: Wesleyan University Press, 1973.

Smith, Kevin. "Superman for All Seasons." *TV Guide,* December 8, 2001, 24.

Sontag, Susan. "The Imagination of Disaster." In *Liquid Metal: The Science Fiction Film Reader,* edited by Sean Redmond, 40–47. London: Wallflower Press, 2004.

Spanakos, Anthony Peter. "Exceptional Recognition: The U.S. Global Dilemma in *The Incredible Hulk, Iron Man,* and *Avatar.*" In *The 21st Century Superhero: Essays on Gender, Genre and Globalization in Film,* edited by Richard J. Gray II and Betty Kaklamanidou, 15–28. Jefferson, NC: McFarland, 2011.

_____. "Super-Vigilantes and the Keene Act." In *Watchmen and Philosophy: A Rorschach Test,* edited by Mark D. White, 33–46. Hoboken, NJ: John Wiley & Sons, 2009.

_____. "Tony Stark, Philosopher King of the Future?" In *Iron Man and Philosophy: Facing the Stark Reality,* edited by Mark D. White, 129–43. Hoboken, NJ: John Wiley & Sons, 2010.

Spangler, Bill. "Fighting Princesses and Other Distressing Damsels." In *Star Wars on Trial: Science Fiction and Fantasy Writers Debate the Most Popular Science Fiction Films of All Time,* edited by Jeanne Cavelos and Bill Spangler, 329–38. Dallas, TX: BenBella Books, 2006.

Staub, Dick. *Christian Wisdom of the Jedi Masters.* San Francisco: Jossey-Bass, 2005.

_____. "On the *Star Wars* Myth." *Christianity Today,* May 16, 2005, http://www.christianitytoday.com/ct/2005/120/22.0.html, accessed May 26, 2005.

Steiner, George. *The Death of Tragedy.* New York: Oxford University Press, 1961.

Stone, Bryan P. *Faith and the Film: Theological Themes at the Cinema.* St. Louis, MO: Chalice Press, 2000.

Stover, Matthew. *Star Wars Episode III: Revenge of the Sith.* London: Century, 2005.

Stoy, Jennifer. "Of Great Zeitgeist and Bad Faith: An Introduction to *Battlestar Galactica.*" In *Battlestar Galactica: Investigating Flesh, Spirit and Steel,* edited by Roz Kaveney and Jennifer Stoy, 1–36. London: I.B. Taurus, 2010.

Taylor, Vicki, ed. *The DC Comics Encyclopedia: The Definitive Guide to the Characters of the DC Universe,* updated and expanded ed. New York: Dorling Kindersley, 2008.

Telotte, J. P. *Science Fiction Film.* Cambridge: Cambridge University Press, 2001.

Thomson, Iain. "Deconstructing the Hero." In *Comics as Philosophy,* edited by Jeff McLaughlin, 100–129. Jackson: University of Mississippi Press, 2005.

Tiffin, Jessica. "Digitally Remythicised: Star Wars, Modern Popular Mythology, and *Madam and Eve.*" In *Inter Action 6: Proceedings of the Fourth Postgraduate Conference,* edited by Hermann Wittenberg, G. Baderoon and Y. Steenkamp, 99–114. Bellville, Cape Town: University of Western Cape Press, 1998.

Tindall, George Brown, and David E. Shi. *America: A Narrative History, Volume Two,* 4th ed. New York: W.W. Norton, 1996.

Turner, Bryan S. "Globalization, Religion and Empire in Asia." *International Studies in Religion and Society* 6 (2007), 145–165.

_____. "Islam, Religious Revival and the Sovereign State." *The Muslim World* 97 (2007), 405–418.

Tuveson, Ernest Lee. *Redeemer Nation.* Chicago: University of Chicago Press, 1968.

Tylor, E. B. *Primitive Culture: Researches into the Development of Mythology, Philosophy, Religion, Art, and Custom,* 2 volumes. London: Murray, 1871.

Vidal, Gore. *Perpetual War for Perpetual Peace: How We Got to Be So Hated.* New York: Thunder's Mouth Press/Nation's Books, 2002.

Vinci, Tony M. "The Fall of the Rebellion; or, Defiant and Obedient Heroes in a Galaxy Far, Far Away: Individualism and Intertextuality in the *Star Wars* Trilogies." In *Culture, Identities and Technology in the Star Wars Films: Essays on the Two Trilogies,* edited by Carl Silvio and Tony M. Vinci, 11–33. Jefferson, NC: McFarland, 2007.

Volf, Miroslav. *Exclusion and Embrace: A Theological Exploration of Identity, Otherness, and Reconciliation.* Nashville, TN: Abingdon Press, 1996.

Wagner, Rachel, and Frances Flannery-Dailey. "Wake Up! Worlds of Illusion in Gnosticism, Buddhism, and *The Matrix* Project." In *Philosophers Explore the Matrix,* edited by Christopher Grau, 258–87. Oxford: Oxford University Press, 2005.

Wartenberg, Thomas E. "*Passions of the Christ*: Do Jews and Christians See the Same Film?" In *Mel Gibson's Passion and Philosophy,* edited by Jorge J. E. Garcia, 79–89. Chicago: Open Court, 2004.

Watkins, Gregory J. "Introduction: Teaching Religion and Film." In *Teaching Religion and Film,* edited by Gregory J. Watkins, 3–14. Oxford: Oxford University Press, 2008.

Westfahl, Gary. "Space Opera." In *The Cambridge Companion to Science Fiction,* edited by Edward James and Farah Mendlesohn, 197–208. Cambridge: Cambridge University Press, 2003.

Wetmore, Jr., Kevin J. *The Empire Triumphant: Race, Religion and Rebellion in the Star Wars Films.* Jefferson, NC: McFarland, 2005.

_____. *The Theology of Battlestar Galactica: American Christianity in the 2004–2009 Television Series.* Jefferson, NC: McFarland, 2012.

White, David, and Robert Arp, eds. *Batman and Philosophy: The Dark Knight of the Soul.* Hoboken, NJ: John Wiley & Sons, 2008.

White, Mark D. "Introduction: A Rorschach Test." In *The Watchmen and Philosophy: A Rorschach Test,* edited by Mark D. White, 1–4. Hoboken, NJ: John Wiley & Sons, 2009.

_____, ed. *Iron Man and Philosophy: Facing the Stark Reality.* Hoboken, NJ: John Wiley & Sons, 2010.

_____, ed. *Watchmen and Philosophy: A Rorschach Test.* Hoboken, NJ: John Wiley & Sons, 2009.

Wilhelm, Stephanie J. "Imperial Plastic, Republican Fiber: Speculating on the Post-Colonial Other." In *Finding the Force of the Star Wars Franchise: Fans, Merchandise, and Critics,* edited by Matthew Wilhelm Kapell and John Shelton Lawrence, 175–83. New York: Peter Lang, 2006.

Wilkinson, David. *The Power of the Force: The Spirituality of the Star Wars.* Oxford: Lion, 2000.

Williame, J.-P. "Religion in Ultramodernity." In *Theorising Religion: Classical and Contemporary Debates,* edited by J. A. Beckford and J. Wallis, 77–89. Aldershot, UK: Ashgate, 2006.

Williams, Rowan. *The Truce of God.* London: Collins, 1983.

_____. *Writing in the Dust After September 11.* Grand Rapids, MI: William B. Eerdmans, 2002.

Willis, Garry. *Under God: Religion and American Politics.* New York: Simon and Schuster, 1990.

Wilson, Veronica A. "Seduced by the Dark Side of the Force: Gender, Sexuality, and Moral Agency in George Lucas's *Star Wars* Universe." In *Culture, Identities and Technology in the* Star Wars *Films: Essays on the Two Trilogies,* edited by Carl Silvio and Tony M. Vinci, 134–52. Jefferson, NC: McFarland, 2007.

Windham, Ryder. *Star Wars: Revenge of the Sith Scrapbook.* London: Scholastic, 2005.

Windham, Ryder, and Peter Vilmus. *Star Wars: The Complete Vader.* London: Simon and Schuster, 2009.

Wink, Walter. *Engaging the Powers: Discernment and Resistance in a World of Domination.* Minneapolis, MN: Fortress, 1992.

_____. *The Powers That Be: Theology for a New Millennium.* New York: Doubleday, 1998.

Winkler, Martin M. "*Star Wars* and the Roman Empire." In *Classical Myth and Culture in the Cinema,* edited by Martin M. Winkler, 272–90. Oxford: Oxford University Press, 2001.

Winter, Karen. "The Politics of Star Wars." http://belladonna.org/Karen/politicsof starwars.html, accessed May 30, 2005.

Wood, Robin. *Hollywood from Vietnam to Reagan.* New York: Columbia University Press, 1986.

Woodman, Tom. "Science Fiction, Religion and Transcendence." In *Science Fiction: A Critical Guide,* edited by Patrick Parrinder, 110–30. New York: Longman, 1979.

Wright, John W. "Levinasian Ethics of Alterity: The Face of the Other in Spielberg's Cinematic Language." In *Steven Spielberg and Philosophy: We're Gonna Need a Bigger Book,* edited by Dean A. Kowalski, 50–68. Lexington: University Press of Kentucky, 2008.

Zelinsky, Wilbur. *Nation Into State: The Shifting Symbolic Foundations of American Nationalism.* Chapel Hill: University of North Carolina Press, 1988.

Žižek, Slavoj. "The Matrix: Or, the Two Sides of Perversion." In *The Matrix and Philosophy,* edited by William Irwin, 240–66. Chicago: Open Court, 2002.

_____. *Violence: Six Sideways Reflections.* New York: Picador, 2008.

_____. *Welcome to the Desert of the Real! Five Essays on September 11 and Related Dates.* London: Verso, 2002.

Zynda, Lyle. "Was Cypher Right? Part II: The Nature of Reality and Why It Matters." In *Taking the Red Pill: Science, Philosophy, and Religion in the Matrix,* edited by Glenn Yeffeth, 43–55. Dallas, TX: BenBella Books, 2003.

INDEX